John Esten Cooke

Colonel Ross of Piedmont

A Novel

John Esten Cooke

Colonel Ross of Piedmont
A Novel

ISBN/EAN: 9783744685160

Printed in Europe, USA, Canada, Australia, Japan

Cover: Foto ©Thomas Meinert / pixelio.de

More available books at **www.hansebooks.com**

A Novel.

By JOHN ESTEN COOKE,

AUTHOR OF

"SURRY OF EAGLES NEST," "MOHUN." "HILT
TO HILT," ETC., ETC.

NEW YORK:

COPYRIGHT, 1892, BY

G. W. Dillingham, Publisher,

SUCCESSOR TO G. W. CARLETON & Co.

MDCCCXCII.

CONTENTS.

PART I.
THE STORY OF A CRIME.

PART II.
COL. ROSS AND DR. HAWORTH.

COL. ROSS OF PIEDMONT.

PART I.

THE STORY OF A CRIME.

I.

BROUGHT TOGETHER.

AT the end of September, 1880, the steamer Argentine Republic, direct from Buenos Ayres, arrived at New York, and one of the passengers, registered as Dr. Haworth, Lima, was driven to a hotel on Fifth avenue, where he made his toilet and dined at his leisure.

Dr. Haworth was a man of about thirty-five, with a face of the American type, brown hair and heavy mustache, a broad forehead and remarkable eyes, which seemed to slumber, but were plainly on the watch. His dress was plain and neat; the carriage of his person erect and firm. As he walked down the avenue in the afternoon, people more than once turned to look at him, which is unusual in so large a town as New York.

Near Madison Square he came into collision with a personage hurrying in the opposite direction—a gentleman of about his own age, dressed in an elegant business suit, with a handsome face, smiling lips, hair parted in the middle, and wearing eye-glasses.

"Why, Haworth! What good wind has blown you to New York?" exclaimed this gentleman.

"The south wind, my dear Burdette," replied Dr. Haworth, cordially shaking hands. "Come and stroll with me, and tell me the news."

"In a moment." And, having called to a person whom he had been in pursuit of, Mr. Burdette exchanged a few words with him, returned, and he and Dr. Haworth walked down the avenue together.

They were evidently old friends, and it was obvious from their conversation that smiling Mr. Burdette had visited Dr. Haworth at his hacienda near Lima, and retained delightful memories of the visit. To his question now what had brought his friend to New York, Dr. Haworth replied quietly:

" To keep an appointment."

" Is it down town ? " asked Mr. Burdette.

" On the steps of the City Hall at seven."

" Well, I am going in that direction, and am glad to have your company. I am looking up an old gentleman whose work on the ' Opium-Habit' I am publishing. I am afraid he is not practicing his precepts, and I think I shall find him at one of the ' joints ' in Mott street."

Dr. Haworth made no comment, and, turning out of Broadway, they were soon near Chatham Square, where, in one of the subterranean opium-dens, they found the person of whom Mr. Burdette was in pursuit. He was a gray-haired man of about 60 in appearance, and of mild and benignant countenance. A simple smile made his old face attractive, and he quietly yielded to Mr. Burdette's guidance, and left the joint. Holding his arm, Mr. Burdette turned to Dr. Haworth and said, in a whisper:

" This is a melancholy business. The poor old fellow came from the South to correct his proofs, and fell back into his vice. I have tried to look after him, as some friends of his placed him in my charge—Col. Ross and Mrs. Maurice."

As these names were uttered Dr. Haworth turned his head suddenly.

" Col. Ross ? " he said.

" Yes ; do you know him ? "

" I believe so."

" Well, the name of this poor old party is Prof. Lesner, and as his friends are back from Canada on their way South, I will turn him over to them. They will no doubt be at the opera to-night, and I will see them."

Dr. Haworth had listened in silence, but it was plain that he was not losing a word.

" Come and go with me," said Mr. Burdette, " and I hope it is distinctly understood that my humble cottage on the avenue is to be your headquarters during your stay in New York. My coupe won't compare with that splendid affair of yours at Lima, but—"

"Thank you, my dear friend ; but I leave New York by the morn-ing train."

"Well, we'll sup after the opera, and I'll try to talk you out of that resolution."

And the friends parted, Mr. Burdette bearing off the poor old Professor, and Dr. Haworth going in the direction of the City Park.

On the steps of the hall a young man of 18 or 20 was standing, evidently on the look-out for some one. He was a slender and graceful youth, with black curly hair and ruddy cheeks.

As Dr. Haworth approached, and the gas-light fell upon his face, the youth rushed up to him, seized his hand, and seemed about to kiss it.

"Excellency!" he exclaimed, with a French-Spanish accent ; "Oh, how glad I am to see you!"

Dr. Haworth's face had softened, and a bright smile made it winning.

"I really believe you are," he said, looking with great affection into the youth's face. "So you expected me ? "

"I knew you would be here between the 20th and 25th, as you said."

"Well, here I am. Now come with me. I have something im-portant to tell you, my dear Jean."

On the same night Dr. Haworth, Mr. Burdette, and Jean were at the opera. Mr. Burdette was evidently in his element, and ex-changed nods with a hundred friends ; but Dr. Haworth was evi-dently waiting for something.

As the curtain rose he turned quickly and looked at one of the loges. An elegantly dressed man of middle age, tall and command-ing in person, had just entered with a lady in black silk, and a young girl with a face full of freshness and attraction. The escort was relieving the young lady of her cloak when Dr. Haworth looked at them, and his air was that of a lover.

"These are old Prof. Lesner's friends," said Mr. Burdette indi-cating the party.

"Yes," said Dr. Haworth quietly.

He touched Jean, who sat beside him, on the arm and said :

"Do you recognize anybody yonder ? "

The youth looked in the direction indicated, and his smiling face suddenly overclouded. His smooth brow contracted and his eyes flashed.

"Sacre!" he muttered unconsciously. "Yes, yes, Excellency! I should be blind not to recognize that man."

"I thought perhaps you might have forgotten him."

"I remember him, as he gave me this."

And pushing back his hair the youth showed an ugly scar on his forehead, apparently a cutlass stroke.

Dr. Haworth nodded.

"Very well," he said, "we may renew our acquaintance with him. We are going in his direction, and as you will be my traveling companion, things might so turn out that you would have an opportunity to get even with him for that cut."

"I would like to have the chance," said Jean, knitting his brows.

"Very well. Remember my instructions. See that all is in order about the carbines. After the opera go to the hotel. I will join you there in an hour."

"Yes, Excellency—don't fear! Oh how glad I am I am going with you!"

The performance was over, and Mr. Burdette went up to the loge and joined the Ross-Maurice party, to whom he bowed with great elegance. It was plain that he was informing them on the subject of their new traveling companion, Prof. Lesner—probably urging them to take him home with them. Then they parted with bows and came into the lobby, where Dr. Haworth awaited his friend.

As the party passed, Col. Ross did not see Dr. Haworth. It was impossible to be certain, but a sudden flash of the dark eyes and flush of the cheek seemed to indicate emotion. As to the face of Dr. Haworth, that indicated nothing. He simply moved his head slightly as if satisfied, and accompanied his friend Burdette in his coupe to his residence on the avenue.

They had an excellent supper, and when his host's charming family retired, the friends remained in confidential conversation. At last Dr. Haworth rose to go.

"I will come and see you again before I leave the States," he said.

"You must not fail; and good luck to you, old fellow!"

"Thank you!"

"You have not told me what takes you South?"

"I should like to see the country."

"That's strictly non-committal. My own impression is that

you aré going to exterminate somebody. Come, tell your friend everything. A man like yourself doesn't travel for mere amusement. You are either going to plunge a gory dagger in the recreant heart of somebody, or your mission—observe the term—is to penetrate some bloody mystery."

Dr. Haworth unconsciously looked at his friend with quite a piercing expression, but said nothing.

" You see I've been reveling in the seaside literature, which is my delight," said Mr. Burdette laughing.

" Do you like that ? "

" Don't dodge the question ! Are you or are you not on—well, say a secret mission ? "

Dr. Haworth made no reply. At last he said as he pressed his friend's hand :

" Did you ever reflect upon the profound significance of one word in the English language ? "

" What is that ? "

" Perhaps."

And without adding anything further Dr. Haworth returned to his hotel.

Jean was waiting for him, and exhibited two carbines in their cases, with a full supply of ammunition.

Dr. Haworth tried the locks, made them click, and was evidently satisfied.

" They may be useful down yonder," he said. " And now to get some sleep."

On the next morning he and Jean took the train for the South.

II.

MAURICEWOOD.

MRS. MAURICE, who had stopped in New York on her way from Canada, was from the South, and resided at a very old country seat in what is called the Piedmont region—that is to say, the eastern slope of the long range of mountains extending from Maryland to Northern Georgia.

The estate, which had been in the family for some generations, was known as " Mauricewood." It was still of large extent and very considerable value in spite of that subdivision which seems to be the fate of all landed property in America. The house stood on a hill rounding off into level fields of great fertility, and a mile to the westward a low range of wooded hills shut in the prospect. In other directions, however, the view was unimpeded. Several additional country seats were visible in the distance, and a few miles off was the Town of Abbeyville, the nearest postoffice.

Mrs. Maurice was the widow of a Mr. John Maurice who had died many years before. She was tall, delicately beautiful, a person of great gentleness, and managed her household with a mild good sense which accomplished a great deal without producing the least friction. She was very much beloved by everybody, especially her old servants, who had all remained with her, their emancipation having apparently produced no effect upon the relations of the members of the household. The footfalls were as quiet, the tones as low and respectful, and it seemed to be the general conviction of man and maid that their old home and mistress were the best home and mistress they would be apt to find.

As to the estate, that was managed by Mr. Timothy Maurice, a bachelor uncle, who had always lived at the place. He was a lively little fellow, devoted to field sports and to the game of chess. He was devoted to his niece, Mrs. Maurice, and a careful manager of her property. What he said was acquiesced in by everybody; he was consulted by all; and indeed what "Uncle Tim" did not know was generally conceded to be not worth knowing. His personal portrait may be drawn with a stroke of the pen. He was about 60, florid, with gray hair, a wiry figure, smiled habitually, and was rapid in all his movements. Every morning he rode over the estate carrying his fowling-piece for the chance of a shot at something. In the evening he played chess with Mrs. Maurice or Miss Cary.

Miss Cary Maurice was a fresh-looking little beauty of about 19, with brown hair, worn in bangs very low on her forehead, large blue eyes set wide apart, a rosy complexion and an air of cheerfulness. She had been thoroughly educated by an excellent governess, residing at Mauricewood, and played and sang very sweetly. She was rather domestic in her tastes, liked horseback riding, read all the novels she could lay her hands upon, and had never cared for anybody but her immediate family, which might have been owing to the fact that there were few young men in the vicinity of Mauricewood who were calculated to impress the fancies of maidens.

One suitor Miss Cary seemed to have, or to be going to have—
a certain Col. Ross, who lived some miles from Mauricewood. He
was a man of from 40 to 45, but he never alluded to his age, and
his estate was ample. He lived in very handsome style, as his elegant drag, driven by a neat servant and drawn by a pair of superb
bays, indicated. In his appearance he was a mixture of the fine
gentleman and the military man. He was punctiliously polite, wore
kid gloves and a jaunty hat, and had a delicate black mustache and
imperial, and smiled and bowed frequently. He was said to have
been in the United States Navy, and then to have resigned and entered the Chilian army. He had returned to the States a year or
so before, on a " mission," it was said, connected with the interests
of a guano or nitrate company, engaged in exploiting the resources
of Peru. He was frequently absent in New York or Washington,
but resided a part of the year on his estate, and having seen Miss
Cary Maurice had been presented to her, and was now a tolerably
constant visitor.

Whether his attentions had made any impression on Miss Cary
was not known. It was not unreasonable to suppose that they had
in some degree flattered her vanity, and when people saw the young
lady and her mother leave Mauricewood, during this summer, under
Col. Ross' escort, they said succinctly in provincial phrase, that it
was " going to be a be."

Mrs. Maurice had been persecuted by Miss Cary for a long
time to take a Northern tour. The young lady was dying, she said,
to see Niagara and the Falls of Montmorenci, and as it was always
a very difficult matter for Mrs. Maurice to deny her daughter anything, she finally yielded, and it had been the intention to carry off
Uncle Tim with them. At this Uncle Tim had uttered outcries and
protests. Everything would go to wrack and ruin ; his presence at
Mauricewood was indispensable. The home would burn down,
general destruction would ensue—which meant that Uncle Tim
abominated traveling, and thought there was nothing worth attention beyond the Mauricewood horizon.

He groaned and consented, however, when to his immense relief
Col. Ross called and casually observed that he was about to visit
Montreal on business. When he heard of the project of the ladies
he promptly offered to escort them. He was entirely at their orders.
His business in Montreal could be attended to in two or three hours.
The best route—the one he had in fact intended to take—was by

way of New York, Albany and Niagara, then down the St. Lawrence by the Thousand Isles, and nothing would please him more than to return by the historic City of Quebec, which he had never visited.

There was no resisting Col. Ross' cordial and urgent offer. Uncle Tim nodded significantly to Mrs. Maurice, and she accepted with thanks. The tour followed. Col. Ross made himself not only useful, but extremely agreeable. and by the time they had returned to New York on their way southward it became plain that the gallant colonel was very much interested indeed in one of his traveling companions. If for any reason Dr. Haworth had been curious on that subject, he might have had his doubts dispelled by the manner in which Col. Ross had wrapped Miss Cary Maurice's cloak around her shoulders at the theater.

When the party reached home, their escort bowed, smiled, and declared that the trip had been delightful to him, pressed the hands · of both ladies with deferential cordiality, and, entering his equipage which awaited him, drove away.

———

III.

NEW FACES.

ABOUT a week after the return of the ladies Mr. Tim Maurice mounted his horse, fowling-piece in hand, to take his morning ride.

He did not return until late in the afternoon, which was very unusual with him, and apologized for keeping dinner waiting.

"The fact is, my dear niece," he said to Mrs. Maurice, as they sat down to dinner, "I have had quite an adventure."

He then turned to Miss Cary, and said in a low tone, obstructed by roast mutton:

"A mysterious stranger, Cadie "—which was his pet name for Miss Cary. As the young lady looked at him inquiringly, he said still more confidentially:

"Two mysterious strangers !"

As this was really too tantalizing Mr. Tim Maurice was ordered to explain himself at once, which he proceeded to do.

His ride had taken him toward the "hill country," as the wooded range west of Mauricewood was called, and just at the foot of the hills he had noticed a hawk of great size perched up in a dead tree. As he had a great antipathy to hawks, he said, owing to his fondness for spring chickens, he dismounted and crept up to get a shot at the enemy. When he thought he was in range he leveled his fowling-piece and fired both barrels in succession, but the hawk spread his wings and soared off with silent contempt.

"And you call that an adventure, Uncle Tim?" said Miss Cary, with derision.

"Wait, my dear—never interrupt. The adventure is coming."

"Did the hawk show defiance or laugh in scorn as he soared away?"

"Interrupting! interrupting! No, he did not even soar away."

"You said he did."

"I said he soared off, which is a different expression from away —a fact you are, perhaps, ignorant of, my angel, owing to your defective education."

"He only soared off, then—"

"When he was suddenly arrested in his towering flight, to use the style of your favorite romances. In other words, he dropped with a bullet through him. It is unnecessary to say that his fall was preceded by the crack of a gun, and I saw a light cloud of smoke rise from some undergrowth near. A gentleman then came out, followed by a youth, who seemed to be carrying a game-bag, and went and picked up the hawk. I joined him and he bowed, after which we indulged in mutual introductions."

"Who was he?"

"A Dr. Haworth, who has stopped for a few days at old Hunter Wilson's—one of the hill people, you know. He is traveling on horseback to hunt and see the country. I invited him to come and visit us."

"That proves to me that he is a gentleman, uncle," said Mrs. Maurice in her gentle voice. "You are so terribly aristocratic."

"A gentleman? Certainly he is; and he shot that hawk with a bullet from a jewel of a breech-loading carbine. I never saw a prettier affair."

"Do you think he will come?"

"He said he would."

"You have not told us about him," said Miss Cary.

"About him? Oh, you mean his looks—that's the first thing you angelic beings think of. Well, he's good-looking, quiet in manner, and well dressed. His companion was a fine-looking young fellow, as bright as day."

" Well, you are evidently pleased with your new friends, uncle," said Mrs. Maurice, " and I shall be glad to see Dr. Haworth."

" I invited him to drop in to-morrow. I think from the expression of his face that he plays chess," said Mr. Tim Maurice, thoughtfully.

" Then you and he will swear eternal friendship," exclaimed Miss Cary—" that is, if he doesn't beat you."

And the subject of Dr. Haworth having apparently been exhausted, the conversation busied itself with other matters.

On the next afternoon Dr. Haworth made his appearance at Mauricewood, and was presented to the ladies. His manners were marked by a courteous composure, and as Mr. Tim Maurice found, to his delight, that he was an excellent chess-player, it seemed probable that the eternal friendship predicted by Miss Cary would be sworn. When the visitor retired, declining the invitation, usual in the country, to spend the night, the general verdict was flattering.

" Dr. Haworth is a very nice gentleman," said Mrs. Maurice, with her sweet smile.

" And very handsome," said Miss Cary.

" There ! I said that was the first requisite," exclaimed Mr. Tim Maurice. " Yes, he is both a gentleman and a fine-looking man ; but he is more than that—he plays a number one game of chess ! "

The acquaintance between Dr. Haworth and the inmates of Mauricewood having begun in this simple manner soon became friendly and unceremonious. The guest was apparently pleased with his sojourn in the upland region, and took long excursions on foot or horseback to places in the vicinity ; but his evenings were generally spent at Mauricewood. He played interminable games of chess with Mr. Tim Maurice, and was very quiet and courteous in his demeanor to the ladies. One evening after his departure Mr. Tim Maurice said :

" I have invited Dr. Haworth to make us a visit, but he has refused."

" We should be glad to see him," said Mrs. Maurice, " he is very agreeable."

" What do you say, Cadie ? "

" It is a matter of indifference to me. He refused, you say ? "

" Yes, he is afraid of giving trouble, though I assured him he would give none at all."

" Very well," said Miss Cary. " I suppose there is an end of it."
" I shall invite him again—shall I, my dear niece ? "
" Of course, if you wish, uncle," said Mrs. Maurice.
" What do you say, Cadie ? "
" If you choose," said Miss Cary, with the rising inflection on the word choose.

IV.

THE CRIME.

ONE day Dr. Haworth rode to Mauricewood and found Mr. Tim Maurice just back from his morning ride. The ladies had driven out, and the duties of host having thus devolved solely upon Mr. Maurice, he received his visitor with unusual cordiality.

" Glad to see you, my dear Doctor—no one could be more welcome," he exclaimed ; " come in. Sorry the ladies are not at home, but they will soon return."

Dr. Haworth bowed courteously, and looked up at the old mansion with its stacks of chimneys, its long rows of stone-capped windows, and the nearly encircling veranda.

" These old houses have a great attraction for me," he said. " I was admiring the grounds and old oaks as I rode up. There is the charm of age and permanence about such places ; the interior arrangements only are sometimes defective."

" Mauricewood is a very well-planned establishment," said Mr. Tim Maurice, " and if you wish I will show you through it."

" I confess I should like to look at it," said Dr. Haworth, "if it would not annoy the ladies."

" With pleasure—nothing would please me better."

And taking Dr. Haworth's arm the old gentleman entered the house.

" You see the general plan is an L," he said, " only the base line is to the left. On the right here you have the drawing-room, and behind it the dining-room. To the left are two chambers, a large one in front and a small one in rear, and the winding staircase in rear of the hall leads to the second and third floors, on which other chambers open."

" An excellent arrangement, as the main hall is left unincumbered," said Dr. Haworth.

" Excellent—there is nothing I like more than a good, broad hall, with a lofty ceiling, oak cornices and oak floor scrubbed until it shines. We manage to keep up the scrubbing. The old people there on the wall would turn pale if it was overlooked." He laughed and rubbed his hands. " There is a great deal of fine wainscoting and other woodwork in the various rooms," he said, " particularly in that to the left of the hall."

" I should be pleased to look at it," said Dr. Haworth, walking with a matter-of-fact air toward the room in question, and laying his hand on the knob. The door was locked.

" I am sorry I cannot show you that room," said Mr. Tim Maurice rather sadly. " It is never opened."

" Never opened ? "

" My poor brother James was murdered in that room."

" Your brother—murdered ? "

" Yes, yes, my dear Doctor—a melancholy family affair. The room has been closed for nearly twenty years—no human being has entered it."

Dr. Haworth remained silent, and his companion wiped his forehead with a red bandana handkerchief, as if endeavoring to remove some unpleasant memory.

" I see you are surprised," he said, " and nothing is more natural. But the fact is just as I state. My elder brother, James Maurice, was murdered in that chamber during his sleep, and it has never been occupied by any one since that time."

" You interest me deeply. I need not say that I am also a little shocked," said Dr. Haworth. " Who was the murderer, and what was his motive ? "

The old gentleman shook his head sorrowfully, and replied :

" The whole affair is a mystery to this day."

" Was no one suspected ? "

" Yes, unhappily. I say unhappily because I do not believe that the person charged with the crime had anything to do with it."

" Who was the person ? "

" A Mr. Ducis of the neighborhood, one of the most honorable men I have ever known."

" How could such a person have been accused of murder—and cowardly murder, since you say that Mr. Maurice was murdered in his sleep ? "

" It is an old story and a very sad one, Doctor," said Mr. Tim

Maurice, sighing. " None of our family ever believed that Mr. Ducis was guilty."

" Was he formally charged with the crime?"

" Yes."

" Tried?"

" Yes."

" And ——?"

" Found guilty on what seemed to be very strong circumstantial evidence."

" Well, that is a gloomy incident of your family history, Mr. Maurice," said Dr. Haworth. " I have always felt an interest in such things—but it would perhaps be painful to you to dwell further on the subject."

" Not at all," said Mr. Tim Maurice, " it is rather sad, but I will tell you the circumstances—it will not take long. The owner of Mauricewood at that time was my brother James, and the household consisted of himself, his wife, and daughter—the present Mrs. Maurice, who kept her own name by marrying her first cousin, John Maurice. I was also one of the family, as I never cared to marry. Well, my brother was a man of about 60 at the time, and of very social temper, but, when aroused, his passions were hot. He lived with great elegance and was careless in money matters; so it happened that when his daughter Ellen came to be married he was very much troubled about her dower. Young John Maurice, her intended husband, was only moderately well off, and my brother was anxious under the circumstances to assist the young couple in beginning life."

" A natural wish," said Dr. Haworth, who listened with attention.

" Certainly. Well, there was trouble about that. My brother had no ready resources, and a mortgage on his land was not to be thought of—it was opposed to all the traditions of the family. He therefore had recourse to a friend who had borrowed a considerable sum of money from him, a Mr. Ducis."

" Yes."

" Mr. Ducis, it seems, resented this, or perhaps took offense at some fancied slight conveyed in the tone of my brother's note to him. However that may be, he had an angry interview with my poor brother on the subject, and was said to have denounced him as a skinflint, or in some other insulting manner. He would pay the amount, he said, if he was compelled to sell every acre of his land;

and he did dispose of a considerable tract, it seems, and paid the amount of his indebtedness in gold and bank-notes. An unfortunate altercation occurred on this occasion. From words the old friends came to blows, and then some bystanders dragged them apart."

"An unhappy affair."

"A most unhappy one, considering the characters of the two men, and their long friendship. Mr. Ducis was universally respected. He was a man of elegant culture and an enthusiastic student of mineralogy and geology; most amiable, like my brother, when nothing occurred to irritate him; and here the two old friends had come to a personal struggle, calling names and striking blows at each other. Well, well, Mr. Ducis went away in a rage, declaring that he would have my brother's blood."

"An unfortunate expression."

"Yes; but to end my sad story. The scene between my poor brother and Mr. Ducis occurred a few days before the marriage, and the day for the ceremony came. As Ellen was very popular she had received many presents, a portion of which were laid out in the apartment yonder, now closed, and in the evening the ceremony took place.

"A great number of friends attended, and the house was full of merriment to a late hour, when the guests finally departed. Well, everybody had retired, and the whole establishment was silent, when, just as I was going to bed, about 2 in the morning, I heard a cry from the lower floor. I ran hastily down, and hearing groans from the room yonder, hastened toward it. I knew they must proceed from my brother. During the afternoon the bride's chamber had been changed—she preferred one up stairs—and my brother, who habitually slept in this room, returned to his own apartment."

"Yes."

"I ran in and saw a fearful sight. My brother was stretched groaning upon the bed, with the clothing thrown about as if in a violent struggle—his wife had started up, shaking with fright, and well-nigh paralyzed, it seemed, by what had occurred. The glimmering night-taper showed me all this."

"It must have been shocking."

"It was really frightful. I ran into the dining-room for some brandy, and I was hastening back when I met a person coming out of the room. This was a Mrs. Pitts—a woman who performed the functions of a sort of head servant, and was kept because she was useful, not because she was much liked. When she saw me she stopped and stared at me in silence. I noticed that both her hands were under her apron.

"'What do you mean by standing there in that idiotic way?' I said.

"She only made some muttered reply as I hurried by her into the chamber. My brother was dead."

The old gentleman drew a long breath as if the memory of the scene oppressed him.

"But what was the manner of his death—and who was the murderer?"

Mr. Tim Maurice shook his head.

"One question is nearly as difficult as the other. But there was reason to believe that my poor brother had come to his end in a peculiarly barbarous manner."

"Barbarous?"

"That he was struck heavily with an iron instrument on the temple or behind the ear—such an instrument was found on the floor."

"What was it?"

"A small hammer, such as amateur geologists use in their excursions."

"Geologists?"

"Yes, and the only one in the country was Mr. Ducis'. He habitually carried such a hammer in his rides to chip off specimens of rock, and the one discovered on the floor was supposed to belong to him."

"That was fatal."

"It was not all. The murderer had evidently entered from the veranda—the window was open. On the veranda was found a buckskin riding-glove such as Mr. Ducis generally wore."

Dr. Haworth shook his head.

"That ended all reasonable doubt, I suppose."

"There was even more. The amount paid in gold and banknotes by Mr. Ducis to my brother, which had been placed on a table, had disappeared."

"Murder and theft combined," said Dr. Haworth.

"The only question was, who had committed the murder and the theft."

"Could there be any doubt?" said Dr. Haworth, in a tone showing some surprise. "You stated, sir, I remember, that your family never believed Mr. Ducis to be guilty—but how could they doubt it? I concede that the evidence was purely circumstantial, but then circumstantial evidence, when it is cumulative, is of irresistible force. It is a chain which grows stronger with every link which is added."

Mr. Tim Maurice sighed and said :

"That appears reasonable, but—"

"Consider, sir," said Dr. Haworth, interrupting him with the air of a man anxious to establish his point, "two friends have an altercation; a violent quarrel follows; one is heard to say that he will have the other's blood; and the murder follows, committed by means of a weapon the ownership of which is traced to the man who has made the threat. Then his glove, too, is found near the spot, and the money paid by him in the morning has disappeared. Is it possible to doubt that Mr. Ducis is the criminal, and that he meant what he said when he uttered the word 'blood'? He no doubt knew that his enemy habitually slept in that room, which was accessible from the veranda, and duly committed the murder and robbery."

Mr. Tim Maurice sighed again:

"What you say is very much like the reasoning of the prosecuting attorney on the trial," he replied, "but—"

"The evidence justified his theory—did it not?" said Dr. Haworth with an air of conviction.

"Well, the array of circumstances, I am afraid, was very strong. It was shown that poor Mr. Ducis had been obliged to sacrifice his property to raise the money; that he had spoken with violence when he said that he would have my brother's blood—and had even used similar expressions to others after the quarrel."

"The only weak point," said Dr. Haworth, thoughtfully, "is the improbability that a person of the character you attribute to Mr. Ducis—an honorable gentlemen—would have disturbed the money."

Mr. Maurice sighed again.

It seemed that sighing was to be a stated performance of Mr. Tim Maurice's during the interview.

"Unfortunately there was evidence as to that, too," he said.

"As to the theft !—the money?"

"Mr. Ducis was heard to say that he would recover the amount."

Dr. Haworth shook his head.

"I am afraid that concludes the matter," he said. "It is true

Mr. Ducis may have spoken hastily, and in a moment of passion—or may have merely intended to say that he would 'recover at law' from some one, on the plea of a forced and unfair sale of his property. But the conjecture is vague, and could have had little force."

"It was urged by his counsel, who stated that such was his meaning; and further, that the threat to have my brother's blood meant a personal encounter—a duel."

"A natural explanation—but the hammer and the glove?"

"He denied that the glove belonged to him."

"And the hammer—the murderer's weapon?"

"He acknowledged that it was similar to one he was in the habit of using—he had two or three like it—but was unable to explain how his own—if it was his own—had got into my brother's chamber."

"A fatal circumstance. Was no other defense set up but this general denial of the charge?"

"One strong plea—an alibi."

"Ah! an alibi? That is a very strong plea, indeed, Mr. Maurice, as it makes all others unnecessary. Was it established?"

"Unhappily it was not. Mr. Ducis alleged that on the night of the murder he was in an adjoining county. He had ridden to a warehouse on the railway, about fifteen miles distant, to purchase some fertilizers, and after doing so, as it was late in the evening, he had spent the night with a friend in the neighborhood."

"If he could show that his innocence was established. Could he?"

"He failed to do so—I will explain. When sworn on the trial, the friend with whom he had spent the night was unable to testify positively as to the day."

"But the warehouse man—the purchase of the fertilizers? Some record must have been made of the transaction."

"Yes—Mr. Ducis stated that he had made the purchase on the evening of the 7th of May, the date of my brother's murder, which took place the same night. When the ledger at the warehouse was examined, the date of the purchase was found to be the 8th.

"That was conclusive, unless—"

Dr. Haworth stopped and seemed to be reflecting.

"What do you mean, Doctor?"

"A curious idea occurred to me. Observe that the question is the guilt of Mr. Ducis or some unknown person—since the fact of the murder was established. If Mr. Ducis did not commit the crime, somebody else did."

"That is unanswerable."

"Well, now, adopt the theory that this some one wanted to shield himself by sacrificing Mr. Ducis. He obtains possession of or provides himself with the glove and hammer and places them near the scene of the crime. Then discovering afterwards that Mr. Ducis could prove an alibi he takes steps to defeat that. The real murderer learns the object of his victim's absence from home—follows and ascertains the purchase of the fertilizers—obtains access to the warehouse books, and alters the date. Erasure is easy, and when skillfully executed is difficult to detect."

Mr. Tim Maurice sighed once more.

"The ledger was produced in court, and there was no sign of any erasure," he said.

"Then the plea was necessarily of no effect—it was probably the last resort of a desperate man. All was traced home to him—his motive accounted for. Who other than himself could have had any inducement to commit the crime? Were there any other arrests?"

"Two—the woman Pitts, and my brother's manager, a man named Wilkins."

"Indeed! On what grounds?"

"That the woman, who was noted for her avarice, had known of the presence of the money in my brother's chamber, and had concealed herself with the view of robbing him. You will remember that I saw her come out of the chamber apparently concealing something under her apron."

"But the murder? She could scarcely have committed that."

"It was supposed that Wilkins was her confederate, and executed that part of the plan. He and my brother disliked each other, and the man was about to be discharged. The supposition was that he had entered into a conspiracy with the woman Pitts to murder my brother and carry off the money; that each had borne their part—he had entered the window and struck the blow, while she had seized the money on my brother's night-table; then that, hearing me coming, he had escaped and she had hidden behind the bed-curtains, and was attempting to get away when I came back with the brandy."

"The theory was plausible. What proofs were there?"

"None at all. The woman stated that she had heard my brother cry out, and hastened to the room, which she was leaving in horror when she met me; and the man's presence was not shown. Accordingly, connection in any manner with the murder was not established, and the two persons were discharged."

" And Mr. Ducis ? "

Mr. Tim Maurice uttered a deeper sigh than any that had pre-ceded it.

" He was convicted, and on the day succeeding his conviction was seized with paralysis, the effect, no doubt, of mental anguish, and this terminated life a few weeks later."

Dr. Haworth remained silent for some moments, evidently re-flecting upon this singular tissue of events.

" Well, that is a gloomy story," he said at length, "and I am not surprised to find that the chamber yonder is closed. The associa-tions with it must be painful. The elder Mrs. Maurice, I suppose, never again occupied it ? "

" Never. The murder of her husband had a fatal effect upon her. She was an invalid at the time and went into a decline, from which she never recovered."

" She could give no testimony in relation to the murder? "

" None—when she started from sleep she saw her husband was dying, and no one was in the apartment."

" A curious and tragic affair. It is not to be wondered at that it profoundly shocked her."

" It even produced an unfortunate effect upon her daughter Ellen—I mean my niece, the present Mrs. Maurice—and the death of her husband was an additional blow."

" Of Mr. John Maurice ? "

" Yes, he died a year or two afterwards. An unlucky family, you see," said the old gentleman mournfully. " But then, time does its work, and the sun has come out again. My niece and little Cary take a cheerful view of things, and my own temperament is sanguine and hopeful. Perhaps it would have been better not to tell you these old troubles; but you asked me about them—there is the carriage coming back."

The family vehicle was seen mounting the hill, driven by its sedate old coachman, and Dr Haworth went out and politely assisted the ladies as they emerged from it. As Miss Cary gave him a bright glance, he seemed well repaid for his trouble.

V.

CARY MAURICE.

DR. HAWORTH spent the day at Mauricewood, and his quiet courtesy made an agreeable impression. In the afternoon he and Miss Cary Maurice conversed on the veranda.

She was leaning back in a camp-chair, her rosetted slippers just emerging from the skirt of a painfully pulled-back dress, and with her large blue eyes under her brown bangs she looked very pretty.

"So you like our country?" she said to Dr. Haworth smiling.

"I like it very much," he said.

"I think uncle told me you lived in South America."

"Yes, near Lima, in sight of the cordilleras of the Andes. The country is peculiar, and differs from this."

"But you prefer it, I suppose, as it is home?"

"South America can hardly be called my home. I have no ties there, and am a native of the United States."

"If you have no ties I think you ought to come *home* then," said Miss Cary, smiling.

"I shall no doubt do so sooner or later," he said. "I am not specially fond of Peruvian society, and see very little of it. My chief resource is reading."

"A delightful resource!" exclaimed Miss Cary. "You prefer novels, of course?"

"I prefer criticism and biography. May I ask what you read?"

"Chiefly trash," said Miss Cary, laughing.

"Do you like it?"

"I am wrapped up in it! I have piles and piles of those dear 'library' books—I mean those *cheap* ones! They are full of Sir Edwards and Lady Evelyns, and my tastes are properly cultivated. I am strictly English!"

"Then you are not American? Why not read American literature?"

"There is none, or it is so stupid! That is, it is so dreadfully— well, American! Think of the delightful *ruins*, and the haunted towers, and mysterious strangers! My dear English novels are full of that! Of course it is all fearfully absurd, but it serves to pass the time."

"I see you are romantic, Miss Maurice. I am a stranger, but what a pity it is I am so commonplace and unmysterious."

"It is unfortunate," said Miss Cary, smiling; "but you know real life is always commonplace."

"I am not so sure of that," said Dr. Haworth; "you make me think of what your uncle told me this morning—the strange story of the locked-up room here."

"It is very sad," said the young lady. "So uncle told you?"

"Yes."

"It was before I was born, but I have often heard about it."

"What conclusion did you arrive at?"

"What conclusion?"

"Who was the real criminal—Mr. Ducis?"

"Oh, no! I am sure he was not. Mamma says it is impossi-. ble. She was acquainted with him, and very fond of him."

"But there was a criminal—who was he?"

"I do not know."

"You are certain Mr. Ducis was innocent?"

"Perfectly certain. I never believed a word of it."

"That proves, at least, that you have a generous nature; almost all women have."

"But I am not a woman!" protested Miss Cary. "I am an ex-school-girl only!"

"Yonder is the proof that you are not regarded in that derogatory light," said Dr. Haworth.

Miss Cary looked in the direction indicated by her companion's finger and saw Col. Ross coming into the grounds. His elegant drag, driven by a liveried servant and drawn by a very fine pair of horses, was just passing through the gate, flanked by its lofty white posts with ornamental tops.

"Col. Ross is a friend, I believe?" said Dr. Haworth.

"Yes," returned the young lady, with the rising inflection.

"No more? But the question, I confess, is unceremonious, and I hope you will pardon it, Miss Maurice."

Miss Cary Maurice made a little salute with her bangs in return for Col. Ross' bow—he was nearly at the door. She then turned to her companion and said innocently, "Did you ask if Col. Ross was a relation? None in the world. I have never heard of any connection between the Rosses and the Maurices."

Dr. Haworth said no more. and as Miss Cary rose to receive

her visitor, who was now on the veranda, her companion rose also.

Dr. Haworth's expression was entirely composed, Col. Ross' very different. A sudden glance indicated that the two men were not strangers.

"A pleasant evening," said Miss Cary, who had held out her hand.

Col. Ross bowed low as he received it and said:

"Very pleasant, indeed—I really enjoyed my ride."

"Dr. Haworth, Col. Ross," said Miss Cary.

The two gentlemen bowed, and as Mr. Tim Maurice made his appearance at the moment, general conversation followed. Miss Cary seemed to be in excellent spirits, and concentrated her attention upon Col. Ross, having apparently forgotten Dr. Haworth's existence. That gentleman, however, did not seem to observe the fact, conversed for a while with Mr. Maurice, and finally took his leave. As he rose to do so, Miss Cary turned quickly and said with a charming smile:

"You are not going?"

"I regret to be compelled to do so," said Dr. Haworth, bowing.

Miss Cary's face expressed mild regret, and the visitor then departed. As he rode away he said in a cold voice:

"I wonder if she cares for that man? I saw that he recognized me."

VI.

TWO HILL PEOPLE.

IN a gash of the hills some miles west of Mauricewood was a poor and mean-looking house, in a small yard surrounded by a dismantled fence, with a pig-sty near the door, a cur in his kennel, an ashbank beside it, broken utensils lying about, and some soiled clothes hanging out of a window with broken panes.

In the single room of this house, which conveyed an impression of utter pauperism and steady decay, sat a woman whose appearance accorded with her surroundings. She was tall and gaunt, with long gray hair falling in tangled masses upon her shoulders, her dress faded and slatternly, her huge feet thrust into list slippers bursting open at the seams. She was seated upon a low stool, resting her bony chin upon her two long hands, and her bony elbows in turn on her knees. Beside her was a wash-tub under the window, in which there was scarcely a fragment of glass. She was watching some bacon frying in a pan in the stone fireplace.

"You, Job Wilkins!" she shrilled.

No reply came.

"You worthless hound!"

Still silence.

"Now, you make out you don't hear me! Come here, I say!"

Steps approached; a snarl came from the cur and a shadow ran across the floor which the woman evidently observed, for she growled in great ill-humor:

"You are not worth your salt! What do you mean by slinking off whenever my eye's not on you to that doggery—and sponging on people for liquor to drink and leaving me here to do your work?"

She turned round to add the fire of a pair of bloodshot eyes to the force of her invective, but the newcomer was not Mr. Job Wilkins, but a well-dressed stranger—Dr. Haworth, in fact.

"Good morning, madam," he said, bowing.

Women never cease to be women—that is to say, something good remains in them. The surly face relaxed, and the woman rose with an expression of surprise.

"I have been hunting in the hills," said the visitor, who carried a carbine under his arm; "and am thirsty."

In response to this appeal to her hospitality the woman presented him with a gourd of water taken from a bucket on the window-sill, and with an attempt to suppress the natural gruffness of her voice, asked him if he would not sit down and rest.

"Thank you, madam," he said, taking a chair with a broken leg, which cracked as he seated himself. A commonplace colloquy of a few minutes followed, the woman having resumed her stool.

"Your place here is rather lonely," said the visitor. "I suppose you rarely hear any news."

"Not much," said the woman.

"There is very little stirring at present. The only topic of interest has been the great murder trial in Pennsylvania."

"A murder trial?"

"Yes, a curious case."

The visitor put his hand into his pocket as if reaching for something.

" I have left my newspaper at home," he said, " but I can tell you the substance of it. A Mr.—, Mr.—, well, the name is not important—was charged with the murder of a friend of his, who had just received a large sum of money."

The woman turned her head and listened attentively.

" The owner of the money was waylaid, it seems, as he was riding along a wood road and killed by a blow on the head, apparently with the butt end of a riding-whip."

" You don't say ! "

Dr. Haworth, who glanced carelessly at his companion, saw her turn a little pale—that is to say, as pale as her dirty complexion permitted.

" Yes—there seemed to be no doubt that his death took place in that manner, as there was a bruise on his left temple ; but an additional circumstance supported the idea."

The woman was looking at him with eyes wide open, unwinking.

" A riding-whip with a heavy leaden handle was found not far from the corpse. Whether dropped by the murderer or wrested from his hand by the murdered man, in the struggle, was not known. It was ascertained, however, to be the property of a neighboring farmer, who was thereupon arrested."

" He was the man, was he ? " the woman said, in a low voice.

" The strange fact is that he was not," replied Dr. Haworth, in a matter-of-fact tone.

" You don't tell me—! "

Listening carefully he could perceive that the woman was full of suppressed excitement.

" The owner of the whip was proved to be innocent. It was shown that on the day of the murder he was twenty miles off, and could not have committed it."

The woman had again rested her chin on her hands and her elbows on her knees, half turned away from her visitor. As she made no reply he went on.

" The real murderer was discovered by the merest accident," he said, " and the facts brought out on the trial proved that he was a skillful fellow. He had an enemy—the man first arrested—and meant to throw suspicion on him. He therefore bought a riding-whip precisely like that always used by his enemy, and cut the first letters of his enemy's name on the lead butt. He left this whip at the spot after committing the murder—the innocent man was of course arrested—and if he had not been able to prove the alibi, as it is called, he would have died on the gallows, for he and the murdered man were known to have quarreled a short time before, and he had been heard to make threats that he would have his blood."

The woman's face was now of a dead-ash color, and she was shaking a little.

" Well ? " she said, in a guttural tone.

" I see you are interested," continued her visitor, " and perhaps you would like me to tell you how the real murderer was discovered."

" Yes," the single word was uttered in a whisper.

" It was very simple. The murdered man had drawn the money from the bank on the same day—part in gold and part in notes. As he intended to make a large payment to one of his creditors he took one hundred dollar notes, and for safety requested the bank cashier to take down the numbers. You may not have observed, madam, but every bank-note has a particular number, and can be tracked if it is stolen. Say that I have a bundle of such bank-notes, and you or any one murder and rob me, then if the numbers are known, and you try to pass the notes, an officer of the law asks : ' Where did you get these notes ? ' "

The woman got up to turn the meat without looking at her visitor.

" That was just what happened in this case," he said ; " the bank-notes were traced by their numbers to the real murderer, who attempted to pass them ; he was arrested, and other circumstances were discovered which brought home the crime to him."

As Dr. Haworth said this a man came in, looking sidewise at him. This look was so sullen that the visitor unconsciously moved his carbine in such a manner as to be able to use it promptly. The new comer was, in fact, a most unpleasant-looking personage. He was tall, strong, slouching, with a hang-dog look, a wide mouth fouled with tobacco juice, and had the watchful eye of a beast of prey. As he had approached in mute silence it was probable that he had heard a part or the whole of the conversation.

" Sarvant, sir ! " he said, ducking his head and taking off a brown rag which served for a hat.

" The gentleman came for some water to drink," said the woman, in her gruff voice, but Dr. Haworth discerned a tremor in it. His attention, however, seemed to be concentrated upon the man, whose hooked fingers, with their dirty nails, resembled the talons of a hawk. He knew that this man was the former manager of Mr. James Maurice, and that the woman—now his wife apparently—was the former Mrs. Pitts, who had been seen coming out of the chamber of the murdered gentleman with her hands under her apron. He had tried the self-possession of the woman—he proceeded now to test that of the man.

The conversation which ensued lasted for half an hour. It resulted in nothing. The man Wilkins was either innocent, or a master of dissimulation. In the most natural manner he alluded to his poverty-stricken condition. The worst of it was that he couldn't please his wife. He had been well-off once—manager for a 'Squire Maurice, who was the best gentleman in life, but so hot-tempered and hard to please that he had to leave. Not that he had anything against 'Squire Maurice—he had nothing against him, and when some villain murdered him, which was done, he, Wilkins, had been struck all of a heap. He didn't mind telling that he himself had been charged with the murder, but some low folks done it, which the court discharged him immejiately. Then Mr. Wilkins looked with interest at the frying meat.

There was nothing to be gained by remaining longer, and Dr. Haworth got up and went away with his carbine under his arm toward his horse. Something was meantime passing in the cabin. The man had gone to a closet under the stairs in a corner, caught out a gun, and said to the woman, as he cocked the weapon—

" What do you say to givin' him a bullet ? "

" I say no ! You are a fool," growled the woman. " There's been trouble enough."

" As you say," the man replied, putting the gun back. " 'Twould be the shorter way. Who is he ? "

" How do I know ? "

" Well, mark what I tell you—trouble'll grow out of this."

" Mind your business and turn the meat," grated the woman. " I'll attend to matters."

Dr. Haworth had meanwhile gone into the thicket and mounted his horse to return to his temporary home in the hills. His face was gloomy and expressed mingled hatred and disgust. Were these creatures guilty of the murder ? There was nearly everything to support the supposition, but it was quite clearly a supposition,

VII.

AN AGREEABLE ENCOUNTER.

To reach his home in the hills, Dr. Haworth followed a road through the woods, along the foot of the range, catching a glimpse now and then of Mauricewood, two or three miles distant. He was riding on slowly with head bent down, when hearing hoof-strokes in front he looked up and saw Miss Cary Maurice, who had come out of a by-road and was galloping in the same direction which he himself was taking. He hastened to join her and bowed.

" Dr. Haworth ! " she exclaimed, with evident pleasure, " I am fortunate ! I have found an escort—and armed to protect me ! " she added, laughing, and looking at the carbine under his arm.

" I am glad to be of any service. I was out hunting," he said.

"And I am going to see a friend who promised me some ferns. Don't be shocked to find me riding without an escort. Our neighborhood is very orderly, and then everybody knows me. So you see it is the pleasure of your company, not the want of a protector, which inspired my friendly speech."

" It is good to be friendly," returned Dr. Haworth. " We are nearly strangers, but I hope on better acquaintance you and your family will find me worthy of your regard—that our relations will be cordial."

" Why should they not be ? You are quite a friend of the family already."

Miss Cary uttered the words in a cheerful manner, and with a dangerous glance. She was an attractive object in her black riding-habit, defining the graceful figure with her roses, her brown curls, and her little head inclined sidewise. As he glanced at her, Dr. Haworth seemed to forget his harsh emotion, and his face relaxed.

" Thank you," he said. " I am glad to be regarded as the friend of your family, and then there is nothing I like so much as friendly expressions."

" I prefer flattering ones ! " said Miss Cary.

Dr. Haworth looked at the bright face and said :

" Then I will tell you what I thought when I saw you riding in front of me a moment ago."

" What you thought ? "

" I was thinking how beautiful you were."

" What a delicious speech ! " cried Miss Cary, with the least possible increase of color.

" I will venture to add that you recalled to me two passages in a book I have been reading."

" Was it trash ? "

" No, it was a volume of Count Pontmartin's, the great French critic, who is a favorite of mine."

" Well, do tell me the passages you thought of when you saw me. I hope they were complimentary ? "

" You shall judge for yourself. The critic is speaking of an author whom he admires, and says that his works have an attraction only to be described by the word ' charm.' "

" That is—well, charming ! "

" He then defines this charm. It is what the Italians mean by the term sympathy—the indefinable something, which charms, but cannot be described."

Miss Cary made a bow, blushing a little under his glance.

" Shall I now tell you the other passage ? "

" If you please ! "

" This time it is Prosper Merimee. He writes to his ' unknown,' describing a lady whom he has just met. She is beautiful, faultlessly dressed, a queen of the salon, he says ; but he adds, addressing his fair unknown : She has not that inexpressible something, which you have, and which I cannot express—except by saying that it is a something which makes people love you."

" That is really exquisite," Miss Cary said, laughing a little hastily, " but I am afraid I am taking you out of your way."

" Out of my way ! I have no business," said Dr. Haworth, composedly.

" But you were going home—"

" There is nothing to attract me there."

" But you have been hunting—I am sure you are hungry ! It would be wrong to impose upon you ! "

It was obvious that Miss Cary Maurice considered that the conversation had taken a dangerous direction.

" I am not hungry," he said.

" But—really—it is not to be thought of."

" Allow me at least to accompany you as far as your friends,"

This proposition seemed to relieve Miss Cary.

"Thank you, I will accept your escort so far with pleasure. Yonder is the house," she said.

They were opposite a small lodge in an opening of the woods— a cheerful establishment, nearly overgrown with creeping vines, and surrounded by nicely-trimmed sward, scattered through which were borders of autumn flowers in full bloom. The place indeed was a bower of verdure, flowers, and bees, which were humming merrily in the sunshine

"I won't detain you," said Miss Cary to her companion, as he assisted her to the ground.

"I should like to know your friend."

As it was impossible to refuse, Miss Cary said:

"I will introduce you with pleasure.".

"What is his name?"

"Professor Lesner."

VIII.

PROF. LESNER.

AT the name of Prof. Lesner Dr. Haworth turned his head quickly. Miss Cary, however, was arranging the skirts of her riding-habit at the moment, and did not observe his surprise.

He was very much surprised, indeed. Nothing could have been more unexpected than the singular chance which was then about to throw him again with the friend of Mr. Burdette, the opium-smoker of the "joint" in Mott street. He was aware of the fact that on Mrs. Maurice's Northern tour she had been accompanied by Prof. Lesner, but it had never occurred to him that the Professor resided in the Mauricewood neighborhood—he had, in fact, forgotten his existence. Now it seemed they were about to meet again, and Dr. Haworth asked himself if the old scholar would recognize him. It was improbable. When they met in Mott street he was in no condition to remember anything. It was much the most probable supposition that he would not connect Dr. Haworth, the friend of Miss Maurice, with the unknown stranger of New York—and so it proved.

Prof. Lesner came out of his house in a dressing-gown and slippers, with his gray hair upon his shoulders, and smiling kindly. The visit of Miss Cary evidently delighted him.

"It does my old heart good to see you, my dear little rosebud," he said, squeezing her hand.

"Thank you, dear Prof. Lesner—you always make charming speeches," returned the young lady. "This is my friend, Dr. Haworth—Prof. Lesner, Dr. Haworth."

"I am glad to know any friend of Miss Cary's," said the Professor, bowing courteously.

It was plain that he had not recognized him. There were no indications of opium about the old scholar, and Dr. Haworth hoped he had discontinued the evil habit when once beyond temptation.

"But come in," he said hospitably; "I was reading, but not much interested."

"I generally find you among your flowers and bees when you are not with your birds," said Miss Cary.

The Professor sighed, looking around him sadly. "My poor flowers have nearly all left me," he said, "and my bees, too. I have lost twenty swarms and have now scarcely a hundred. Then my pets, my canaries, are dying in some mysterious manner. I have only two hundred left. Come, little one!"

He held out his finger and a beautiful canary darted from a window and perched upon it, turning his bright head from side to side.

"That is my aviary. I thought I would give them a little sunshine to-day. They are too good to fly away," said the Professor, smiling and caressing the canary.

Miss Cary Maurice laughed.

"Scarcely a hundred swarms of bees, and two hundred canary birds left—just listen, Dr. Haworth! We shall next be told that the mice have devoured all your folio volumes but one hundred thousand."

"I have not so many, Miss Cary—you know I am a poor scholar, only. But I have many things to cheer me in my lonely life—your bright face is one of them."

"Well, I told you before that you were charming, Prof. Lesner! Have you the ferns you promised me weeks ago?"

"Oh, yes. I would have brought them, but my health has been so bad."

He went into a little sitting-room on the right of the entrance, the walls of which were nearly covered by books, and brought to the porch a large portfolio filled with delicate ferns.

"These are all arranged with both their scientific and common

—I will not say vulgar—names beneath them. I fear you will find the portfolio cumbersome."

" Oh, no. I can easily take it."

" You are very welcome. Always try to find something that I can do to please you."

And Prof. Lesner beamed on the young lady, who renewed her thanks, and then rose to go.

" You will not leave me so soon!" he protested.

"'Thank you, but I am afraid I shall have to go now. You are very good—come and see us soon."

And the amiable Professor, having declared that as soon as he could stir out, his very first visit should be to Mauricewood, Miss Cary shook hands and was assisted to her saddle by Dr. Haworth. He had brought out the portfolio of ferns and Miss Cary now extended her hand to take it, but Dr. Haworth responded by mounting, with the portfolio still beneath his arm.

" It would be impossible for you to carry such a load," he said, " and it is too late for you to return without an escort."

Dr. Haworth then touched his horse, whose head was turned in the direction of Mauricewood, and Miss Cary was obliged to follow. If she expected the conversation to take a romantic turn, she was mistaken.

" A curious person," said Dr. Haworth. " I mean Prof. Lesner. Is he a friend of yours?"

" Oh, yes; we have known him all our lives."

" Then he has always lived here?"

" Ever since I can remember. He was once professor in some college, I believe, but retired, and spends his life in studying and writing. I think he has written some work which is to be published in New York, but I do not know upon what subject."

Dr. Haworth knew, but respected the Professor's secret.

" You describe a scholar and recluse," he said. " Your friend is evidently devoted to country life and innocent pleasures."

" You mean his birds and bees. He is devoted to them ; and it is the most rational life, is it not ? I mean, to live quietly and happily ? "

" I can hardly say. My own life has passed mainly in action of some description, and not always happily," said Dr. Haworth.

" I am sorry—in action? "

" In laboring for my livelihood and otherwise. I was poor."

"That is said to be the test of character and the preface to distinction, Dr. Haworth," said the young lady earnestly.

"It has tested mine if not given me any distinction. But perhaps Prof. Lesner's is the truest philosophy—repose is best—where one can enjoy it."

"I hope you are able to do so."

"No, I have an object in life still unaccomplished."

His grave, almost cold, tone indicated that he was not uttering a gallant speech, and Cary Maurice said earnestly:

"If I were a man I would offer to assist you if I could."

"You cannot—but you can do one thing."

"What is that?"

"You can hope for my success. It is a worthy object I have in view."

"I am sure it is, and I do hope you will succeed in it."

He went on for some moments in silence, and then said in a low voice:

"I am glad you have given me that assurance. My life has been rather sad—I have not had many persons to sympathize with me—thus I value your regard and would like to have an opportunity to prove my own—that I am your very faithful friend."

"I am sure you are," said Miss Cary Maurice in an earnest tone.

"Then we understand each other, we are friends?"

He held out his ungloved hand.

"Yes, with all my heart."

She drew off her own glove and gave him her hand; he felt its soft and warm pressure. At the same moment the horses stopped. They were at the Mauricewood gate.

Dr. Haworth looked up—on the veranda of the Mauricewood house stood Col. Ross, and his superb riding-horse was at the rack near.

"Shall I go further, or do you wish me to leave you now?" said Dr. Haworth.

"How coldly you say that! What is the matter?" exclaimed the young lady, looking up at him impulsively.

"You have a visitor. One of the greatest blunders a man can commit is—to be *de trop*."

"You will not be *de trop*! The idea!"

"Do you wish me to come?"

"Certainly! You know how very glad we all are to see you,"

" Col. Ross may remain all night."

" Why should not Dr. Haworth remain also, then ? " said Miss Cary, smiling.

" Because one is a stranger—myself I mean ; and the other an old friend. He is more than a friend, perhaps."

" More ? " she said quickly. " I assure you you are mistaken, sir ! "

" No more ? " he persisted, looking steadily at her.

" Not the least bit ! " said Miss Cary, laughing.

" Well, to be frank, I am glad to know that," said Dr. Haworth coolly, " but I find, after all, that I shall be obliged to return home."

And as they had reached the house now, he assisted the young lady to dismount, bowed and departed.

IX.

COL. ROSS TAKES A NIGHT RIDE.

COL. ROSS didn't remain at Mauricewood later than about 8 in the evening. At that hour he rose, bowed deferentially, and alleging business in Abbeyville on his way home, took his departure.

The moon was shining, and he rode on slowly with an expression of decided discomposure. He had not been able to exchange more than a few commonplaces with Miss Cary Maurice in the midst of the family circle ; but that hardly accounted for his expression of moody displeasure. In fact, Col. Ross was thinking of something very different, as some muttered words now and then indicated.

What had occurred was this : On his arrival at Mauricewood he had found Mrs. Maurice confined to her room by a headache, and Miss Cary absent, but Mr. Tim Maurice received and entertained him. They had entered into a conversation, and a chance allusion by the old gentleman to Dr. Haworth had naturally led Col. Ross to say :

" He is a visitor in the neighborhood, I believe ? "

" A gentleman traveling for his pleasure, and a very agreeable man, I assure you," replied Uncle Tim.

Col. Ross inclined his head politely, but said :

" My experience, Mr. Maurice, is a little opposed to putting too much confidence in strangers—unaccredited people. I do not mean, of course, to say anything to the prejudice of your friend Dr. Haworth, for he seems to have become a friend of the family."

"Why, yes; he is very intelligent, and plays the best game of chess I ever saw!"

"I know that you consider that an admirable trait in anybody," said Col. Ross; "but it is not a guarantee of character."

"I believe Dr. Haworth to be perfectly open and honorable."

"No doubt, and you say he is intelligent?"

"Extremely so. I was much struck by his acuteness the other day, when I was telling him of our unfortunate family tragedy—my brother's death, you know."

"Ah! you told him about that old affair?"

"Yes, he seemed curious to hear the details, and, I observed, listened with the closest attention. Afterwards in discussing the question of Mr. Ducis' connection with the murder he indicated great acuteness of intellect. He suggested as Mr. Ducis' probable defense the one actually set us by his counsel—even to the possible erasure in the warehouse ledger by the real criminal. You will remember the case."

"Yes," said Col. Ross, speaking slowly with his eyes fixed upon the opposite wall, "I believe I remember."

"I have some reason, you see, for speaking of Dr. Haworth as a man of intelligence," added Mr. Tim Maurice.

"Yes."

"I should call him a man of great penetration. All his comments on the case proved that."

"He had a theory, of course, as to the real murderer?" said Col. Ross.

"Yes. He was clearly of opinion that Mr. Ducis was guilty—if not, then Wilkins and the woman Pitts; that one struck the blow and the other carried off the money."

Col. Ross made no reply to this for a moment; he then said:

"So strange a story must have interested Dr. Haworth."

"He seemed very much interested. Such puzzles, he said, had always had a great attraction for him."

"They have for most people—and your friend inquired into every detail?"

"Minutely. If he had been a detective he could scarcely have been more curious," said Mr. Maurice, smiling.

"He is not probably a detective," replied Col. Ross coolly, "but then you will not think me intrusive, I hope, Mr. Maurice, if I add that he is—a stranger."

" Well, stranger or not, he is a delightful fellow !" cried Uncle Tim, with friendly warmth ; " quiet in his manners, thoroughly well-bred, and plays a superb game of chess."

As Miss Cary had made her appearance at this moment the discussion of Dr. Haworth's merits and demerits proceeded no further, and Col. Ross had concentrated his attention on the young lady. She had not received him with much warmth. His quick eye detected an almost imperceptible alteration in her manner. It was perfectly courteous, but the *riante* ease which habitually characterized it was absent, and Col. Ross, moodily reflecting, attributed the change to Miss Cary's riding companion.

Hence the impression of displeasure on his face as he rode back toward Abbeyville through the moonlight. As he reflected, his eyebrows steadily contracted and a sullen fire kindled beneath them.

" What is this man's errand here ? " he muttered. " Who is he ? I know his name and heard of his visit to the United States, but what brings him here ?   What is he trying to find out ? "

He reflected for a moment and added in the same tone :

" He may only be interested in a puzzle—a ' mysterious crime,' as the newspapers head their reports.   But there is the chance—it is possible—whatever his motive is he may make trouble."

Col. Ross drew rein as he said this, and his horse stopped. Looking toward the hill country west of Mauricewood, he hesitated, reflected and said at length :

" I will put them on their guard.   That old. chatterbox yonder has given him the names, and he will be sure to hunt them up—he may have already done so."

Col. Ross then turned into a side road winding through woods, went on at full gallop and in about three-quarters of an hour was in front of the cabin occupied by the man and woman visited by Dr. Haworth.   The presence of the horseman was announced by a violent barking from the cur.   At this the slatternly woman came to the door and peered out.   Col. Ross had dismounted, and as he was within a few feet of her, she had no difficulty in recognizing him.

" Has a stranger been here ? " he said, in a brief and abrupt tone.

" Yes."

" Heavy brown mustache, sunburnt, middle height, and looks straight through you ? "

" That's him."

" What did he want ? "

" A gourd of water—he was out hunting."

" It was a mistake. He was hunting for *you*."

The woman changed color, but made no reply.

" What did he say to you! " continued Col. Ross, in the same abrupt tone.

" He talked about a murder trial somewhere—and tracking up some bank-notes."

" Well ? "

" The man that murdered the other one was found out by the figures on the notes."

" Well ? "

" And he was hung," said the woman, with a slight shiver.

" Well ? "

At each repetition of the word " well " the voice of the speaker seemed to grow colder and more threatening.

" Then he left," added the woman, " and Job wanted to put a bullet in him."

" The best thing he could have done," said Col. Ross, coldly. " Is he in there ? "

" Yes."

" Call him here. I have something to say to him—and you."

" Better come in and say it quiet. There's never any certainty that nobody's near by."

She looked around her as if suspecting the presence of some eavesdropper, but there was only the mangy cur in his kennel, the pig-sty, the ash heap, the broken fence and the scraggy thicket.

" You are right," Col. Ross said. " What I have to say had better be said without listeners."

He then went into the house and the door closed. After about half an hour he came out again and mounted his horse. The man Wilkins had followed him to the fence.

" Remember what I told you," Col. Ross said in a low tone. " Be on your guard. This man is cool, strong, rich, and it will not do to try to frighten him. That means he is dangerous. If he comes back here take care what you say."

" If he comes back I'll put an ounce of lead into him."

" Well—that's your affair."

He touched his horse, set forward, and reaching the main road was heard galloping toward Abbeyville. The man Wilkins had gone back into the house and shut the door.

It seemed that the woman with the dishevelled hair had given Col. Ross some very good advice. As soon as the cabin door closed, something which resembled a moving shadow detached itself from the rear of the cabin which was opposite the moon and gained the thicket in which it disappeared. This shadow was Jean Baptiste, and his presence can be accounted for in a very simple manner. He had grown a little uneasy about Dr. Haworth, who had not returned at nightfall, and fearing that some accident had happened to him in hunting, Jean, who had nothing else to do, followed the hoof-prints of his horse. This was not difficult, as a slight rain had fallen the night before, and there was little travel on the mountain roads. He traced the hoof-prints to the cabin of the two hill people, and was about to approach and inquire if any one had seen Dr. Haworth when Col. Ross made his appearance. As Jean was quite concealed from view in the thicket he remained quiet, listened to the colloquy between the woman and her visitor ; and when they went into the house gained the rear where there was a small window. Through this he had cautiously looked, but could only see that the three persons were in earnest conversation. As they spoke in a low tone it was impossible to hear them.

After the departure of Col. Ross, Jean, knowing that his further stay was useless, stole away and went back rapidly to the home in the hills, where he found Dr. Haworth, who had just returned from Mauricewood.

X.

DR. HAWORTH DISCOVERS A LIKENESS.

WHEN Dr. Haworth rode to Mauricewood some days after these incidents and was told that the ladies had again driven out, his expression of disappointment might have revealed a great deal to Mr. Tim Maurice if he had been a person of curious disposition. In truth, with Cary Maurice absent there was no longer any sunshine at Mauricewood, and even Mr. Tim Maurice's cheerful talk did not seem to entertain his guest. It was only when the old gentleman said : " We had a visit from Col. Ross last night," that Dr. Haworth seemed to arouse himself.

" He is a tolerably frequent visitor, I believe, Mr. Maurice ? " he said, speaking in his habitually composed tone.

" Yes, he has become quite regular in his attentions to—my niece Ellen and myself," replied Uncle Tim, jocosely.

" You mean, I suppose, to Miss Maurice ? "

" Yes, I mean that."

" He is paying her his addresses ? "

" I think there can be no doubt of it."

" Is she going to marry him ? "

" Well," that is rather a puzzling question. Women are wondrous in their way, and wondrous uncertain—also, unfathomable. Books say so. I don't know much about them myself."

" Will you permit me to ask you a question, Mr. Maurice ? It may appear a little unceremonious."

" Certainly. Do so without ceremony."

" Do you and Mrs. Maurice approve of Col. Ross' attentions ? "

" Well," said Uncle Tim, dubiously, " I never meddle in such matters myself, and Ellen—Mrs. Maurice—has great confidence in Cary. I suppose I may say that what Cary thinks will probably decide the matter."

" Pardon me for saying that you have not answered my question."

" Your question ? "

" If Miss Maurice's family approve of an alliance with Col. Ross. Frankly, I do not particularly admire him."

Mr. Tim Maurice laughed heartily.

" Well, do you know that it is pretty much my own senti.nent," he said. " It is curious, but there is something about our friend the Colonel which rather jars on one at times. It is hard to say what it is—but there it is."

Dr. Haworth reflected for a moment—then he said :

" I have no doubt Col. Ross has made me the subject of conversation, and asked what brought me to the neighborhood."

" Yes, he asked me the question."

" Well, then, I am fairly entitled to ask you who he is, in my turn."

" He is the son of a gentleman of this county who died about twenty years ago. Young Ross was educated for the navy, and spent some years cruising, I believe, but afterwards resigned and entered the Chilian army or navy, I think. He is now a guano or nitrate contractor or agent, I hear."

" He is rich, I believe ? "

" He is said to be very rich."

" Well, I presume he acquired his wealth in South America, and where I understand you to say he has always lived when not on his cruises, until recently."

" He has not always lived there. When he was a young man of from 20 to 25 he succeeded to his father's estate, and was frequently at home."

" You were no doubt acquainted with him at that time."

" Yes, but the acquaintance was slight. He was rather—well, what is called wild."

You mean dissipated."

" That is the polite word. But it is rather too polite to express the exact idea. Young Ross was what is vulgarly called a ' hard case.' I remember an unlucky affair of his in which my poor brother was concerned."

" Your brother, Mr. James Maurice ? "

" Yes, he was a magistrate, and young Ross was brought before him in Abbeyville for some drunken misconduct. My brother was anxious to let him off with an admonition, but he openly insulted the court, told my brother in fact that he was an ' old fool '—and was committed to jail for contempt."

" Ah ! Then your brother and the present Col. Ross were possibly not very good friends ? "

" Very naturally they were not. My brother felt that he had been unwarrantably insulted, and young Ross professed to regard his commitment to jail as a gross outrage ; he went so far, it is said, as to swear that my brother should smart for it."

" Ah ! " Dr. Haworth said once more. His companion's reminiscences seemed to interest him very much.

" If that incident occurred about twenty years ago," he said, " it must have been about the time of Mr. James Maurice's death."

" I think it just preceded it."

" I suppose there was little intimacy between young Ross and your family ? "

" None at all."

" He was not acquainted with the present Mrs. Maurice ? "

" It is possible—yes ; I remember seeing him at Mauricewood, but not more than once or twice, I think."

" And Mr. John Maurice was also a stranger to him ? "

" Yes—no. Really, I anr remembering a number of things. It was said that the two young men had not only known each other, but had a quarrel about a woman—in South America. John was attache there, and I remember there was some vague talk of a duel, or quarrel at least, between him and our friend the Colonel, who was then a naval officer."

" Ah ! a quarrel ? "

" About some woman, as I said. Yru see, they make all the trouble—which makes me keep clear of the dear creatures, Doctor. Yes, there was certainly a quarrel of some sort between young Ross and John Maurice, and that may have explained his absence from the wedding."

" Mr. John Maurice's wedding ? "

" Yes. I remember he was not present."

Dr. Haworth nodded.

" After all, you are better acquainted with Col. Ross than you think, Mr. Maurice," he said ; "and as he is received at Maurice-wood now in so friendly a manner, it is a proof that he has reformed the objectionable traits in his character—if there were such."

" I have no doubt that he has done so."

" Then you will not oppose his matrimonial views ? "

Mr. Tim Maurice made a dubious movement with his lips and said :

" Well, I should be sorry to see Cary marry him, with all his wealth, as he and poor John were enemies. It is natural to take up the family dislike, you see."

" You were no doubt attached to young Mr. Maurice ? "

"·Attached to him ! I was devoted to him. He was a splendid youngster ; as brave as steel, as firm as a rock, and you had only to look at him to see that he was a noble fellow."

" You speak with enthusiasm."

" Well, not extravagantly. We have his portrait."

" Ah ! "

" Would you like to see it ? It is in my niece's chamber, but she will not mind my taking you up."

" I should be very glad to see it."

" Then you need only follow, Doctor."

Mr. Tim Maurice led the way up the winding staircase with the elastic step of a boy, followed by Dr. Haworth, and they reached the second floor, where a neatly-matted hall, corresponding to that down stairs, gave access to the numerous apartments. Mr. Maurice opened a door on the right and entered a chamber of lofty pitch, with lace curtains, an old-fashioned bedstead, with tall posts and a tester, and many easy-chairs disposed in front of a wide fireplace, where a wood fire was burning on ancient brass andirons. Over the narrow, carved mantelpiece was a fine oil painting representing a very handsome young man of about 25, with blue eyes, short, black curls, and a frank and open smile.

" There is poor John's picture," said Uncle Tim.

Dr. Haworth looked up at it. It was the most remarkable likeness of Jean Baptiste.

At the same moment the voice of Miss Cary was heard calling from the hall below :

" Where are you, Uncle ? "

XI.

PROF. LESNER'S THEORY.

DR. HAWORTH rode away from Mauricewood a little before sunset. Cary's hand had remained in his own a moment as he bowed and took leave. She was charming as she leaned back in her arm-chair, looking up at him out of her great blue eyes, with a little color in her cheeks and a happy smile. His own fixed look made the roses redder, and then the following dialogue ensued :

" You have forgotten the portfolio, Miss Maurice."

" Oh, you must not trouble yourself to take it."

" It is no trouble."

" I can return it to Prof. Lesner by a servant."

" He may wish it—it is scarcely a quarter of a mile out of my way."

" You are very kind then."

And Miss Cary delivered the portfolio, after which Dr. Haworth rode away. He went on in profound thought and reached Prof. Lesner's just at sunset. That gentleman was seated on a rustic bench with a canary singing beside him, a bunch of autumn blooms in his button-hole, and reading a folio volume which rested on his knees.

" Dr. Haworth, if my poor eyes do not deceive me," he said, rising courteously.

His visitor bowed.

" Miss Maurice requested me to return your portfolio, sir—that which contained the ferns."

" It was unnecessary; I had quite lost sight of it. Sit down, Doctor, sit down."

And the benignant old Professor pointed to the rustic bench, which was large enough for two or three persons.

" I was reading—it is nearly my only amusement," he said. " I am a little lonely now and then, as I have never married—a great mistake—but I manage to pass the time."

" Reading is occupation," Dr. Haworth said. He had taken his seat resolving to remain a few moments.

" A great resource," returned the smiling old Professor.

" But a more effectual means still of killing time is writing—I mean literary composition."

" I have found that true, Doctor."

" You write, then ? "

" Yes, a little on scientific subjects."

" On physical science, perhaps ? "

" Yes; I know of no other."

" There is the psychological."

Prof. Lesner looked at his visitor. The title of his work about to be published by Mr. Burdette was the " Psychology of Opium."

Prof. Lesner, seeing only a composed face opposite to him, which indicated nothing, shook his head and replied :

" I am afraid the term psychological, as applied to science, is misleading. The soul—if there is one—is a mystery, and we know nothing of it."

" Do you doubt the existence of a soul in man ? "

Prof. Lesner did not reply for a moment. He then said mildly :

" Is it proved to exist ? The body exists."

" Are you certain ? "

" I think I am," said Prof. Lesner smiling. " My senses prove its existence."

" The senses are not trustworthy. You are no doubt aware of the phenomena accompanying hallucination ? "

" Yes."

" That certain excellent people distinctly see the dead come into the room where they sit ? "

" Yes, Doctor ; but these excellent people have diseased senses.

In a normal state these same senses are reliable, and the only reliance."

" You attach no faith, then, to the inborn sentiment of the existence of a soul and a future life ? "

" I am obliged to repeat, Doctor, that nothing is proved. Evolution—development—that is demonstrated."

" That man descends or ascends from the monkeys ? "

The Professor laughed.

" That is one of the popular phrases which obscure scientific discussion."

" Phrases often have a rude truth in them," said Dr. Haworth, " as where Mr. Carlyle calls the development theory the 'Gospel of dirt.' "

" A hardy adversary, my dear Doctor ! But Mr. Carlyle was not a sound thinker. He was all his life tormented by dyspepsia. That clouds the mind."

" No doubt—he was a sufferer like Heine, though, unlike Heine, he never resorted to anodynes."

" Heine was a very great genius," said Prof. Lesner.

" And believed in nothing but the agony in his spine. It is not surprising that he lived on opium."

" It is not surprising," said Prof. Lesner, sighing ; " and he was much more excusable than Coleridge."

" You blame Coleridge ? "

" Of course, Doctor. Poor Heine was incessantly wracked with pain, but it is not said that Coleridge was. He fell a victim to the drug from weakness of will and the force of circumstances."

" I have forgotten the details. Did he smoke or use the drug in the form of laudanum ? "

" The latter, I believe."

" Smoking seems to be the method preferred by the Chinese—at least, the papers say so of the Chinese population of New York." '

" I—think so," said Prof. Lesner sadly.

Dr. Haworth, who had directed the conversation to the opium subject more from inadvertence than design, felt a sentiment of compunction as he looked at the sad face and gray hair of his companion. He had no desire whatever to make the application of his views personal, or reveal his knowledge of the scene in Mott street. Here was an old scholar, who had, no doubt, accidentally contracted the habit of using opium, probably like De Quincey, to relieve physical pain at first, and finally as a source of mental enjoyment in his lonely condition. It was unfortunate—there all ended.

"Well, I believe it is conceded, sir," he said, "that the opium habit, under whatever form, is unfortunate. It is said to subjugate the will and destroy a man's energy. But let us change the topic. I am returning from an agreeable visit to Mauricewood."

"A delightful place!" said old Prof. Lesner, brightening up.

"You know the family—the rest as well as Miss Maurice?"

"Oh, yes! They are all my attached friends."

"I congratulate you upon having such attractive neighbors."

"Yes, I always feel as if the sunshine were coming out when I am in sight of the house," said Prof. Lesner cheerfully, "though I seldom leave home."

"That is very poetical and very just—your description. The family deserve some credit, too, for their cheerfulness under the circumstances."

"The circumstances?" said the Professor, with a puzzled look.

"I referred to the unfortunate affair which took place, you know, at Mauricewood—the murder of Mr. Maurice."

The Professor sighed and said:

"I suppose Mr. Tim Maurice mentioned it. Yes, it was a touching affair. But time wears away the memory of almost everything, Doctor. Miss Cary was not born and her mother has, I think, nearly forgotten it. It occurred, I think—yes—fully twenty years ago."

"A very singular affair. I confess it has puzzled me completely to arrive at any satisfactory conclusion in reference to it."

"You mean as to the real person who committed the crime— yes, that is still a mystery."

"Have you ever framed an hypothesis?" said Dr. Haworth. yielding to the temptation to discuss what had become his possessing idea. Prof. Lesner shook his head.

"None that satisfies me," he replied.

"I understood that you doubt whether Mr. Ducis was the criminal?"

"I could never believe it. His character contradicted the very idea. In spite of the terribly circumstantial evidence, I could never convince myself that Mr. Ducis was in any manner connected with the crime."

"Was the woman—the servant or housekeeper?"

" That also seems improbable. Women are not apt to commit murder by means of deadly weapons."

" There was a man, a manager, I believe, with whom Mr. Maurice had quarreled. I think he was arrested and charged with the murder."

" Yes, but both he and the woman were discharged, as there was no proof against them."

" Still, the crime was actually committed. Mr. Maurice died by violence, and some one must have been concerned in the event."

Prof. Lesner nodded and seemed to reflect. He then said:

" This is the first time in many years that the subject has been recalled to my mind. . I remember, however, the drift of my speculations at the time. You will probably differ with me in my conclusion, however; it has not much, I confess, to support it."

" You came to a conclusion, then ? " said Dr. Haworth, turning his head quickly.

" Yes."

" I should be very much interested if you would state it."

" I will do so with pleasure, though it will probably appear absurd. After reflecting upon the whole matter, I concluded in my own mind that Mr. Maurice was not murdered at all."

" Not murdered ? "

" That he himself was the author of the accident which resulted in his death."

" He himself ?—the accident ? "

" Yes—an accident so simple that from its very simplicity it never occurred to anybody. If you have observed the floors at Mauricewood you must have admired their high polish which is the result of continuous scrubbing. There was formerly, and I believe is still, in the South, a great preference for bare floors, which are much cooler in the summer than those covered with carpeting or matting. The only objection to them is the defacement produced by grease or other stains; and this has always been counteracted by laborious scrubbing with a heavy block of wood to the face of which is affixed a stiff brush or a mat of corn ' shucks,' as we call them. A long handle is inserted into the block, and by dragging it to and fro a very smooth surface and high polish is produced by the friction."

" Yes, yes, I understand, sir. But—your theory——"

" I will proceed to state it, my dear Doctor. If it seems fanci-

3

ful it will do no harm. My theory, then, is that the chamber occupied by Mr. Maurice on the night of the marriage was thus scrubbed
to a degree which rendered it slippery. He probably rose during
the night, possibly to close the window, which may have been left
open, and putting on his slippers attempted to do so."

" And—"

" You understand me, I see. He slipped and lost his balance,
and in falling struck his temple against an angle of the carved bedstead, uttered a cry of pain, and staggering to the bed groaned so
that he waked his wife—the whole resulting in his death from syncope."

Dr. Haworth, who had listened attentively, shook his head and
said :

" I fear that theory is what you call it—fanciful. How are we
to account for the disappearance of the money, and the hammer
and glove ? "

" I have never been able to do so. Everything is pure conjecture. As to the first—the sum in gold and bank-notes which Mr.
Maurice was supposed to have placed on his night-table when he
undressed—the evidence, I think, was rather vague. It was shown,
if I remember aright, that he did place it there. If so, it was, of
course, stolen—possibly by the housekeeper—or it may have been
knocked from the table by Mr. Maurice in regaining the bed after his
fall, and afterwards found by some dishonest servant under the bed."

" That is possible, but not probable."

" But we are driven to conjecture, and I grant you all this is
pure supposition. It seems tolerably certain that some one must
have stolen the sum, unless Mr. Maurice used it, of which there is
no proof."

" And the gloves and hammer ? "

" As I said, I could never account for either. The hammer was
apparently of the sort only used for chipping rock specimens. I
examined it, I remember. But it was utterly unreasonable to convict Mr. Ducis merely on the strength of so trifling a circumstance."

" But the buckskin riding-glove ? "

" That was more absurd still. The hammer was a hammer and
the glove was a glove, and they were both found near the scene of
the crime, that was all. To prove that they were the property of
Mr. Ducis or some other murderer was essential, if that was all the
evidence."

"Your view is singular," said Dr. Haworth thoughtfully. "I can scarcely say that it convinces me."

"It is merely suggested in reply to your question what I thought of the affair, Doctor."

Dr. Haworth bowed.

"I am much interested in this enigma," he said, "a common weakness in the case of idle people. I see you regard Mr. Ducis as an innocent man—what is your opinion of the question of the alibi set up by the defense?"

"I have always thought that Mr. Ducis was really absent at the time of the murder, and that the register on the warehouse books was simply a clerical error."

"A clerical error?"

"Yes, Doctor. Mr. Ducis, I remember, stated that he had made some purchases on a certain day—the day of the murder— and not returned home until the next day. The warehouse ledger contradicted him, but it is probable that the clerk or proprietor had neglected to make the entry of the purchase on the day before, and possibly seeing Mr. Ducis pass on his way home was reminded of his forgetfulness, and from oversight made the entry as of that date. This, you see, would allow for the fact that the warehouse ledger did not establish the alibi."

"A trifle involving a man's life!"

"Yes, unhappily, what are called trifles very often do. I am only trying to establish an hypothesis, you see, consistent with Mr. Ducis' innocence. The ledger seemed to show that he had not made the purchases on the day of Mr. Maurice's death, but on the day succeeding. There was another hypothesis that you may regard as the most fanciful of all, but it really occurred to me."

"What was that?"

"That Mr. Maurice's death was the result of a deep design conceived by some secret enemy of Mr. Ducis, who entered the warehouse and changed the date."

"As we are wandering on the ocean of conjecture," said Dr. Haworth, "that, also, was possible."

"It was shown, I think, to be a mistake. There was no erasure such as would have been necessary, in altering the date in the ledger. I am, therefore, forced to adopt the clerical error theory."

Prof. Lesner then sighed, and said:

"These old neighborhood matters occurred a long time since.

I seldom recall them, as they are rather saddening, and only puzzle my poor brains. As I said, I never believed that Mr. Ducis was guilty, but human nature is a strange mixture. He was a man of the highest character, but it must be confessed appearances were terribly against him. Now, let us converse of something more cheerful, Doctor. Do you make any stay in the neighborhood? If I were as young and good looking as yourself I should find it difficult to leave the vicinity of—Mauricewood."

The Professor smiled rather slyly, and as Dr. Haworth rose to go, said:

"Come and see me whenever you have leisure, though there is not much to attract you in the society of a poor old scholar like myself. I have been quite interested in our talk."

"And I also, sir."

"I am glad we touched on the subject. I never omit an opportunity to say that I believe Mr. Ducis was innocent; he was one of my kindest friends. True, all the Maurice family were the same, but I shrink from injustice. I am sure Mr. Ducis was innocent."

"I am not certain I do not have your view," said Dr. Haworth, "and am much obliged by your invitation. I will be glad to avail myself of it."

"He then bowed and rode away in deep reflection. He was no doubt revolving in his mind the simple hypothesis suggested by Prof. Lesner—that Mr. Maurice's death was the result of accident. Could that have been true? It was possible—but Dr. Haworth shook his head.

"I do not believe it!" he muttered.

XII.

JEAN BAPTISTE.

ON this evening, about dusk, Jean Baptiste was seated on a bench in front of the modest house of "Hunter Wilson," in the hills, amusing his noisy children who had gathered around him, by telling them wonderful stories. They were listening in open-eyed astonishment, and a little girl who was perched on his knee looked at him with open mouth and the profoundest admiration.

At the approach of Dr. Haworth, however, the wonders came to a sudden end. Jean let down the little girl, and ran to meet the Doctor with a smile of pleasure.

" Your Excellency is just in time for supper—broiled venison," he exclaimed, taking the horse.

" And you are hungry, no doubt, Jean ! " he said, looking kindly at the boy.

" Not so hungry," laughed Jean.

" Will you throw my bridle over that bough, then, and come and talk with me a few minutes ? "

Dr. Haworth went to a knoll about fifty yards distant where a ledge of rock jutted from the sward, and sat down, pointing to the place beside him. Jean took the seat and looked at his master inquiringly.

" I have never told you how much you have interested me, Jean," said Dr. Haworth. " At your age young fellows are generally mere boys. You are a prudent and acute man, as when you repeated to me every word uttered by Col. Ross to those people."

Jean colored slightly and said :

" Do you know what makes me cool ? "

" What ? "

" Devotion to your Excellency."

" Very well. Devotion is a trait which is apt to be repaid in the same coin. Now, to come to another matter. I want you to tell me all you know about yourself—your history."

" My history ? "

" The story of your life—in South America, before I became acquainted with you."

" When I was a boy ? "

" From your childhood ; you have told me something, but it was not much. I found you roaming about Lima ; a young fellow with a bright face, ready to turn an honest penny, and a penny of no other sort. So I took you into my service. I liked your face."

" You were so kind ! You were always so good to me ! "

" Leave that aside, and tell me your story."

" There is none to tell. My first recollection of myself is traveling on the high road to Callao, slung behind old Mother Pinza's shoulders in a sort of pouch. She was not my mother—she was an old half-breed, and lived a lonely life, so I ran off one day when I was about 10 years old and went to Lima."

" Who were your father and mother ? "

At this question Jean Baptiste shook his head.

"I really do not know," he said. "I often tried to find out something about myself, but old Mother Pinza couldn't tell me. She was very ignorant. All I could get from her amounted to very little."

"What was it?"

"Well, I could only make out that I had been left with her when I was a baby by some one or other."

"She could not tell you the names of your parents, then?"

"She either could not or would not. I think she could not."

"And you never discovered any traces of them?"

"No, Excellency. I only remember hearing vaguely in some way that my father was an American."

"A South American?"

"No, a native of the United States."

"And your mother?"

"I do not know who my mother was, but I think she was a French woman. You know my name is Jean Baptiste."

"Possibly; so this is all you can tell me?"

"All, Excellency—you see it is almost nothing."

"Are your father and mother living?"

"I think they are dead."

"When did they die?"

Jean again shook his head and said:

"I know nothing at all about it, Excellency. I know it was very foolish in me to be so indifferent on the subject. I was not really indifferent, but I am sure I might have found out more if I had been more persevering. But you know how it is in South America. People live a careless life under the blazing sun. They eat and sleep and don't think much. I was too ignorant to take the right steps, and have always been too thoughtless and light hearted."

"Your heart may have been light, but it has always been in the right place," said Dr. Haworth. "So you have told me all you know?"

Jean reflected before replying.

"There was a ring," he said suddenly. "I remember playing with it when I was a child."

"A ring?"

"A gold ring—I am sure it was my mother's."

"Where is it?"

"Mother Pinza must have sold it. I don't know. She was very poor and loved money better than everything else on earth. I remember the ring perfectly well, but she denied all about it when I asked for it just before I left South America."

"She, no doubt, sold it—at Lima or Callao, which are not far, you know, from her cabin."

"Your Excellency knows where Mother Pinza lived!" Jean said.

"Yes," said Dr. Haworth.

"You have seen her?"

"Yes."

Jean said nothing more, but he was evidently puzzled.

"I know Mother Pinza," said Dr. Haworth, "and possibly more about yourself than you have told me. To be plain, the object of this talk was to find whether you had discovered anything after our last conversation at Lima. You don't know when your mother died?"

"I do not, Excellency."

"Well, that is all I have to say now, Jean. Supper is waiting."

They went back and supped with the hunter and his family, after which Dr. Haworth went to his small chamber, in one corner of which was stretched a pallet for the boy. There were writing materials on a table, and he sat down and wrote a letter. This he folded and directed to Senor Espartero, Notary, Calle Plateros, South America, and then leaning back in his chair reflected for a long time. At last he muttered: "Espartero is not a man who fails in anything or loses time where bank notes are concerned. I shall soon have his reply."

Jean came in and sat down beside the fire. His master looked at him thoughtfully and said:

"I wish to caution you more than ever, Jean, to be on your guard during our stay in this country. I have said, and repeat, that you are one of the most discreet young men I have ever known, but I caution you again in spite of the fact."

"You need not," said Jean simply.

"Well—open and close that door."

Jean reached the door with noiseless feet, opened it, looked out and again closed it.

"There is no one—your Excellency can say what you wish to say."

"It is only a few words," said Dr. Haworth, speaking in a low tone. "I am here to discover something which I mean to know at whatever risk. There is risk—from three people. You have seen them all; or at least two of them. They are the man you know, the woman you heard him talking with at that house, and the woman's husband."

Jean, looking intently at his watch, made a quiet movement with his head and said:

"Yes, Excellency, but Col. Ross is a long way the most danger-ous of the three."

"You really seem to have a great prejudice against our poor friend, the Colonel," said Dr. Haworth, grimly.

"A prejudice, Excellency? The man is a snake! Carrajo! How I hate him! He sent that torpedo boat to blow us up in Cal-lao Harbor, and he gave me this cut on my head! I was off my guard. He was about to cut at me again. Your Excellency saved me by cutting at him!"

"Well, I see you don't like him, and your instinct in the matter is a true instinct. To be plain—I told you that I meant to trust you implicitly—this man has done much worse than cut down an enemy in fair fight. If he has not committed a murder in which I am interested, he has been concerned in it. I have come here to discover all about it, for the gratification of my personal curiosity. He knows my object without knowing what motive I have; and I need not tell you that a struggle with such a man is a matter of life and death."

"To both of us—yes, Excellency."

"No—not to you."

"Does your Excellency think I care for my life? It belongs to you."

Dr. Haworth looked at the boy and smiled, which made his grave face an attractive spectacle.

"Gratitude!" he murmured; "then the definition of the term is not only 'a word found in the dictionary!'"

Jean looked at him with an expression of the deepest affection, and as if inquiring what he had said.

"I was muttering to myself, you can see, Jean—a bad habit, the result of living in solitude. What I said was that the sentiment called gratitude is a conventional illusion rather than an actual trait of human nature. People talk of it, but rarely meet with it in real life—you have it."

"Have it? Why should I not have it?" cried Jean, impulsively. "Your Excellency took me when I was a poor child in the streets and gave me a home! You not only gave me a home, but educated me and made me your companion. I was proud to be your servant, to wait on you and do all that I could to please you. But that did not satisfy you—you are such an exacting Excellency! You must make me your secretary and almost a gentleman!"

"I did not make you that. You became such of your own motion, and not 'almost,' either—wholly."

"Your Excellency is so good! Well, you saved me—not my life only, when that man's cutlass was going to cut me down—you saved me from becoming a mere vagabond. Thanks to you, I am educated, well dressed; I hope I am what is called respectable!"

"In every sense, and more."

"Well, I owe all to you."

"And you left me," said Dr. Haworth, smiling.

Jean Baptiste exclaimed:

"I had to, Excellency! There was some one who—I thought I would go away for a year or two—and try to forget her."

"Well," said Dr. Haworth, smiling, "what is the result? Have you gotten over the effect of your sweet honey-poison?"

Jean's color deepened.

"I can't say I have," he replied with a rueful laugh; "but I keep up my good spirits. Some day I may meet her again."

"I see you are not cured. When a young lover talks in that way he has not given up all hope. Well—patience and shuffle the cards. We are going back to Lima soon; for you will return, will you not?"

"I was thinking of it when you came to New York."

"Very well; that is assured, then. Keep up your spirits."

"They keep up of themselves," said Jean, with a light laugh.

"Very well; then we will return together, and you will see her again."

On the next day Dr. Haworth rode to the Town of Abbeyville and mailed his letter to Senor Espartero. He then returned homeward, and either designedly or unconsciously followed the road leading by Mauricewood. About a mile from the town he heard hoof-strokes behind him rapidly approaching, and turned his head. The person following him was Col. Ross.

XIII.

COL. ROSS.

COL. ROSS rode as usual a very fine animal and was elegantly dressed. His light brown ulster of the finest cloth half covered his superb riding boots, on which he wore silver spurs. His black riding cap was trimmed with fur, which also decorated the cuffs of his kid gauntlets. With his tall person, his erect seat in the English saddle, his delicately curled mustache and his ready smile, Col. Ross was the model of a " gallant cavalier."

"Good morning, Gen. Haworth," he said as he rode up. "We seem to be riding in the same direction. A charming day."

Dr. Haworth, as we may as well continue to call him, in spite of the title of general thus applied to him, bowed and said : " A delightful morning," after which the two men rode on side by side.

" In the very first place," said Col. Ross, with a courteous smile, "let me make you an apology, General."

" An apology ? You owe me none," replied Dr. Haworth, in his composed voice.

" For meeting you so formally at Mr. Maurice's. I had not anticipated the pleasure of seeing you, and supposed that I was deceived by a resemblance. This must be my excuse for so ungracious a reception of an old friend."

When Col. Ross said "old friend," he showed a row of very fine white teeth under his black mustache.

" It was unpardonable ! " he added.

" Nothing was more natural," said Dr. Haworth.

" I am glad you are so charitable. I was annoyed by the idea that you might suppose our little differences down yonder had made me unfriendly." This time Col. Ross laughed. " The little affair in Callao harbor, you know ! " he said.

" A trifle," replied Dr. Haworth. " A difference of flags does not necessarily make men enemies."

" Surely not. I was in the Chilian service, and you in that of Peru. As a consequence, when we chanced to meet sword in hand, we fought as a matter of course."

" As a matter of course," said Dr. Haworth, who seemed willing that his companion should bear the burden of the conversation.

" It has always struck me as somewhat singular that two officers of the land forces should have been engaged in that affair," said Col. Ross. " A soldier ought to be contented with the amount of fighting which falls to his lot in his proper place—to avoid volunteering."

" You are right. I had myself gone on board the Peruvian steamer on a mere matter of business when that ingenious attempt was made to blow up the vessel. Were you aware of it ? "

" Well, I was not the author of it. Like yourself I was on board ship by mere accident."

" The device was not your own, then ? "

" Mine ? No, indeed. I confess I should never have imagined such a thing !" The Colonel laughed and added : " It was worthy of those Chilian people, who, between you and me, are a bad lot. Our American people would never have thought of fitting a market-boat with a submerged torpedo, filling it with bananas and clusters of white grapes, and turning it adrift in the direction of your war vessel."

" As you say, the invention was original."

" It was only explained to me after its execution by the commander of the Conquestador, with whom I was conversing on the deck of that ship. He pointed to the boat as it drifted toward your steamer and said : ' There is a prize our Peruvian friends are going to haul in with a boat hook.' And then he explained that the submerged torpedo at the prow of the boat would blow you sky-high !"

" He was nearly right."

" Unfortunately. I say unfortunately because such things are repugnant to my instincts as a North American. I protested, but, of course, had no right to give orders on the ship. I had no choice, but to return to shore, or take part in the fight which followed."

" That is plain."

" So, when the Conquestador bore down on you, I thought I would stay and see the affair. One of your sailors, you will remember, threw a rope and boat hook to catch the boat, with its load of fresh fruits and vegetables. It sheered off as it exploded, which was all that saved you, and then we came to close quarters."

" In which I can testify that you bore your share."

Col. Ross bowed politely.

" I am able to bear the same testimony in regard to yourself, General. You were a thunderbolt ! Excuse my grand language. You know it is the fashion with our dear South Americans, who invariably cry ' God and liberty !' when they are about to thrust their hands into anybody's pockets. I had the honor, I remember, of meeting you sword in hand."

" After cutting down some of my best men, including a favorite young body servant."

" I had forgotten that. In fact, the result of things was so unpleasant as to obscure my recollection of particular incidents. You captured your assailant, the Conquestador, and I had the pleasure of a brief residence as a prisoner at Lima, when I was exchanged. I had nearly forgotten all this, but seeing you again has reminded me of it."

" Naturally. Do you make any stay in the United States ? "

" Well, I really do not know. I have a little business."

" Take care! I shall understand what it is without being told."

" Ah ! " said Col. Ross quietly.

" Every North American who has business with South America at this time is either a railway contractor or an agent of the guano or nitrate claimants."

Col. Ross laughed and said :

" I have heard much of these latter."

" Landreau and Cochet are the French claimants, I believe."

" I think so—or rather their representatives ; the men themselves are dead."

" Will the United States interpose ? "

" I really do not know—but see that vista through the oaks ! Decidedly, there is no comparison between North and South America."

Dr. Haworth evidently acquiesced in the change of topic.

" I prefer this country," he said, " but shall probably return to Lima at the end of autumn. I find the climate here too agreeable to leave it before I am obliged to do so."

" It is charming, like the society. I see you have made the acquaintance of my friends at Mauricewood."

" I have had that pleasure," said Dr. Haworth.

" You could not have been more fortunate. I had the honor of escorting the ladies this summer on a tour to Canada, and greatly enjoyed their society ; in addition to which I had the conviction that I was performing a good action."

" A good action ? "

" By relieving Mr. Timothy Maurice of the necessity of escorting the ladies. He wished to remain at home; and nothing pleased me more than to be able to do something to oblige him."

"I see you are a friend of his. He is an interesting gentleman. I have seen him frequently, and have been much interested in his reminiscences—especially by his account of the singular death of his brother, Mr. James Maurice."

"Yes, that was a sad affair, and surrounded, as you say, by very singular incidents," replied Col. Ross.

"It strangely impressed me, even the narration of it. It must have terribly shocked Mr. Maurice's friends and family?"

"Terribly."

"As you are a resident of this neighborhood it is possible that you were acquainted with the murdered man."

"Yes, I had seen him frequently."

"I think I remember," said Dr. Haworth, "that Mr. Timothy Maurice spoke of your intimacy with his nephew, John Maurice—in South America, was it not?"

Col. Ross looked sidewise at his companion, just sufficient to bring his face within the range of vision.

"Yes, I was acquainted with Mr. John Maurice—in South America," he said. Dr. Haworth listening, keenly discerned in the tone of his companion the caution of a swordsman standing on guard.

"So you were not intimate with him?"

"I was not."

"I only asked," said Dr. Haworth indifferently. "The degree of our intimacy with people naturally measures our sympathy when any misfortune befalls them. Mr. Maurice, the younger, must have been shocked by the mysterious death of his uncle and father-in-law."

"Very naturally."

"I say mysterious," continued Dr. Haworth, "because, so far as I have ascertained, there has never been any satisfactory demonstration that the affair took place as it was supposed to have done."

"I think some doubt still exists," said Col. Ross.

"I mean that the question who really committed the murder has never been answered."

"It was answered in one sense by the verdict of the jury," said Col. Ross.

"But you think there is still doubt?"

" I think the affair has never been wholly cleared up."

" To what view did you incline—that Mr. Ducis, the person con•victed of the crime, was the really guilty person ? "

Col. Ross did not look sidewise this time—his eyes were fixed upon the mane of his horse. He mused apparently for a moment, and then said :

" Well, I really have never been able to come to any distinct con•clusion on the subject. The case is altogether a labyrinth. If I re•member there were three or four persons charged with the crime, but the fact remains that Mr. Ducis was convicted while the rest were discharged."

" Do you think he was guilty ? "

" It is hard to believe it. He was a most honorable gentleman."

" Why, then, did the jury convict him ? "

" Well, my impression is that they were forced, as they supposed, to bring in a verdict in accordance with the evidence."

" Which traced the murder to Mr. Ducis ? "

" They seem to have taken that view at least, but I think I have heard that it was meant as a form only."

" A form ? "

" I think it was the general impression that the Executive would pardon Mr. Ducis, and the jury were reported to be ready to sign a petition to that effect."

" Did they do so ? "

" I believe not. The death of Mr. Ducis from paralysis, the re•sult of mental excitement, is said to have forestalled it."

Dr. Haworth rode on in silence. After a while he said :

" As Mr. Ducis was convicted, the other persons accused of the crime were discharged, I suppose."

" No doubt."

" Well, I fear I weary you with the prolonged discussion of this curious old affair. I can only say that it has presented itself to me in the light of an interesting puzzle. There is a great attraction in such incidents when we meet with them in real life, instead of in fic•tion. And yet the writers of fiction are sometimes valuable detect•ives. If we could resuscitate Edgar Poe and put him on the scent of this affair, I think he would unravel it."

" Do you think so ? "

" Yes ; his powers of analysis were wonderful, and I think he would reach the conclusion that I myself have reached."

Col. Ross turned his head slightly.

"Then you have formed a theory on the subject?" he said.

" A distinct one."

" May I ask what it is ? "

" It might weary you."

" You need have no such fear, General. I am really anxious to hear your view."

" I will state it then," said Dr. Haworth.

There was a moment's silence; the footfalls of the horses going at a steady walk were heard keeping time to each other. Dr. Haworth seemed to be reflecting; Col. Ross was looking sharply ahead apparently, but with the corner of his eye watched his companion's face. It was, however, a perfectly calm face and expressed nothing.

XIV.

DR. HAWORTH'S IDEA.

IT was in the midst of this silence that Dr. Haworth said in a composed voice :

" The simple question is who entered the Mauricewood house on the night of May 7, 1860, and put to death Mr. James Maurice—is it not ? "

" Yes."

" That is the precise date of the crime, I believe."

" You are no doubt correct. It had escaped my memory."

" My information is derived from Mr. Timothy Maurice."

Col. Ross inclined his head, but made no reply.

" The crime of murder having thus been committed," continued Dr. Haworth, " the interesting point to be ascertained is the author of the crime. Such an author was supposed to be found. He was a neighbor who had had an altercation with the murdered man a few days before—had threatened to have his blood—and the weapon with which the blow was struck was apparently shown to belong to him."

"Yes."

" One of his riding-gloves was also found near the spot."

" Yes."

" And he failed to prove an alleged alibi."

"That is correct, I believe."

"Thus the murder seemed to be brought home to him, but there was a serious objection to the theory of his guilt. He was a gentleman of the highest character, and the very family of the murdered man refused to believe that he could have committed the crime. He protested his innocence, but was convicted, when the tragedy ended in a manner not usual in the case of hardened criminals—the accused died of paralysis produced by despair at having been thought capable of the commission of so cowardly a crime."

"In other words," said Colonel Ross coolly, "Mr. Ducis was not guilty, you think. Concede the fact. Who was? The woman-servant or the manager?"

"There was little or nothing to support such a view. Women rarely commit murder, and the man was afraid of his employer."

"Well, that clears the way for your own theory, no doubt?"

"Yes; the way, as you express it, is clear. Mr. Ducis did not kill James Maurice; the criminals were neither the woman Pitts nor the man Wilkins. Who, then, you ask, was the murderer? I reply that I cannot tell you who he was, but I think I can tell you what he was."

"Ah!" said Col. Ross, with an air of interest.

"He was a personal enemy—a cowardly assassin who, fearing to attack in open day, resolved to steal on his victim unawares and put him to death under the shadow of darkness without risk."

"The affair was then what is called a secret vengeance?"

"Yes! You employ the exact phrase to describe it—a secret vengeance. Secret since it was committed at midnight; a vengeance, not a mere burglary and robbery complicated with murder."

"Well," said Col. Ross quietly, "who was this man in pursuit of blood, not money?"

"I have said that I do not know."

"What was he—that is to say, what was his character? You have your theory, you say."

"A fully developed one. It was neither a vulgar robber, nor a bungling manslayer blinded by passion or fear. He was a man of brains and precaution. He had resolved to attain his object, the death of his enemy, without personal risk, without chance of discovery, and he matured and executed his plan in the most skillful manner."

"I am not sure I understand."

" I will endeavor to explain my meaning clearly ; and as nothing is better to convey one's idea than a resort to illustration, I will adopt a simple one to define my hypothesis. Say that I or you—I bring the matter home to ourselves, you see—resolve to put an enemy out of the way. But we are men of intelligence, of forethought, and perfectly aware that murder is a dangerous proceeding ; that a vengeance which draws down vengeance in turn on the head of the avenger is a very poor business—badly arranged, in a word."

" Well."

" You are then a man of intelligence, I say, for you will allow me for the sake of argument to suppose that *you* were the real murderer of Mr. James Maurice."

" It is rather an unflattering hypothesis," said Col. Ross, with a slightly grating laugh, " but you may assume it if you fancy doing so."

" Well, then I assume it. You have your motive, which may be this or that. Your personal cause for hatred is known only to yourself and is not a necessary part of my theory—such hatred exists, let us say."

" Yes."

" You hate your enemy then, and resolve to destroy him as secretly, as silently as possible, in such a manner that no suspicion should point to you; so that afterwards you might walk openly before all men with head erect, enter the court room where an innocent man was arraigned for committing the crime committed by yourself, listen calmly to all the testimony, see the innocent man convicted, and go home laughing in your sleeve at the farce called justice."

" That is rather fanciful," said Col. Ross, attempting to laugh.

" You are aware that it is only a fancy employed for the purpose of illustration ? "

" True."

" Well, to proceed, say that such was your plan—the path you had traced out for yourself—the path beginning with a secret murder and ending in profound security."

" I conceive your idea," said Col. Ross in a satirical tone, " but it seems to me rather forced. Why not waylay your enemy—instead of entering his house and striking him in the midst of his household ? "

" Waylay him ? "

" In some hollow of the woods, let us say—fire on him and gallop away ? "

" Nothing would be more absurd. The body is found and an inquest is summoned; there are one, two, three persons who are anxious to testify."

" They are unable to testify to anything, since they witnessed nothing."

" They are able to testify to more than you suppose. One remembers that your enemy, whose body is lying yonder with a hole through it, rode in the direction of the spot where the murder took place, about 5 o'clock in the evening. Another remembers you about the same hour going in the same direction. A third heard a pistol shot, and a few moments afterwards observed you riding at full speed past the field in which he was at work. Under the painful circumstances the coroner or magistrate would regret the necessity of arresting you on suspicion."

Col. Ross laughed in the same grating manner.

" Your fancy is vivid," he said, " but I call your attention to the fact that your highly intelligent criminal would have his explanation ready. He would know nothing about the pistol shot—for I suppose the murder would be committed by means of a revolver. He would acknowledge that he had been in the vicinity—he had been going to visit a friend, say; but, remembering that he had forgotten to mail an important letter, had hurried back to do so. Any simple explanation would serve to explain everything."

" And any simple circumstance would serve to contradict everything. The wisest man overlooks something. The least trifle would convict you. The prints of hoofs are found in the road, stopping at a certain spot, and then returning. They are measured, and found to be those of your riding-horse—so you turned back to mail your letter at the very spot where the body was found."

" And you would hang me on the strength of that ! " said Col. Ross.

" There would be more—there is at least the possibility. You employ a derringer, not a revolver, and in loading use a wad of paper. The wad is carried into the wound inflicted, extracted, unrolled—it is the envelope of a letter with your name upon it."

" Well, then I see I am done for. I would be wrong, I acknowledge, to waylay my enemy ! "

"It would be dangerous, and you would reject the idea. You would resort to something safer and more skillful to reach your end."

" To burglary and homicide?"

" Yes."

" That seems to me much more desperate—the risk of discovery a thousand times greater."

" If unskillfully executed—but remember that you are a skillful man—a man of brains, as I have said. You would so arrange matters that no one would ever suspect you."

" We are coming, now, I think, to the details of your theory."

" Yes."

" I confess I do not understand precisely."

" I will explain. You will resolve to throw suspicion upon another person."

" Ah, I—I begin to see."

" You would reconnoitre the house and ascertain where your enemy slept—discover that his bedchamber was on the ground floor and could be easily entered. Then you would endeavor to secure some weapon belonging to some one—to be afterwards identified. Fortune might favor you; you might get possession of a hammer of peculiar shape known to be the property of a particular person. You might secrete this weapon; steal into the house at midnight, commit the crime. Drop a glove similar to that worn by the owner of the hammer, and erase the figures in a warehouse ledger establishing an alibi in favor of the innocent man."

" There was no erasure!" exclaimed Col. Ross. " That is to say—pardon my interruption—there seemed to be none, if I was rightly informed."

" I am merely supposing a case," said Dr. Haworth.

" And such is your theory of the murder, sir? You think that Mr. Ducis was innocent?"

" Yes," answered Dr. Haworth.

" That some mysterious unknown, as the romance writers say, was guilty?"

" Yes—that he planned the crime, gained possession of the deadly weapon, stole to the sleeping mansion, raised the window-sash of his victim's bedchamber, approached the bed without noise, and struck the blow on his temple, under which he started up, struggling and groaning in the death agony!"

Col. Ross made no reply.

"Then the rest duly followed. The murderer dropped his murderous weapon beside the bed, where it was to be found—the glove outside as he escaped through the window—you could defy the keenest detective then to show that you had any connection with the transaction."

"Really, that is a flattering supposition that I could be so skillful!" said Col. Ross with the same harsh laugh.

"If you were like some human beings I have known you would be proud of your skill. You would feel that you had outwitted everybody. Your enemy would be dead; an honest man, innocent of the offense, would be convicted in your stead; his name would be dishonored, his family overwhelmed with disgrace, while you—you who committed the crime—you, the real murderer, moved about unsuspected, attended the funeral of your victim, the trial of the accused, saluted the court, talked with the constables, heard the verdict and went home in triumph! No one would dare to utter a whisper against so respectable a person. You would remain an ornament of society; people would take off their hats to you, women would smile upon you, you would appear in your pew at church, you would drink your wine, utter your jest, laughing in your sleeve as I have said—you, the bloody assassin, the murderer of two human beings, the hypocrite and whited sepulchre, who ought to feel around your neck in place of your silk cravat the hangman's rope."

Col. Ross rode on, sitting erect in his saddle, but a slight shudder passed through his vigorous frame. They went on for some moments in silence. Then he said in a perfectly cool voice:

"Very well; that is rather a curious theory. You will allow me to compliment you on your acuteness at least, Gen. Haworth."

Dr. Haworth had turned his head and was looking at him.

"You regard it as a mere theory, then?" he said.

"I venture to regard it in that light. It is scarcely necessary to point out the objections which suggest themselves to such an hypothesis. There was no such enemy of the Maurices in the country that I have ever heard of; and then the theory, you will allow me to repeat, resembles rather what we find in romances than in real life."

"Real life is quite as curious as any romance I have ever met with."

"Well, that may be true, possibly, and I have at least been much interested in your discussion of this strange affair. I am not sufficiently familiar with criminal matters to form an opinion, and I was absent from the country when this affair took place. At least, there is no longer any feeling of distress at Mauricewood in regard to this tragic occurrence. It is happily forgotten, and the real criminal, whoever he may have been, is no doubt dead. I am going to visit our friends to-day. I see we are in sight of the house. Do you come in?"

"I shall be obliged to return."

They were soon at the white gate by which the country road passed. Col. Ross bowed and entered, while Dr. Haworth rode on in the direction of the hill country.

He had no sooner turned his back on Col. Ross than his face, which had remained perfectly composed during their conversation, assumed an expression indicative of great disgust.

"That man makes me sick," he muttered. "Is he the real criminal—I never was so tempted! When he said: 'There was no such enemy of Mr. Maurice in the country,' it was on my very lips to say, 'Which Mr. Maurice do you mean? Mr. James Maurice, the uncle, or Mr. John Maurice, the nephew?' It was not the elder Maurice who was struck at, but Maurice the younger. He was to have slept in that chamber; for days the bride's presents were exhibited in it upon the bridal couch. The change was only made on the night of the marriage. Who then struck at John Maurice there? Was it or was it not the man who had fought with him about a woman, and who hated his successful rival? He may not have struck the blow himself—may have been really absent. Did he not suborn others to do so—the woman Pitts or the man Wilkins —and was not this the meaning of his night visit to their house in the hills, the suborner of murder going to caution the tools of his crime?"

Dr. Haworth rode on in deep thought. His acute and penetrating mind saw here and there a flaw in this apparently flawless theory. It was improbable that a man so intelligent as Ross would have put himself in the power of those degraded creatures—conceived a project so hazardous—that he would not have preferred to quarrel with his enemy on some pretext and shoot him. But there was the obstinate fact that he *had* ridden by night to warn the murderers—if they were the murderers.

A last subject of reflection to Dr. Haworth was the singular fact that if Col. Ross had procured the death of John Maurice, he was now paying his addresses to John Maurice's daughter!

"Men are vile enough for anything when they listen only to their passions," he muttered. "This one is of that sort, and I have only to keep my hands off of him to let him succeed. Am I apt to do that?"

A grim smile came to Dr. Haworth's lips, and a latent fire in his eyes showed a powerful organization moved and strung for action.

"It is not probable," he muttered harshly. "If I had no other motive for bringing everything connected with this black business to light, I would do almost anything to prevent that!"

PART II.

COL. ROSS AND DR. HAWORTH.

I.

DR. HAWORTH IS AFRAID.

IT was about the middle of autumn, and Dr. Haworth and Jean Baptiste had been, for some time, inmates of Mauricewood.

Having been urged anew by Mr. Tim Maurice to make them a visit—ostensibly for the pleasure of his society, but quite as much to secure an adversary at chess—Dr. Haworth had ended by accepting the invitation, and had come with Jean to take up his residence for a short time at the old manorhouse.

For this he had his reasons. Among them was an incident of a rather curious character, which had taken place soon after his interview with Col. Ross.

He had gone out hunting one day—or rather to wander in the solitude of the hill country, and reflect—when his meditations suddenly ended.

A bullet whistled by his head, and looking up quickly—for he had been seated upon a ledge of granite with his carbine resting easily upon his knee—he saw a puff of smoke rise from the woods about 200 yards in front of him.

Dr. Haworth was a man of great promptness and had an ardent curiosity to ascertain why he had been fired at. That was difficult, but seemed practicable. The spot where he had seated himself was nearly encircled by laurels, and entering them, he made a circuit, and reached the point from which he had observed the puff of smoke rise. No one was to be seen there, and nodding his head as if the fact did not surprise him, Dr. Haworth went straight toward the cabin of the man and woman Wilkins, about a mile distant.

The woman, looking as slatternly and as disheveled as ever, was washing soiled clothes in an old discolored tub near the door of the house, and at the sound of the cur in the kennel turned around and saw the visitor.

"Is your husband at home to-day, madam?" asked Dr. Haworth.

"He's away somewhere," she replied with a side look.

"Hunting, perhaps."

"I don't know."

Steps were heard approaching—some twigs cracked under them in the thicket.

"He is coming back," said Dr. Haworth, quietly.

The man Wilkins make his appearance at the moment, in the edge of the thicket, rifle in hand, and seeing Dr. Haworth, made a movement to conceal himself. As he saw that this was impossible, he came forward and coolly ducked his head by way of greeting to the visitor.

"I see you have been hunting," said Dr. Haworth, looking at the rifle.

"After a deer seen in these parts lately."

"Did you get sight of him!"

"I thought I seen him in the bushes, and fired at him, but it were nothing."

"Nothing?"

"I went there and there was no hoofprints. I spect it was a trick of the light. That ofting happens."

The explanation seemed perfectly satisfactory to Dr. Haworth. Nothing was more natural than that a huntsman should fire upon what he supposed to be the game he was hunting. There was only one flaw in Mr. Wilkins' statement. He had not been near the spot where he, Dr. Haworth, had been seated. On the contrary it was plain that he had rapidly retired in the opposite direction.

Any discussion on the subject did not seem necessary, apparently, to the visitor. He remained a few moments longer conversing in a commonplace way, and then took his departure, with the air of a man who has no special object beyond a ramble with the view of getting a shot at something. Having gained the woods, however, he went straight home. Jean Baptiste saw him approaching and came to meet him, when Dr. Haworth stopped and made a sign. The boy hastened toward him and Dr. Haworth said:

"I am afraid you find this place rather lonely, Jean."

"The home in the hills here, Excellency? I like it of all things."

"It strikes me as rather a solitary retreat—the fact is, I want society. On the whole, I think I will accept an invitation I have received to Mauricewood—Mrs. Maurice's, you know, where I visit frequently."

"Would you like that better, Excellency?"

"I think so."

"Then I like it better," said Jean, smiling. "Am I to go, too? I hope so."

"Certainly, the invitation includes you. The family are aware that you and I are inseparable. I have informed them that you are my friend and traveling companion."

"Your Excellency is so good!"

"I see no proof of goodness in that. Then the matter is arranged. Pack the valise—I will go to-morrow."

"The horses?"

"We will take them, of course."

Jean nodded and walked back with Dr. Haworth, who retired to his chamber.

"Well, all that is plain enough," he said. "War is declared, it seems, and the first gun has been fired. These people are playing a bold game—it is a proof that they are awake to their danger. Did my friend, the Colonel, suggest that deer hunt to his friend, Job Wilkins? It is possible, but not probable. I think it was a brilliant conception of Mr. Wilkins himself. Does he mean to shoot me to prevent my hanging him? If so he has been concerned in one hanging affair, at least!"

After saying this Dr. Haworth reflected for about half an hour without moving in his chair. He then muttered:

"Yes, I will go away from this lonely place—it is too convenient and I am afraid. A bullet better aimed than the last would leave my friend, the Colonel, free to carry out his programme—of matrimony. I am an obstacle. I think he would like to remove me—he or his friend, Mr. Wilkins. There is no guarding against such skillful people as long as I am in this hill country—if they hold the trumps they will play them. As I am afraid, therefore, I will move my quarters."

On the same afternoon Dr. Haworth rode to Mauricewood and

4

said to Mr. Tim Maurice, who met him with a hospitable smile, on the veranda:

" I have resolved to accept your obliging invitation, sir, and make you a short visit with my young friend Jean."

At these words Mr. Tim Maurice beamed with satisfaction. He saw before him unending games of chess.

" Nothing could give us more pleasure, Doctor !" he exclaimed with a cordial pressure of his guest's hand.

" Are you sure it will not inconvenience you ?"

" Inconvenience us—in this large house ? There are countless spare chambers."

" I accept one, then, with many thanks, for myself and Jean, my young traveling companion. At home he is my private secretary, with his seat at my table and his pallet in my sleeping-room."

" He will be as welcome as yourself at Mauricewood, Doctor. You will come to-night I hope."

" I shall not be able to do so until to-morrow."

" I am sorry. To-morrow, then, without fail, remember."

And as Miss Cary Maurice floated down the staircase at that moment Mr. Tim Maurice exclaimed:

" Dr. Haworth has promised to make us a visit, Cary."

Miss Cary received this announcement with polite smiles.

" I am very glad."

" And I am delighted," exclaimed Mr. Tim Maurice. " I am certain that if I only get a fair pull at you I can checkmate you, Doctor !"

" I will try to prevent you from doing so," said Dr. Haworth, bowing.

After which, friendly conversation ensued and he took his departure.

On the next day Dr. Haworth and Jean bade good-by to honest Hunter Wilson, who promised to send their traveling valises after them, rode to Mauricewood, and were installed in an up-stairs chamber affording a view of the lawn in front. The chamber was a model of comfort and neatness. Miss Cary Maurice had seen to it in person.

II.

COL. ROSS MAKES A MORNING CALL.

THE days at Mauricewood succeeded and resembled each other.

The autumn was slowly fading; the yellow leaves floating to the green carpet beneath, and the red turning, hour by hour, to a richer russet. Often not a sound disturbed the silence but the lazy caw of a passing crow. The year was going, wrapped in balmy airs and golden mist.

The outer world is unimportant, however, when the inner is full of attractions. Dr. Haworth found Mauricewood a pleasant place after his lonely sojourn in the hills. The family, consisting of Mr. Tim Maurice, his niece Mrs. Maurice, and Miss Cary, had received an addition to it in the person of a young seamstress, Miss Burns, from the neighboring town of Abbeyville—but as Miss Burns only appeared at meals, with the rest of the family, Dr. Haworth saw very little of her, and had not advanced beyond a bow.

He was apparently quite satisfied with the society of the two ladies and Mr. Tim Maurice. He and Mrs. Maurice conversed a great deal upon South America and other topics, and the pleased smile on the gentle face indicated that the lady had conceived a sincere regard for her visitor. Mr. Tim Maurice was chiefly solicitous about his darling hobby. "Well, Doctor, a delightful day," was almost always followed by, "Shall we try a game?" and the game almost always took place.

As to Miss Cary, that was different. She and Dr. Haworth did not have many interviews—private interviews, that is to say. In some manner these seemed to be prevented. When they were in danger of being left alone together, Miss Cary always discovered that she was obliged to run up stairs for a moment—that household matters required her attention—that she had forgotten something—she would soon be back. But her engagements had a mysterious fashion of prolonging themselves, and preventing her from returning to enjoy Dr. Haworth's society until some other member of the family appeared, when she returned at once.

What was the meaning of all this? Dr. Haworth asked himself the question, but gave it up in despair.

Then, after a while, he asked himself another question—Was he going to fall in love with Miss Cary Maurice? Had he not done so in a measure already?

When he faced this problem his face clouded over, and a cold light settled in his eyes. One day he muttered:

"That would be idiotic. I am a mere acquaintance, a passing stranger, with a glum face and nearly twice her age. And that's not all. I have not come here to make love to a girl. Something very different brings me—I have no time for fooling."

This something occupied his mind at all hours of the day. He was far from social. He took solitary walks in the grounds under the oaks, so old now that they were dying at the top; and whoever chanced to pass him could see that his brows were knit together, his thoughts busy with some problem. If Miss Cary Maurice had made an impression on him he was not pursuing a judicious method of agreeably impressing her.

He was thinking eternally of Col. Ross and his probable connection as principal or accessory with the crime at Mauricewood. Up to a certain point everything seemed clear, beyond that point all was vague. Was this smiling gentleman the real criminal? It was impossible! Human nature could not be unfathomably vile. The man would never have been able to discuss the affair so coolly; would have shunned coming near Mauricewood; would have shrunk from the very idea of paying his addresses to John Maurice's daughter. But there were the undeniable facts. He had warned these people to be on their guard. He had quarreled and fought with John Maurice; doubtless hating him for supplanting him with the woman both had loved. There was sufficient motive, and once or twice in their conversation Dr. Haworth had heard the voice of Col. Ross indicate a secret apprehension.

"I will know all sooner or later," he said one day as he was taking one of his lonely walks. "I wonder if that bullet that grazed my head was fired by his order? I doubt it—but nothing is certain in dealing with such a man. That is a trifle; the main point is to take him unawares; to force him into a corner where his crime, if he committed the crime, will confront him; to watch him and decide the question, in my own mind at least. How am I to do that?"

He reflected for a quarter of an hour, walking slowly and looking at the ground. Then he exclaimed:

"If I could—! Well, that might be done with a little skill! I think it might be arranged. I'll try, at least!"

One day Col. Ross drove to Mauricewood. If he came to see Miss Cary Maurice, which was probable, the fates were against him. The young lady was suffering from a severe headache, and, after hospitably receiving Col. Ross, Mrs. Maurice smiled and returned to her daughter.

Col. Ross was evidently very much disappointed—the headache was apparently bona fide, and might confine Miss Cary for the rest of the day. Courtesy required, however, that he should not go away abruptly, so he sat conversing in a friendly manner with Mr. Tim Maurice and Dr. Haworth.

" I congratulate you," he said to the latter, " on your pleasant quarters here. You must find them more cheerful than the hills."

" A great deal more cheerful," replied Dr. Haworth. " I am fond of hunting, but found there were some drawbacks. There was very little society and some risk."

" Risk ? "

" The danger of being shot."

Col. Ross looked a little puzzled.

" Shot by accident, I mean," said Dr. Haworth. " That is not unusual in wooded districts where separate parties or individuals are out hunting."

" I think I understand your meaning."

" There is danger of being taken for game. You push aside the bushes in passing through some thicket, and a hunter at his stand takes you for a deer or a wild turkey. He therefore puts a bullet through you, and when he rushes forward to secure his prize, is much shocked and deeply regrets having shot you, and hopes you will pardon his awkwardness."

Col. Ross laughed and said :

" That's rather a poor consolation."

" Very poor. You accept his apology, of course, with your last breath ; but a more agreeable state of things would be not to be shot."

" Yes ; I think I have heard of such accidents."

Col. Ross uttered the words so naturally that Dr. Haworth's doubts were dispelled, or nearly. It was improbable that he had had anything to do with the affair. When Wilkins had suggested it, on the night of the ride, Col. Ross had not dissuaded him, but it was more than probable that Wilkins had acted from his own impulse to get rid of a dangerous adversary.

" Well, your change of quarters to Mauricewood," said Col. Ross,
" is defensible on every ground.   It is safer and far more agreeable."

" Much more so.   All is cheerful and attractive with one exception."

" One exception ? "

" Perhaps I ought not to have referred to it, as the subject is, no
doubt, painful to Mr. Maurice."

" Oh ! you mean the locked-up room," said Mr. Tim Maurice.

" Yes, sir."

" It is a somewhat sorrowful feature of the house, I agree."

" I fear I was indiscreet."

" Not at all, Doctor."

" But the subject has a morbid attraction for me.   Perhaps the
fact that this room has been closed for twenty years has made me
curious to see it."

" To see it ?   Would you care to see it ? " said Mr. Maurice.

" I confess I should like to."

" There is no objection, whatever, to showing it to you, and perhaps Col. Ross might also be interested."

Dr. Haworth did not look at Col. Ross, but he listened acutely
to the tones of his voice as he replied :

" I—cannot say that my curiosity is quite as keen as our friend's,
but—I should be glad to see the place."

" Then I will go and get the key.   I can do so without the knowledge of my niece, who is in her chamber.   It might sadden her to be
reminded of it.   I shall not mind it myself.   I will be back in a moment, gentlemen."

Mr. Tim Maurice then went up the staircase with his rapid step
and disappeared in search of the key.   Dr. Haworth looked in a
casual and unconcerned manner at Col. Ross, who was standing
within a few feet of him.   Their glances met.

" So you are really interested in this old affair, General—or Doctor, as you appear to prefer that title," said Col. Ross.

" It is simpler and attracts less attention," said Dr. Haworth,
replying to the last portion of the sentence.

" Then, you do not wish to attract attention ?   It is a somewhat
uncommon virtue."

" I do not.   I have always preferred passing through life quietly
—the *degito moustrari* has no charms for me."

" Well, everything is a matter of taste.   Most persons prefer as sounding a title as possible, especially when traveling. The hotel keepers bow lower, and put you in better quarters."

It was obvious that both men were best pleased to converse on other subjects than the locked room. As Mr. Maurice returned at this moment that subject was resumed.

"I found the key, after a short search," he said, "and have said nothing to the ladies of our intention. It is quite unnecessary."

He then inserted the heavy key into the brass lock and pushed open the door. It creaked on its hinges, and a cloud of dust fell from the upper edge.

"This is the room," said the old gentleman, entering.

Dr. Haworth followed him, not looking towards Col. Ross, but listening to be certain that he was behind him. His firm tread was heard striking the hard floor in a measured manner, and when the rest stopped he stopped also.

It was a chamber of lofty pitch, with a shining bare floor, two large windows opening on the veranda ; a wide fireplace, in which some blackened embers were leaning against the brass andirons ; a tall mantelpiece of blue-veined marble surmounted by two vases, in which were some withered flowers ; and scattered about were easy-chairs, a lounge, and other accessories looking to comfort. Between the windows was a toilet-table crowned with a handsome mirror, in front of which stood a pair of silver branches with half burned wax-lights. The bedstead was old-fashioned, with heavy curtains, tall carved posts and a tester. Beside it was a night-table. The clothing on the bed was in disorder as if it had been tossed about by a sick man laboring under fever. Nothing had been set to rights. The occupants of the apartment seemed to have just left it—only every object was covered with dust, the dust of twenty years.

III.

IN THE LOCKED ROOM.

"This is the scene of the unhappy affair, gentlemen," said Mr. Tim Maurice. "It is rather dark. I will open one of the windows."

"Will you wait a moment, Mr. Maurice !" said Dr. Haworth, who was looking around with an expression of deep interest.

Mr. Tim Maurice turned his head as if these words puzzled him.

" I really think this dim light suits the place and the tragedy," said Dr. Haworth. " It aids the fancy—for one of my objects in requesting you to show me this room was to attempt to reconstruct the scene, if I may so say, and understand the details."

" I think I see your meaning, Doctor."

" The crime was committed, no doubt, in darkness, or semi-obscurity. If we mean to follow the movements of the assassin, and understand how he went to work, we ought to subject ourselves to the same conditions. Am I wrong ? " asked Dr. Haworth turning to Col. Ross.

" I think you are perfectly right," said Col. Ross quietly.

" Then we may as well leave the window closed, at least for the present, Mr. Maurice."

" Certainly."

" Here are all the objects then connected with the murder ? "

" Yes ; just as they were. Nothing has been touched. There is the night-table upon which my brother placed the money, and the disordered bed clothes. You may see the mark of his head on that pillow."

" Yes."

" The lights in the branches yonder on the toilet-table are half burned, you see, just as they were put out when he retired ; and there are the charred twigs in the fireplace—a slight blaze had been made, as I remember it was rather chilly."

" Yes ; spring evenings often are."

" Yonder is the window through which the murderer entered. It was either open by accident or he raised it."

" He probably raised it. It is singular that he was not heard."

" No doubt it was done quietly by a skillful person."

" You don't mean Mr. Ducis ? "

" No, indeed ; I have already said that I have never thought for a moment that Mr. Ducis was really guilty."

" By simply a skillful person let us say then ; but, however cautious he may have been, there is another singular fact—that his steps on the bare floor did not wake the sleepers."

" He probably walked with precaution."

" That is supposable, but then there was an additional danger."

" What was that ? "

" The danger of falling. Look at the floor. It is as slippery as glass."

" The result of the old-fashioned habit of scrubbing—yes."

. " The assassin then was in danger of slipping, unless he was on his guard. That accident, indeed, might have befallen Mr. Maurice himself."

" My brother ? "

" Yes."

Dr. Haworth took a step forward, and suddenly slipped, nearly falling against the carved edge of the tall bed-post.

" You see, sir ! " he said, regaining his erect attitude. " An accident has nearly happened to me. I came near striking my temple against that carving there."

" That might have been dangerous."

" It might even have been fatal. A sudden blow on certain parts of the head often results in death, you know."

" My poor brother was an instance."

" Your brother ? " Well, a curious idea occurs to me, Mr. Maurice. Is it not possible after all that no murder was committed in this room ? "

" No murder ? "

" That the death of James Maurice was simply the result of accident ? Why not conclude that he rose in the night, placed his feet in his slippers, slipped on this smooth surface and fell against that post ? A fatal contusion might have been the result."

Mr. Tim Maurice shook his head.

" I believe that theory was broached at the time," he said, " but I have never had any faith in it."

" It is possible."

" Yes ; it is possible. A little thing will sometimes kill a man ; but there are difficulties in the way of that explanation which I have never been able to get over."

" What are they ? "

" My brother was found in his bed."

" He may have staggered back to it."

" His slippers, I am sure, were not on his feet."

" They may have fallen off."

" But the money—that was gone."

" True, but you yourself have told me that you suspected the housekeeper of stealing it."

" I certainly did."

" But not of committing the murder ? "

" I don't think she did."

" Very well, then, consider for a moment. Your brother rises during the night, slips on this smooth floor, strikes his temple against the post, cries out so that you are startled up-stairs and staggers back to bed, where you find him dying in a fainting fit— that happens to people."

Mr. Tim Maurice shook his head again.

" I do not think your idea has any real foundation, Doctor," he said.

" And what is your opinion, sir ? " said Dr. Haworth, turning to Col. Ross, who had been standing with his left arm across his breast, the hand supporting his right elbow and his chin resting in his right hand.

" My opinion ? " he said. " Well, I think your idea is very ingenious."

" And that is all ? "

" I am unable to say how the affair really took place," said Col. Ross.

" Naturally, sir, but we are at liberty to indulge in conjecture. To revert then to the theory that Mr. James Maurice was murdered.. How did it take place ? "

" I really cannot inform you," said Col. Ross coolly.

" We are here on the spot—the actual scene is under our eyes; there is the window, the bed. Let us fancy, if possible, the movements of the assassin. Let us even do more—you might assist me ? "

" Assist you ? " said Col. Ross, looking fixedly at Dr. Haworth.

" Yes, we have nothing better to do this fine morning. As our aim in entering this room is to form as accurate an idea as possible of the real occurrence, why should not you or I personate the murderer, and go through all his probable movements ? "

Col. Ross made no reply.

" You would possibly succeed better than myself," said Dr. Haworth. " I am a bad actor."

" I have no more ability in that particular than yourself," said Col. Ross stiffly.

" Your modesty probably deceives you. I think Mr. Maurice will join in my request."

"I see nothing unreasonable in it, Doctor, and think I take your idea."

"I decline, sir," said Col. Ross coldly, with a flash of the eye which he seemed unable to hide.

"Then," said Dr. Haworth, "I will take your place. Is that the window, Mr. Maurice?"

"Yes—it is bolted inside."

"Will you be good enough to unbolt it?"

With which words Dr. Haworth went out of the room and was heard walking along the veranda. Mr. Tim Maurice had meanwhile unbolted the sash and venetians and returned to the side of Col. Ross. They stood waiting.

For a moment there was a dead silence in the room. Then the venetians opened quietly, the sash was raised, and Dr. Haworth entered through the opening. He stood for a moment looking around him, fixed his eyes upon the curtained bed, advanced and leaned across it, half hidden by the curtains.

Any one glancing at Col. Ross would have seen him shudder slightly.

Mr. Tim Maurice was looking on with sorrowful attention—the curious pantomime seemed to bring back vividly all his gloomy recollections.

In the midst of the dead silence Dr. Haworth uttered a slight exclamation. Was he personating in turn the victim to give more reality to the scene? It did not seem so. The exclamation was low and indicated surprise. Neither of the other occupants of the room was aware of the fact, as his back was turned to them, but he had thrust something, apparently discovered in the bed, into his breast between his waistcoat and shirt. He then turned round quietly.

"You see, gentlemen," he said, "the assassin must have entered in that way and reached the bed without discovery. The curtains were sufficient to hide him from Mr. Maurice even if he had been awake."

He looked from Mr. Tim Maurice to Col. Ross.

"Yes," the latter said without lowering his eyes.

"I will not take trouble to make my exit in the character I have assumed," said Dr. Haworth, "and you may as well close the window, Mr. Maurice. I would make a request of Col. Ross if I was not afraid he would object."

" A request, sir ? " said Col. Ross.

" I have done my part in the first act of the drama. Is it too
much to ask that Col. Ross will now permit me to become one of
the audience ? "

" One of the audience ? "

" That you will take the part of the chief actor in the denouement," said Dr. Haworth quietly. " That is to say, that you will
advance, strike the fatal blow, and make your escape. I have done
my part—let us assume now that *you* are the assassin ! "

Col. Ross turned away muttering : " It is unpleasant—I must
decline, sir," and as Mr. Tim Maurice had now closed the sash and
venetian they left the room, which was again securely locked. The
bright day without was like a cordial after their confinement in the
gloomy chamber, and Mr. Tim Maurice said :

" Really, Doctor, if I had known what a melancholy place that
was I think I would have sent you gentlemen in by yourselves.
Well, well—you have seen the place, at least. Let us forget it and—"

Mr. Tim Maurice looked fondly toward his chess-board on the
center-table of the drawing-room. To play chess with Dr. Haworth
was, however, to treat Col. Ross with scant courtesy, and nothing
followed the word " and."

The ladies not reappearing, Col. Ross finally bowed and went
away. His face indicated no emotion of any description.

IV.

SOMETHING HAPPENS.

WHEN Col. Ross reappeared at Mauricewood, which he did two
or three days afterwards, he was in a perfectly cheerful mood, and
inquired with an air of interest if Miss Cary had recovered from her
headache.

As she had not wholly recovered, but still felt a little badly, she
said, her visitor suggested a horseback ride, and she smiled and
assented.

They were away the whole afternoon, and when Col. Ross assisted the young lady to dismount on her return he did so with an
air of devotion, which seemed to indicate a great deal. It was
plain, he said, with deferential courtesy, as they were all seated on

the veranda, that horseback exercise was an absolute cordial for Miss Cary. And as Miss Cary agreed, and said that she really felt like another person, Col. Ross suggested that she should attend church next Sunday in that manner—he would be glad to escort her. Miss Cary replied that she would accept his escort with pleasure. And then, after tarrying an hour longer, Col. Ross rode away in the highest spirits.

On Sunday they rode to church together, and afterwards it was noticed that they did not take the direct road home. Doubtless this arose from the fact that a slight detour brought them to a hill which commanded a very fine view of the surrounding country—of the beautiful champaign, the wooded hill country and the faint blue mountains beyond.

People smiled and nodded when they rode away from the church together. The matter was plain, and it really did seem to be.

When he went away that evening Col. Ross said that he would not forget Miss Cary's request. As a matter of fact the request was his own—that she should amuse herself with an excellent novel he had just read—but the discrepancy was unimportant. He brought the volume two days afterwards, and when Mr. Tim Maurice hospitably invited him to remain to dinner faintly objected, acquiesced and remained.

After dinner Miss Cary Maurice and Col. Ross took a walk on the lawn. Dr. Haworth, who was seated on the veranda engaged in conversation with Mr. Tim Maurice, saw them stroll away slowly in the evening sunshine—the erect form of the gentleman bending graciously toward his companion, and that companion looking up with her head inclining a little sidewise, her cheeks rosy, her brown curls fluttering and her exquisite figure assuming new attitudes full of grace at every step. Light laughter indicated, it seemed, that the Colonel was making himself agreeable. After a while they disappeared behind the oak foliage.

" As I was saying, Doctor, the practice of plowing in the winter has a thousand advantages. The clods freeze, and when the thaw comes the frost in them reduces them to powder, and—but, really, you are not listening."

" Pardon my bad habit of abstraction," said Dr. Haworth. " I follow your theory and am convinced it is sound, sir."

" I am certain of it."

And Mr. Maurice flowed on, after which he proposed chess. His

companion promptly acquiesced, and they were thus engaged when
Miss Cary Maurice and Col. Ross returned. All his smiles had
disappeared and his figure was as rigid as a ramrod. As to the
young lady, she paused a moment to glance at the chess-board as
she passed, and then quietly left the room and tripped up-stairs.
Col. Ross, whose face was harsh and gloomy, bowed stiffly, regretted that he was compelled to return home, and despite Mr. Tim
Maurice's polite remonstrance, rode away.

"Our friend, the Colonel, seems out of sorts," said Mr. Maurice.
"Checkmate, Doctor!"

The checkmate had evidently driven Col. Ross and his expression of countenance quite out of Mr. Tim Maurice's head.

Dr. Haworth rose and said:

"I am a mere tyro. I ought not to play."

"You are not a tyro, by any means. You play a superb game!
But why on earth did you check with your knight? The obvious
move for you—"

But the obvious move was never indicated. Miss Cary came
down stairs with a celestial smile upon her lips, and entered the
drawing-room.

"At chess yet, uncle?" she said. "You gentlemen are really
incorrigible."

"Well, we thought you were amusing yourself with our friend,
the Colonel. Why did he rush away so?"

Miss Cary quietly declined to meet Mr. Tim Maurice's look.

"I think he mentioned that he had an engagement. He will
have a pleasant ride this delightful evening. Come to the parlor
and see the sunset, uncle."

"After I look at the position of these men on the board."

"Oh, no, come now, you dear old uncle!"

And linking her arm affectionately in that of Mr. Tim Maurice,
Miss Cary said, with a smile, looking over her shoulder at Dr. Haworth,

"You'll come too?"

"With pleasure."

As Dr. Haworth said this he looked at the young lady. Was
she resolved, by dragging out her uncle, to avoid a private interview
with himself? It seemed so.

Col. Ross had become so frequent a visitor that his non-appear-
ance now suggested comment.

"What's the matter with our friend, the Colonel?" said Mr. Tim Maurice one day when Dr. Haworth was present.

"The matter?" said Miss Cary, with dove-like innocence.

"We never see him now. Why does he stay away?—perhaps you can tell us."

"Indeed, I don't know," said Miss Cary without flinching.

"Are you certain?" retorted her uncle with a slight movement of his eyebrows.

"How should I know?"

"I thought something might have happened to him," said Mr. Tim Maurice—"perhaps during that walk that you and he indulged in on the lawn."

"What *can* you mean? Dr. Haworth, do you know what Uncle Tim is talking about? He is the absurdest person."

"Oh, yes, I am absurd!" exclaimed Mr. Tim Maurice, with scorching irony.

"You are dreaming, sir."

"Like other people! Behold, the dreamer cometh—or formerly came—previously to going away after his afternoon promenade."

Miss Cary pouted and looked outraged.

"Dare to tell me you have not refused our friend, the Colonel!" exclaimed Mr. Tim Maurice.

"*Refused!* How could I refuse a person who never asked me."

"Dare to say he didn't ask you! His face told the story!"

"Pshaw, uncle! you are too absurd."

"You and our friend, then, have not—well, had a misunderstanding?"

"Of course not!" cried Miss Cary.

"Then, I suppose we may indulge the hope of seeing him back very soon?"

Miss Cary for reasons best known to herself could not repress a covert smile.

"Why not," she said, with an air of heavenly innocence; "you know he is in the habit of—calling now and then."

"Yes, I believe I have discovered the fact, my child," said Mr. Tim Maurice, with a paternal air. "Now go and dress your doll—most innocent young thing! Dr. Haworth and myself propose to try a game."

Having uttered these words with deep seriousness, Uncle Tim

slowly closed one of his eyelids, and bursting suddenly into hearty laughter turned his back on Miss Cary.

As Col. Ross did not reappear at Mauricewood again, Miss Cary Maurice's character for truth seemed to have suffered shipwreck.

V.

DR. HAWORTH AND CARY MAURICE.

MISS CARY MAURICE seemed to be pursuing a somewhat singular course toward Dr. Haworth. She would never be left alone with him if she could prevent it. What was the meaning of that?

Men rarely understand women, who understand men very well. The maxim is sound, though some superior beings may dispute it.

Dr. Haworth did not understand Miss Cary Maurice in the least. His brain was a vigorous one, but he was puzzled.

The young lady was no longer so frank and unreserved as at first. The change had begun on the ride to Prof. Lesner's that day —from the moment when he had in effect told her that there was a "charm" about her which made people love her. Was that simply the idle compliment of a gentleman to a young lady? The mere words were little, but Dr. Haworth's look was a great deal—or Miss Cary seemed to think so.

What followed was a little reserve. If that was the sudden beginning, the ending might be as sudden and more emphatic. So the young lady had discovered that it would be unreasonable to take Dr. Haworth out of his way, or to trouble him to escort her home when he came to visit them at Mauricewood; a system was inaugurated —it has been mentioned. There were to be no private interviews. If there was danger of that, the peril was to be evaded. Miss Cary had forgotten her thimble. "Was that mamma calling?" So the private interview didn't take place.

There was absolutely nothing to complain of. Miss Cary's demeanor toward Dr. Haworth before others was the perfection of cordiality. It was plain that she liked him, if smiles and tones of voice mean anything. What did it all signify? Dr. Haworth saw it, and had not the least idea.

There really seemed to be no grounds for Miss Cary's apprehensions, if she indulged any. Was she fearful that the utterance of certain words by Dr. Haworth would terminate or unpleasantly modify their friendly relations; that to have a certain question asked, and to be compelled to reply to it in a certain manner, would raise a barrier of constraint between them, and dispel the charm of the little romance? If that was the explanation of Miss Cary's tactics it might be that she was putting herself to a great deal of unnecessary trouble. Why resort to all that strategy of dragging Mr. Tim Maurice out to the portico after Col. Ross' last visit? Dr. Haworth, it seemed, was capable of exchanging intelligent observations on the weather without directing the conversation to the subject of his private feelings.

Two or three times Miss Cary had found herself beaten—the victim of circumstance. She and Dr. Haworth had been left alone together. On these occasions nothing had occurred. The conversation had been friendly, and Dr. Haworth had not indulged in rapturous remarks. He was quite as grave as ever, and spoke easily and simply. This had reassured Miss Cary, and it was plain that she had lost sight at such times of her "system." He had been speaking on one of these occasions of the charm of home and home faces, which so many human beings lacked.

"You say that very feelingly," said Miss Cary, crossing her hands in her lap with an air of reflection, and looking down.

"Yes, I feel it. I have never had what people call a home."

"I am so sorry—but gentlemen have friends—you have one in your young Jean."

"Yes, but they are a poor substitute. Do *your* friends take the place of your home circle, Miss Maurice?"

"Oh, no! What you say is very true—it must be very sad to be without a home. Have you always been? But that is impossible."

"Nearly always; I am a native of this country, and lost my mother and father when very young. I went to South America, and since that time have been roving—and rovers, you know, are not domestic people."

"But you liked it."

"A little when I was young. I am now weary of it."

The grave voice seemed to excite Miss Cary's sympathy.

"But you have not always been roving about—have you lived in South America all the time?"

"No, I spent some years in Europe, and have visited the United States."

"Were none of your family living?—but you must forgive me for asking you so many questions."

"I am flattered by your doing so; it is an evidence of friendly interest."

"I take a very sincere interest in you," said Miss Cary, raising her eyes and looking into his.

"Thank you—we make each other friendly speeches," he said, "as I did that day when I met you riding to Prof. Lesner's."

"Did you?" said Miss Cary, innocently.

"I think I told you that you were beautiful, and that everybody must love you," he said. "It was a little unceremonious, but then it was sincere. You have the charm of friendliness and vivacity."

Miss Cary looked at her slippers, with her eyelashes resting nearly upon her cheeks, and twisted a lace cuff between her fingers. Dr. Haworth, however, seemed the farthest possible from designing to add anything more enthusiastic.

"If I spoke a little too plainly," he said, in a perfectly grave tone, "I hope you will pardon it, and attribute it to my fashion of speaking frankly on all subjects."

"There is nothing to pardon," said Miss Cary, still looking down.

"I have seen little of women, and scarcely know how to address them."

"What you apologize for is said to be a very acceptable way," said Miss Cary, forcing a laugh.

"It is honest, at least, and you know honesty is a great deal."

"Indeed, it *is*!"

She raised her eyes and looked at him. She had forgotten all about systems, and spoke like the good country girl that she was.

"I can't bear affectation, and pretense, and stopping to consider before every word!" she exclaimed. "Why *won't* people be natural!"

"Perhaps the explanation is that they are afraid to appear what they really are."

"You are not!"

"I am not; you know very little about me, my life, I mean—but you shall know. As to myself—my character—you know that, if you have taken the trouble to interest yourself in it. I am honest in my instincts, and my life if not gay has been respectable, which is a good word."

"A very good one."

" Not a gay life; just the reverse, and that has perhaps made me a little hard."

" You are not at all hard. It is a very unfair term to apply to yourself."

" It is just. I am not soft or romantic. You may not believe me, but I have never loved any woman. If I had children I should be different, I am sure, and I wish I had them. I am rather a lonely person, and a lonely man generally becomes hard, but I do not complain; repining is weakness. It is better to make the best of things."

" Yes, indeed," said the young lady, thoughtfully and a little sadly. I see now what you meant when you spoke of home, and your longing for one."

" I should be happier," he said. " There is nothing so dreary as to sit on a South American veranda toward evening—to hear no sound but the cries of the night-birds from the mangroves, and have no desire even to go in and look at the new books and journals lying on the table. The glimmer of the lamps is funereal—the portraits stare at you—in a word, you are alone—or rather I am—and it is not gay."

" It is very sad. You live near Lima, however?"

" A few miles from it, but I have never had any great fancy for the society there."

" But your books?"

" They are my only companions, nearly. I receive the new works from London and Paris. When I am tired, I hunt and sleep. It may be a philosopher's life—it is not a cheerful one."

Miss Cary mused. She was plainly figuring to herself this lonely existence of the pampas, and it seemed to touch her. Her head drooped, and she gazed sadly at the floor. She looked up at last and said, laughing,

" I think you ought to marry."

Dr. Haworth shook his head.

" It is not probable that I shall ever marry," he said.

This matter-of-fact response seemed to embolden Miss Cary.

" Why not?"

" I should not marry without love, and I have never loved any woman."

Miss Cary was aware of a sudden sentiment of pique.

" You may!" she said.

" It is impossible."

A little laugh greeted the words.

" Pride goes before a fall ! "

" It is not pride with me—it is the result of another trait."

" What is that ? "

" I am not impressible."

Miss Cary was thus openly defied.

" I see you are a woman-hater," she said, with a laugh, " and I suppose there is nothing more to say."

" I have a very great regard and respect for women—good ones."

" Then I hope I may inspire you with regard and respect, sir ! " laughed the young lady.

As she spoke, a servant was seen leading out two riding-horses, followed by Jean.

" Are you going to ride ? " said Miss Cary.

" I thought of doing so with Jean."

" He is very handsome," she said, looking at the youth.

" And a very good boy."

" Is he from South America ? "

" Yes."

" He is very refined in his manners, and we are all struck by his curious resemblance to the portrait of papa."

" Mr. Maurice showed it to me one day during your absence."

" You must have observed the resemblance. I notice it at every meal."

" There is certainly a resemblance, but you know that is not un-common."

Soon after which Dr. Haworth rode away with Jean.

Miss Cary remained on the veranda looking after them and musing. Having no means of reading the minds of young ladies by the expressions of their face, the present writer is unable to state what this lady was thinking about. But after a while she rose and sauntered slowly into the house. As she did so she said in a low voice:

" Poor, dear fellow ! How sorry I am for him. He says I have the charm of friendliness and vivacity. He has the charm of repose."

VI.

THE FAMILY PHYSICIAN.

WHAT Dr. Haworth had discovered in the bed in the locked room and thrust into his bosom, was a twisted cord, with a stick thrust through it—in other words, a *garrote*.

He was perfectly familiar with this primitive Spanish instrument for the infliction of capital punishment; and had instantly, at the very first sight of it, connected it with the murder. An end of the cord had protruded from between the bed-clothing, the rest being concealed. Dr. Haworth had drawn it out, and by an instinctive movement had hidden it in his breast under his waistcoat.

As soon as he was alone in his chamber, where Jean Baptiste was seated upon a cricket at a corner of the cheerful blaze—for the nights were growing chill now—Dr. Haworth took the twisted cord from his breast and said to the boy:

" Do you know what this is, Jean ? "

" Certainly, Excellency ; it is a garrote," was the reply.

" I thought you would recognize it."

" There is nothing strange in that. I have seen them often, and that is a good tough one."

Dr. Haworth looked at him quietly and said:

" Do you know you have not asked me a single question ? "

" A question ? "

" Of a hundred youths of your age ninety-nine would have asked me where I found this. You have not."

" Your Excellency's business is your own, not mine," said Jean.

" In other words, you are a person of discretion, Jean. Well, I give you a proof of my confidence now. I have told you about the murder that took place in this house. Here is the instrument with which it was committed."

" With that ! Mr. Maurice was then garroted ! "

" Yes."

Jean said nothing, but his eyes were fixed upon Dr. Haworth with the deepest attention.

" I will explain to you another time how I came to find this," he said ; " take it and lock it up in the valise."

Jean rose quietly, took a key from his pocket and locked up the twisted cord in the valise.

"Now, I have something to say to you, Jean," said Dr. Haworth. "From this moment real war begins between the man you know and myself, and you are a valuable ally."....

They talked in a low tone for about an hour, and then retired—Jean Baptiste to his pallet in the corner and his master to his bed.

On the next morning Dr. Haworth made himself agreeable generally, turned over Miss Cary's music, conversed with Mrs. Maurice, and at length joined Mr. Tim Maurice on the portico as he was about to take his morning ride.

"A pleasant day," he said.

"Really glorious!" exclaimed Mr. Tim Maurice, "and I feel as lively as a boy."

"Your health is excellent, I am happy to see."

"Excellent—owing to my scorn for people of your profession, Doctor!"

"You never take medical advice, then, since you never need it."

"Never! Dr. Seabright often denounces me and predicts I'll come to a bad end, but I laugh at him."

"Dr. Seabright?"

"He is our old family physician—and has been for thirty years."

Dr. Haworth mused for a moment.

"Thirty years?" he said. "Then I suppose he was your brother's physician?"

"Certainly—we sent for him immediately when that terrible affair occurred."

"He came, of course?"

"In half an hour, as he only resides a little beyond Abbeyville; but it was useless, of course, to send for him."

"As Mr. Maurice was dead, I understand. But I am detaining you—a pleasant ride."

"Thank you—amuse yourself with the ladies. I'll be back for a game before dinner."

But Haworth did not seem to have made his morning arrangements with a view to chess or the society of the ladies. As soon as Mr. Tim Maurice disappeared, he informed them of his intention to ride to the postoffice at Abbeyville, and his horse having been brought, he mounted and went in that direction. He soon reached Abbeyville, received the Mauricewood mail, and then, instead of returning, inquired of a person passing where Dr. Seabright lived.

The reply was a pointed finger. The house of the Doctor was visible about a mile distant crowning a hill.

Dr. Haworth rode on, and soon reached it. It was a small and very comfortable establishment surrounded by a plank fence and hedge. On the porch was seated a gray-haired man in leather leggins reading a newspaper. His overcoat indicated that he had just returned from riding.

" Dr. Seabright, I believe," said the visitor, approaching him.

" At your service, sir," said Dr. Seabright in brief tones, rising and pointing to a split-bottomed chair opposite his own. He had a ruddy face, penetrating eyes, a large nose and a wide mouth. Behind this composed mask were probably many family secrets.

" My name is Haworth," said the visitor, sitting down. " A member of your profession, sir."

" Glad to see you, Dr. Haworth," said Dr. Seabright, in an unimpressed manner.

" I am visiting your friends at Mauricewood, and thought I would call and pay my respects to a brother physician. Mr. Maurice spoke of you."

Dr. Seabright looked at the speaker with a keen glance from beneath his bushy gray eyebrows.

" Happy to know you. You are the friend from South America I have heard mentioned, I suppose ? "

" Yes."

" You visit our country at a pleasant season, and the Maurice family belong to our best people."

" They are most agreeable. You have known them a long time, no doubt."

" Well; for forty years or thereabouts, and that is quite a long time."

" You were the family physician all this time ? "

" For thirty years or more."

" That establishes a very close relation in our profession, Doctor. A family physician is necessarily thrown in contact, you know, with the joys and sorrows of each and all—unhappily it is the sorrow he sees most of."

" Yes ; he that is whole needs not a physician," said Dr. Seabright with a grim smile. " I like to quote the Scriptures now and then to show my contempt for these modern physical scientists, as they call themselves, though all their science is tomfoolery."

" I agree with you. Yes, the distress in a family is what the family physician sees, and I suppose the Mauricewood household has not been exempt ? "

" They are not often sick, and there has been no death there for a long time—since John Maurice's."

" The husband of Mrs. Maurice, I believe ? "

" Yes. He died nearly twenty years ago—a curious case."

" Curious ? "

" I have always thought—but these are private matters."

Dr. Haworth had turned his head slightly, but made no effort to induce Dr. Seabright to explain himself.

" You are very right, Doctor," he said, " the first duty of a member of our profession is to keep sacred what passes in the sick chamber. In delirium a man reveals what he would not reveal in his right senses. If his physician repeats it he is no longer a trusted friend—he is a spy."

" Right," said Dr. Seabright; " Mr. Maurice, however, did not rave."

" You were present I understand you to say when he died. You may also have been present at the death of his uncle, Mr. James Maurice. I have been told of that sad affair."

" No, I was not present," said Dr. Seabright.

" His death, you mean, followed the blow of the assassin too promptly ? "

" Yes—I see Mr. Tim has told you all about that strange business."

" Everything, and one detail of the murder struck me as remarkable."

" What was that ? "

" The cause of Mr. Maurice's death. I need not say to a gentleman with your knowledge of physiology that a blow in the temporal or parietal region is often fatal ; but it is strange that it should have proved fatal almost instantly, as it seems to have done in Mr. Maurice's case."

" Mr. Maurice was not killed by a blow on his head," said Dr. Seabright.

" Indeed ?—not by the hammer which was supposed to be the weapon used ? "

" A hammer had nothing to do with it ! "

Dr. Seabright uttered the words with the abruptness which marked all that he said.

" You surprise me," said Dr. Haworth.

" I surprised the court also, and all who heard me. I made the post-mortem examination of the body. There was no contusion—but the asses the court summoned as experts said that external indications were not always present. The weapon might have struck the hair. The consequence? I was voted an ignoramus and my whole theory a mere fancy."

" Your theory? "

" It was no theory. It was the fact."

" The fact? "

" James Maurice was strangled—probably by a cord, possibly by the hands of the murderer clutching his throat."

" Strangled! What were your grounds for so singular a supposition? "

" The marks on his throat," said Dr. Seabright coolly, " and they were not marks of hands. I know it as well as I know that I am sitting here that James Maurice met his fate in that way."

" By the garrote? "

" What is that? Oh, I understand."

" The cord used to strangle criminals in Cuba and South America. I am quite familiar with it. I will show you its operation."

He looked around him as though in search of something.

" I have a cord in my pocket," he said.

Dr. Haworth then drew from one pocket the cord which he had found in the locked room, and thrusting his hand into another pocket, produced the stick in which it had been inserted.

" This will serve to show you the operation of the Spanish garrote," he said, placing the cord around a knob of the railing beside him and twisting it by means of the stick.

" Yes," said Dr. Seabright.

" If the cord is sufficiently tough not to break, the man is soon dead, you see."

" I see. Well, that's the way James Maurice came to his death. That cord in your hand was plenty strong enough."

Dr. Haworth restored the cord and stick to his pocket and said :

" Your idea is curious—it appears remarkable that an American should have committed murder in that manner. A Spaniard might have done so."

" It is curious, but it's so," said Dr. Seabright concisely.

" You saw the traces of the garrote? "

"As plainly as I see you."

"How were they explained by the friends of the hammer theory?"

"They were not explained. As the hammer was there and the expert asses had their bosh ready about external indications, the marks on the neck went for nothing."

"The difficulty of removing a preconceived impression, I see. But—who was the garroter?"

Dr. Seabright shook his head and said:

"I have never had the least idea——"

"Mr. Ducis?" said Dr. Haworth.

"Mr. Ducis?" said Dr. Seabright, "the idea is wild! No sane person believes that."

"Who was, then?"

"Dr. Haworth," said Dr. Seabright, solemnly, "you might as well ask that jackass yonder. I am not an expert, and don't know everything. I know Mr. Ducis had nothing to do with it—he was one of the noblest of gentlemen and the best friend I had. The matter has puzzled me for twenty years. If you will clear it up I will present you with the best case of instruments to be bought in the City of London. Come in and join me in a glass of grog. I have been riding and feel a little chilled."

Dr. Haworth joined his professional brother in the glass of grog, and after a little more conversation rose to go.

"I am surprised at your theory of that murder," he said as he shook hands. "Garroted? Was there an enemy of Mr. Maurice who had been to Mexico or South America—who was familiar, I mean, with the process of garroting?"

"I never knew of any."

"No person in the neighborhood had resided in either of those countries?"

"No one but Col. Ross, and the idea that he knew anything about it never entered anybody's head."

"Naturally, as Col. Ross is a gentleman of position and character."

"He was strangled, though!" said Dr. Seabright, warmed up by his grog. "If I was on my death bed and past talking, and anybody said, 'What was the cause of James Maurice's death?' I would try for a last mouthful of air to say, 'He was strangled—the expert asses to the contrary notwithstanding.'"

Dr. Seabright then shook hands, invited his professional brother to repeat his call, and that gentleman, having stated that it would give him pleasure to do so, rode away.

VII.

AN OMEN.

WHEN Miss Cary Maurice went up-stairs, after her interview with Dr. Haworth, she sat down by an open window and looked out at the yellow trees.

Her expression was pensive and a little sad. She was probably thinking of a lonely personage living in a lonely hacienda, and pitying his lot.

"Poor, dear fellow!" she murmured again in a tone of celestial pity. And then Miss Maurice went through a curious performance. She smiled, sighed, got up, and standing in front of the mirror, which was a handsome oval, surmounting a white marble toilet table, looked at herself. The mirror reflected a pretty face just tinted with faint blushes, brown bangs nearly covering the forehead, big blue eyes and lips with a charming smile just indicated. As she looked the smile became fully developed, and Miss Cary uttered a faint laugh. Was she laughing at herself? Her reflections did not seem to concern themselves with the face in the mirror. She said half aloud:

"He must think it strange that I avoid him—and certainly it is not very polite."

This reasoning seemed to have convinced Miss Cary, since, on Dr. Haworth's return, she was sitting upon the veranda and smiled in a friendly manner as he approached. She even glanced in a casual way at a second camp-chair not far from her, and Dr. Haworth sat down.

He was a little surprised. Miss Cary had evidently forgotten nothing up-stairs; had no engagement requiring her presence elsewhere; and was ready to indulge in a friendly *tête-à-tête*.

They conversed for about an hour without interruption—Miss Cary in a happy and riant mood which drove away her companion's gloom; smiles and bright glances are like sunshine and light up all they touch upon. Miss Cary Maurice seemed to have resolved that nothing grave or gloomy should live in her presence; and when a girl as beautiful as herself ever resolves she is apt to succeed. .

Every trace of melancholy disappeared from Dr. Haworth's countenance. He had forgotten all but the fair face at his side; and the eyes fixed upon her own might have told her a great deal if she had needed to be told it.

It is nearly certain that Miss Cary did not need to be told anything about it. A man's face is never full of "strange matters" to a woman—the matters are quite familiar and are read with the utmost ease. Therefore seeing that Miss Cary understood, and realized that this man loved her—whether *he* realized it or not—her happy smiles and caressing tones were an omen.

If the only use of language is to convey ideas, and the business of a writer is to employ the words best suited to express his meaning, it would be better, perhaps, to say that Cary Maurice saw that she had inspired love and meant to say, when the moment came, "You may love me as much as you choose!"

. It was a very long step from that careful avoidance of all private interviews—but Miss Cary had taken the step.   .

When they went into the house after this conversation in the autumn twilight, something happened in the most natural manner.

Miss Cary's companion offered his hand to assist her in rising from her low seat. She at once accepted this polite attention, and the two hands met—which would have been nothing if they had not remained in each other. They did so—apparently they were both unconscious of the fact. Suddenly Dr. Haworth made Miss Cary aware of the state of things, They were at the door, and he impulsively raised the small hand to his lips.

"I think more than ever now," he said, "that you have about you the something I spoke of on our ride that evening."

Miss Cary turned and looked up at him. Her eyes were full of light.

"I am very glad," she said in a whisper almost, smiling and blushing faintly. After which she went up-stairs.

When she came down to tea, Miss Cary was perfectly easy and self-possessed—the model of a charming young person in the bosom of her family. She had never been so gay. Any one looking at her and listening to her would have said that this young lady had heard some good news,

When she retired for the night she made a low courtesy to Dr. Haworth, holding her tight skirts at the side and laughing.

He bowed and said; "I hope you will remember your engagement, Miss Maurice."

"Y—es," said Miss Cary.

"What engagement?" asked Uncle Tim.

"Dr. Haworth was good enough to promise to escort me to see Prof. Lesner. I wish to borrow a book," said Miss Cary.

"Well, take good care of the young thing, Doctor, and come back in time for our game," said Uncle Tim.

Dr. Haworth scarcely heard the words. He was looking at Cary Maurice, whose exquisite figure was just disappearing from the apartment.

As she left the room she turned her head over her shoulder and their eyes met.

The look was another omen—a word signifying, according to Dr. Johnson, "a prognostic."

VIII.

THE RESULT OF AN ACCIDENT.

THE morning was superb—a dying flash of the imperial autumn. The leaves were red-russet or as yellow as gold, the sky of gold-blue, and the woods swam in a rosy mist. It was a day for the youth and maiden of Mr. Browning's poem to take their "last ride together."

Miss Cary Maurice was in the highest spirits and looked charming in her riding-habit. Her brown hair was in a coil on her neck and a small hat was perched like a bird on the summit of her head. If Dr. Haworth's heart did not beat at sight of her, and at the touch of her ungloved hand as he assisted her to mount, he must have been what he called himself, unimpressible.

They rode at a gallop through the woods, and Miss Cary retained her extravagant spirits. Her jests effervesced like sparkling wine bursting into bubbles. In a word, something had evidently pleased her.

They reached Prof. Lesner's in half an hour, and he came out in his dressing-gown, as usual, to receive them.

His smile was as cordial, and he displayed unmistakable pleasure at seeing the young girl, but Dr. Haworth at once discerned the odor of opium smoke in his clothes. The dreamy eyes of the poor Professor were another indication that he had not abandoned his evil habit—it was very sad.

"So you have come to see your old friend before he has returned your last visit, Miss Cary," he said, smiling. "Good day, Doctor, am happy to see you."

Dr. Haworth bowed and shook hands, and Miss Cary cried:

"Returned my visit? I wish you would come, dear Prof. Lesner, but I shall not think anything of it if you do not. Your time is valuable and mine is worth nothing. I came to beg you to lend me a book."

"A book? Yes, indeed—anything I have, my dear ·Miss Cary."

"I thought I would like to read 'Luria' again—he is so grand and kind."

"A great poem—as you say, he is of heroic mold, and so profoundly *true.*"

Prof. Lesner then went into his library and brought out the volume, a canary bird having embraced the opportunity to perch upon his shoulder.

"You see my birds still pet me—poor recluse that I am," he said, with his dreamy smile.

"I think they show their sense—you are their very best friend," said Miss Cary.

"Well, we all need friends—and I have just had a proof that I have some myself. Would you believe it these poor Hill people have insisted on electing me a magistrate?"

"A magistrate?"

"A justice of the peace!"

And Prof. Lesner uttered a slight laugh.

"It was actually without my knowledge," he said, "and I am not at all fit for it. True, I was a law student in early life, but I never practiced. I think the idea of these humble people is to have a good natured old magistrate who will let them off easily."

"Why, of course!" Miss Cary exclaimed. "I am sure that was why you were elected. So you are a justice?"

"Yes, I have been to qualify and have received my certificate. It is absurd, but the poor folk seem to think I am capable. I hesirated to accept, but thought I would not reject what I suppose was meant as a mark of friendly feeling."

"I think you were perfectly right, sir," said Dr. Haworth.

"I am glad you approve, Doctor. But sit down, Miss Cary."

"Thank you; we were only out riding. I think mamma will expect me back."

And after a lively conversation, rather dreamy and fantastic on the part of the poor Professor, they shook hands with him and again mounted.

"It is sad to see such a person so lonely," said Miss Cary, as they rode on slowly.

"Yes—we spoke the other day of lonely lives, I remember. They are not very gay."

"Of yours, you mean."

Miss Cary rode on at a walk—her good spirits seemed to have all effervesced.

"What the Preacher says is true," said Dr. Haworth. "'Two are better than one'—that is to say, sympathy is a necessity to human beings. You will remember the text, 'woe to him that is alone when he falleth.'"

Miss Cary smiled rather faintly.

"That is said of friends only—is it not?" she asked.

"Yes, but the truth is stronger if we apply it to a man and woman who love each other."

"I suppose so," said Miss Cary, in a tone of deep thought.

"I am only sorry that I can not follow the advice of Ecclesiastes, in that sense, and love some one who would comfort me in my hours of depression."

"That would make you happier," said Miss Cary, in the same tone, without looking at him.

"Unfortunately I do not hope to find any such person. I am not very lovable, and then—"

If Dr. Haworth was on the point of adding that his own obdurate indifference would be an additional obstacle, he did not do so. His sentence remained unfinished. Miss Cary Maurice's horse started violently and began running at full speed.

The cause of this was simple. The woods through which they were riding were the resort of "wild hogs," as they were generally called—that is, of hogs which had escaped from their owners and returned nearly to a state of nature. In passing a copse Miss Cary's horse was suddenly startled by a hoarse growl, and one of these animals rushed out. The consequence was that the animal shied violently, ran, and as Miss Cary had dropped the bridle on his neck she had no control over him.

The result was a painful accident. Before Dr. Haworth, riding at his utmost speed, could catch up with her, she was thrown. Her saddle girth had turned and she fell at full length in the road about ten feet in front of him.

He threw himself from the saddle and ran to her She was lying on her side, quite unconscious. Lifting her in his arms and clasping her close to him, he cried:

"Cary!—my own Cary! Good God!—she is not dead?"

Her head fell upon his shoulders, and she was a limp weight in his arms. Every trace of color had disappeared from her face and her eyes were closed.

With a passionate sob Dr. Haworth placed his hand upon her heart. It was beating feebly, and he knew then that she had only fainted from her heavy fall. Had she broken any of her limbs? Neither arm was bleeding, and with the physician's instinct he glanced toward her limbs.

"She will tell me if she revives!" he said in a trembling voice; and again he called "Cary."

She opened her eyes and looked up at him. Her face was lying upon his breast, and she drew closer to him.

"You are hurt—badly hurt, Cary!"

Whereupon Dr. Haworth, scarce aware of what he was doing, and forgetting his professional character, stooped and kissed her forehead, exclaiming:

"I never knew how much I loved you!"

It was plain that Miss Cary's faint was at an end. Her face filled with blushes, and he could feel her bosom resting against his own rise and fall.

"I am not much hurt!" she murmured.

"God be thanked," he said. "If you had been killed I should not have cared to live. I have been a fool! I did not know! I love you dearly—so dearly! Remember what we said—woe to those who are alone when they fall!"

"Yes."

That was all Miss Cary's reply. As she clasped her hands behind his neck, however, no more seemed necessary.

Dr. Haworth assisted her to a fallen tree near the road, caught the horses after a little trouble, and lifted her to the saddle, after which they rode home, nearly in silence. The accident had taken place not far from Mauricewood, and they soon arrived.

As Miss Cary dismounted, and walked rather painfully into the house, she said to Dr. Haworth:

." I will tell mamma."

She was standing in the door and looking at him out of a pair of moist blue eyes.

" Will you tell her all ? " he said.

" Yes."

" That I love you and can not live without you ? "

" Yes."

He bent down and kissed her, and she returned the kiss; after which she went up stairs.

IX.

MAY AND AUGUST.

. THE love of a mature man differs very much from the love of a youth.

The youth loves because it is a necessity with him—because the time has come to love. In the spring the sap pushes, and the ardor of youth requires an outlet—or say the inner impulse is like the subtile gas in new wine and produces an overflow. It is charming, but evanescent, as all momentary impulses are. To the young lover the character of the object of his love is not of great importance. Red lips, rosy cheeks, bright eyes and curls—he is satisfied if he finds these.

It is not to laugh at him to say that he is satisfied, since he sees much more. What is wanting his fancy supplies. The possessor of the curls and roses is necessarily an angel.

Then the natural result follows. When he has forced upon him the conviction after a while that his angel is a doll and not at all angelic, he suddenly cools. There are other angels or dolls he sees. Other roses are fresher, other eyes brighter. The stronger magnet draws him—and then the first love is quickly replaced by another, to yield in due time to numberless numbers.

The world calls the youth fickle. He is not fickle, he is natural.
What comes quickly, goes quickly. The youth's heart is in his
hand; he gives it and snatches it back. When he gives it again, it
is to snatch it again, and transfer it to a new angel. Or his beloved
does the same, and the young lover has the heart-ache. No matter, that will not last. The sap gushes, and the cut heals over.
The sun is shining, the days are long; there are so many other curls
and roses!

When a man passes 30, April is over, and the summer has
come. From that time forward he no longer carries his heart in
his hand, begging every little beauty to accept it. He is pleased
with them, but loves none of them, and they naturally find him far
less attractive than the rosy youths who burst into raptures. Admiration, friendly regard, even affection—yes, but no more. May
and August differ nearly as much as May and December.

But August is settled weather. The spring showers and sunshine rapidly chasing each other have given way to blue skies and
calm. When a storm rises, however, it is a thunder storm. To
drop figures, the love of middle age is a very profound sentiment. It is not given easily nor recalled easily, and when a man
has reached this period of life without really loving any one before, his passion for the person he comes to love at last is absorbing.

Dr. Haworth loved Cary Maurice in this manner now—with all
the strength of a strong nature. He had met his fate. In the brief
space of time between their first meeting and her fall from horseback he had lost sight of his past life and thought only of the face
and voice, the eyes and lips, of this "simple girl" whom he had
never seen before.

It is the old story which the story-tellers find their pens relating
all these years—a man loving a woman, and counting all else worthless unless she loves him in return.

After the ride to Prof. Lesner's he had no longer any doubt.
Cary Maurice loved him! It was the wonder of wonders, but she
actually did love him! Incredible as it might appear, she had not
preferred some ruddy youth, full of rapture and romance; she had
chosen him, with his furrowed brow, sunburnt cheeks and gravity
—unliked of woman.

What was to be the result? Would his whole life change, and
pass henceforth in tranquil happiness beside this angel? It was

too beautiful a dream to be more than a dream, perhaps. Life had its stern work, demanding the service of every faculty—and his own work was before him.

X.

MISS BURNS.

ON the morning after the ride, which had been followed by such unexpected results, Dr. Haworth and Mrs. Maurice remained for some time in private conversation in the drawing-room.

As Mr. Tim Maurice was absent on his daily tour of inspection, and Miss Cary did not make her appearance, they were not interrupted, and conversed at their leisure.

An interruption at one time did seem to threaten them. Miss Burns, the young seamstress from Abbeyville, who had been for some time employed to assist in the household sewing, came downstairs looking around her, perhaps for Mrs. Maurice to ask some directions.

Miss Burns was a handsome young person, of about 20, neatly dressed, with a fine suit of black hair and a rosy complexion. Her face was smiling and her eyes sparkled. She was, in fact, a very flattering specimen of a class which, wanting the grace springing from culture and refinement, often possess physical attractions. Beyond this there was nothing remarkable in Miss Burns' appearance except that she was retiring and giggled occasionally.

As she came quietly down the staircase now, her feet made no noise. Having reached the hall she stopped and listened. The voices of Dr. Haworth and Mrs. Maurice were heard in the drawing-room, and Miss Burns went to the closed door and listened.

This was a little discreditable, but then curiosity is said to be a feminine failing. She listened with her ear at the keyhole for some moments, but seemed to be disappointed. Either the inmates of the apartments were seated on the other side of the room and spoke in low tones, or the keyhole was filled with dust—certainly Miss Burns rose erect with an expression of dissatisfaction.

She then went out and strolled to and fro on the veranda, looking at the landscape. The venetians were open and she did not approach the windows, on the contrary she re-entered quietly and returned up-stairs.

She had not seen Jean Baptiste, who was lying under one of the oaks smoking a cigarette, but Jean had followed all her movements, and uttered a low laugh as she disappeared.

After a while Mrs. Maurice left the drawing-room and Miss Cary came down. As she did not close the door of the room after her, anybody who had been in the hall at the time might have seen her go up to Dr. Haworth and place her hand in his.

Some one nearly observed it. Miss Burns once more came quietly down the staircase and stole on tiptoe toward the door. It really was discreditable; Miss Burns was about to eavesdrop!

Unfortunately, if she were watching others, some one was watching *her*.

As the maiden gracefully inclined toward the door, a low laugh attracted her attention, and suddenly turning she saw Jean in the veranda looking at her.

Thereupon Miss Burns colored, tossed her head, and abruptly ran up-stairs again. Jean remained standing on the veranda, quietly laughing.

XI.

DR. HAWORTH'S CURIOUS FANCY.

SOME days passed. Affairs at Mauricewood followed the ordinary routine. Mr. Tim Maurice regularly took his morning rides; Mrs. Maurice superintended her household matters, going about quietly with her soft step and sweet smile; and Miss Cary, when not assisting her, was apt to be conversing with Dr. Haworth in the drawing-room, or occasionally with Jean.

A great alteration had taken place in Dr. Haworth. His grave face grew, at times, brilliant with a smile which quite transformed it; and whenever his eyes fell upon Cary Maurice their natural sternness melted into the soft splendor which comes to a man's face when he loves a woman.

His whole life had, in fact, changed—his very being seemed to have undergone a sudden transformation. The collected and somewhat weary air which had characterized him in moments of repose had disappeared—he was eager and hopeful. One could see that the man had a future now—that the past had dropped from him like a worn-out garment.

The object of his visit to the Mauricewood neighborhood was perhaps not forgotten, but he had thrust it aside for the moment. It was tolerably certain that a man of his character would not thrust it aside long, but the blue eyes of a girl had dazzled him for the time. He seemed to ask nothing better than to bask in that light to which he was not accustomed, and for some days after his ride with Cary he seemed to have lost sight of all else.

All at once he was brought back to his work. Something was evidently going on at Mauricewood. It was obvious that Miss Burns was *watching him.*

Dr. Haworth was a quiet observer and not apt to take up fancies. There was no doubt at all about it. For some inexplicable reason Miss Burns followed all his movements with the closest attention, looking and listening.

She did not look *at* him, or appear to be listening, and yet he saw that she was doing both. At table she ate her meals modestly with her eyes fixed upon her plate. When she had finished she rose quietly, smiled, and went up-stairs to her sewing. In the evening when her work was done she took a walk for exercise, or returned to her chamber. Her retiring disposition seemed to dictate to her the propriety of not intruding on the family circle, though when she did so she was treated with the utmost kindness and courtesy. Mrs. Maurice and Miss Cary were much too well-bred to make distinctions in their treatment of people, but Miss Burns modestly insisted upon keeping her place.

She did not speak to Dr. Haworth often. Sometimes it was necessary, as when he would ask if he might help her to a dish before him. She then said : " Thank you," or " no ; I thank you sir," in a modest voice, giggling slightly and scarcely raising her eyes. When she did raise them he observed that they were black and laughing, and said to himself that Mrs. Maurice had a very handsome seamstress.

This had been the state of things up to within a few days. Now Miss Burns seemed to be growing somewhat less shy. Living in the home with people naturally banishes ceremony, and human beings become familiarly acquainted. Miss Burns spoke with Dr. Haworth more frequently, and even seemed to seek for occasions to do so. She often met him accidentally on the staircase and giggled in a friendly manner, looking at him out of the corners of her eyes. At such times she blushed, casting down her eyelashes. Once she met him as he was coming out of the drawing-room, and the two faces nearly struck against each other, when Miss Burns blushed violently and exclaimed :

"Oh, *do* excuse me, I am *so* awkward !"

"I am sure the awkwardness is mine, madam," Dr. Haworth said, bowing. But Miss Burns protested that the accident was the result of her own awkwardness, and, looking bashfully at him, glided away.

This was romantic—but unfortunately there was something mingled with the romance. As the hours passed on Dr. Haworth was more and more convinced that Miss Burns was watching him. Then he began to concentrate his attention upon her. He had seen a great deal of human nature, and knew that the first question was always the motive. Why should Miss Burns take so much interest in him ? Having propounded this interrogatory to himself he began to watch *her*.

She became an interesting study. He was himself the least secretive of human beings, as proud people always are, and a profoundly secretive person was a curiosity to him. The generous and open-handed man marvels at the avarice of the miser, and Dr. Haworth, who was straightforward and virile, studied the secretiveness of this feminine diplomat with interest.

The trait seemed ingrained in her being ; she moved about enveloped in a cloud. To speak more intelligibly, she was evidently observing with close attention all that took place at Mauricewood ; was especially interested in Dr. Haworth, and—a fact which came to be noticed—was even curious to know what was going on in the vicinity, unless her long evening walks were constitutionals.

One morning Miss Burns met Dr. Haworth as he was passing through the hall. He had just returned from riding, and was going to his room to make his toilet.

Miss Burns had just indulged in a walk, it seemed, for she had gathered some superb dogwood leaves of a dazzling crimson. She held them up as Dr. Haworth passed her, and said with a smile :

"Ain't they just lovely !"

"They are really beautiful," said Dr. Haworth, bowing.

"Just too lovely for anything," said Miss Burns, who may have found the phrase in a paper novel. "You have been riding, I suppose, sir ?"

Dr. Haworth bowed.

" How I wish I had an escort—I am *so* fond of riding ? " And Miss Burns giggled.

Dr. Haworth looked at her. Was she proposing that he should become her escort ? It seemed so, since she added :

" I only ride once a week—to town ; and then it is just *too* lonely."

When Miss Burns said this she looked at Dr. Haworth in a languishing manner.

" I am going to-morrow," she said, casting down her eyes, picking at the red leaves. Then she suddenly looked up at him.

Dr. Haworth understood now, and expressed himself in a straightforward manner.

" I regret that it is out of my power to offer you my escort, Miss Burns," he said. " I have an engagement to-morrow."

" An engagement ? " sighed Miss Burns.

" To ride with Miss Maurice."

Miss Burns looked sudden daggers, but before she could reply Miss Cary Maurice came down stairs, and Miss Burns went up, passing her. Cary's face was full of smiles and happiness ; that of Miss Burns had suddenly become overcast. At the landing she stopped and listened, looking through the railing.

" I came down to get a book," said Miss Cary. " I suppose your lordship is too tired to help me to look for it."

Dr. Haworth did not reply, but his action was expressive. He took both Miss Cary's hands in his own, drew her to him, and pressed his lips to her forehead.

It was not much, but Miss Burns, witnessing the performance, shut her lips tightly together and looked furious. When Miss Cary and her companion disappeared, hand in hand, in the drawing-room, Miss Burns knit her handsome brows and went to her chamber.

XII.

MISS BURNS' MAIL-BAG.

THE ride with Miss Cary was not a thing invented by the enemy —if Dr. Haworth were Miss Burns' enemy—but an actual engagement.

Miss Cary Maurice was very popular, and liked to visit her

friends. · Her mother could not always go, and it was stupid to go
alone in the family carriage. She was much fonder of horseback
riding, but to ride alone was not precisely regular; so she hailed the
possession of an escort. As he was the escort whom she preferred
to all others that was all the better. So they rode away together.

They returned in the afternoon, and toward sunset Dr. Haworth
lit a cigar—he smoked sometimes—and walked down the hill toward
the gate opening into the grounds.

He was about a hundred yards from the house when Jean Baptiste joined him, and they walked on together until the foliage concealed them from view.

"We are out of sight now," said Jean, "and I should like to have
a few words with your excellency."

"Out of sight?" said Dr. Haworth quietly. "Then you think
that some one is watching us?"

"I think it not improbable—as they can't listen at this distance."

"Listen?—a few words with me do you say, Jean? Why not
say what you wish to say in our chamber?"

"There are too many ears about."

"Ears?"

"There are more ears in the Mauricewood house than you
think."

Dr. Haworth shook his head and replied:

"I am afraid association with me has had an evil effect upon
your character, Jean. You are growing suspicious of everybody and
everything."

"That would be bad," said Jean laughing, "but if one has eyes
and ears, he can't help seeing and hearing."

"What have you seen and heard?"

"I will tell you if you will go a little way—that is, I will show
you."

"A little way?"

"As far as the big ash tree at the corner of the grounds, toward
the town—yonder it is."

They had passed through the carriage gate and were in the
woods, following a path which led in the direction of Abbeyville.
About three hundred yards in front rose the bushy summit of a tall
ash—it was a landmark.

"We will be there in a minute, and I will then tell you what I
mean," said Jean.

"Very well; take your time, my dear Jean. Would you like to smoke?" ·

"Oh! I was dying for it," exclaimed Jean with a boyish laugh. "Your excellency knows I am half-Spaniard."

"I don't know anything of the sort!" said Dr. Haworth looking at him with a curious smile. "Why, smoke, of course! Here is a cigar."

But Jean had already fashioned his husk cigarette with the rapidity of a Spaniard. Dr. Haworth presented his cigar tip, and Jean began smoking with evident delight.

"Here is the tree, excellency," he said.

It was a very large one growing from a rude pile of rock, and the huge roots twisting to and fro had thrust themselves between the crevices and burst the ledges. Under these were dusky hollows —the probable resort of rabbits and such game.

"What is there so very interesting about this tree, Jean?" said Dr. Haworth.

"It is Miss Burns' postoffice," said Jean, laughing quietly.

"Miss Burns' postoffice! What do you mean?"

"It is more convenient than the town. She puts her letters under that big root."

"Miss Burns—her letters?"

"For your friend Col. Ross, or somebody who takes them to him."

"Col. Ross!"

"I am very much mistaken if Miss Burns is not a friend of the Colonel's, Excellency. It is the only way I can explain her watching you and leaving—well, her reports here."

Dr. Haworth seemed greatly impressed and said:

"Are you sure this is not a mere fancy?"

"Well, it may be—you will judge. I can only say what I think is the fact. My idea is this, that your friend the Colonel has a great deal of curiosity, and wanted to know what was going on at the house yonder; so he persuaded this pretty Miss Burns to keep him informed."

"What reason have you to think so?"

"Well, several reasons. Miss Burns came into your room last night."

"Into my chamber?"

Jean nodded,

"I happened to be awake, which is very seldom, as a youngster is apt to sleep sound, and I saw her."

"Saw her?"

"With my eyes. She opened the door—it may have been nearly 2 in the morning—and came in as quietly as a ghost, or rather a girl in her stocking feet. She walked without the least sound, and looked all about her, particularly toward your traveling valise."

"My valise?"

"She did better than look; she tried to open it, but it was locked. You see I always carry the key in my waistcoat pocket and sleep with it under my head."

"Tried to open my valise, did you say?"

"Yes, but she found it would not open. She then searched your clothes and mine, too, for the key and any papers. I suppose she was looking for papers."

"Papers?"

"Your Excellency seems to forget that a certain gentleman is anxious to know all about you. You are here for something, he thinks—something that interests *him*. If he has not found out what brings you, and would like to know, I suppose he would like to see your letters or other papers."

"You are no doubt right," said Dr. Haworth thoughtfully, "and I was not wrong in saying that you would be an intelligent ally, Jean."

"I mean to do what I can to pay you what I owe you."

"You owe me nothing."

"I owe you my life! Your Excellency knows that. To come to business, what I tell you is certain. This girl has an understanding with Col. Ross—I am sure of it."

"Did he place her here for the purpose?"

"I don't think he did. She was here before he thought of it, I think. Up to the time when Miss Cary sent him off he could see for himself, now he uses this girl's eyes—to find out what is going on between you and Miss Cary—and what you are after, too."

Dr. Haworth reflected for a moment and then said:

"Well, that is really ingenious. If you are right, our friend is a dangerous man."

"He learned to work in the dark down yonder," said Jean, succinctly, pointing in the direction of South America. "He sent that torpedo boat to blow you up."

"Well—that is probable. So he has his confidential agent here, has he? How could he arrange that?"

"Nothing was easier. Miss Burns rides on horseback once a week to the town to see her people. Our friend the Colonel could manage the rest—it is only a question of so much money."

"Yes—but does she really communicate with him?"

"This is her postoffice, as I told you," said Jean laughing, "and that hollow under the root there is the mail-bag. I saw her come here and pull out a paper."

"But her own information—?"

"She had forwarded it, I suppose, already. There is some one who comes at night, I think, and gets the girl's letters. If he has any directions for her he leaves them—and she comes and gets them. That is the way. I saw her."

"Well, that seems to end all doubt. Col. Ross is playing a deep game."

"Deep?" said Jean, "well that just describes the Colonel. There is no danger of his being known in the affair, and what his agent writes to Miss Burns, or she to him, is not apt to entangle *him*. There is no doubt that this girl is employed to watch you—and now, as some one might pass and notice us, I suppose your Excellency had better go back. I will follow afterward."

"That is a wise precaution, Jean," said Dr. Haworth without moving, "but before I go I might as well say that I knew all this before."

"Your Excellency knew?"

"I didn't know of this postoffice as you call it—the rest is no news to me."

"You have noticed her watching you?"

"Certainly."

"Listening, and tripping about and putting her ear to the key-holes?"

"I have not seen her do so, but have no doubt that she does that."

"And you knew—!"

"That she came into the room last night? Yes, I was not asleep."

Jean drew a long breath.

"Really, your Excellency does not need my help," he said with an air of disappointment,

"On the contrary it is of the very greatest service to me—I require it. Listen a moment."

Dr. Haworth had remained composed during the whole conversation. His face now filled with blood and he said in the brief, abrupt voice which always betrayed a great deal with him:

"It is useless to try to hide anything. It is open war between this man and myself. He either assassinated James Maurice or procured his assassination. I have come to this country to ferret out all that, and mean to do so if I am not murdered in my turn. That attempt has been made. It will probably be made again. Some day when I am riding through the woods a bullet may put an end to me—or when I am leaning from my chamber window at night. I may drink a glass of water, or wine, flavored with a peculiar powder. Who knows? This handsome Miss Burns may have the powder in her pocket at the present moment. She is placed here to watch me—you are right about that—therefore I am dangerous. When men are dangerous to certain people they try to suppress them; and I think Col. Ross would like to suppress *me*. Well, I come back to what I began with. It is open war—or rather secret. As he prefers that, it suits me too. War is not rose water—it is a question of blood. Ruse is fair against ruse. As this girl is put here to watch *me*, I will watch *her*. As she crept into my room to carry away my papers, I will carry away her own, or you will for me."

"I won't fail to do that, Excellency!" exclaimed Jean, with ardor.

"It is of little importance—a small feature of the real struggle. Since yesterday I have made up my mind."

"Made up your mind?"

"To strike!" said Dr. Haworth briefly. "Up to this time I have been collecting information. The whole affair I came to investigate was a mystery. That was natural, since it occurred twenty years ago—what remained unknown then is necessarily ten times harder to discover now. I will tell you more at another time. I have now what amounts to a conviction—I will act upon it."

Dr. Haworth then went back to the house by the path which he had taken in coming, and half an hour afterward Jean Baptiste appeared from the direction of the stables.

It was not probable that Miss Burns, if she had seen them walk away together, suspected anything.

XIII.

THE MAIL.

MISS BURNS did not take her weekly ride to Abbeyville, having a bad headache, which confined her to her chamber.

Having then no sewing to do she had recourse to her pen, and seemed to be much interested in the letter she was writing. She wrote quite a good hand, and appeared to express herself without difficulty; in fact, she had received a fair public school education, and had a cultivated taste for reading dime novels.

Toward sunset she announced with pathetic sweetness to sympathizing Mrs. Maurice that her headache was nearly gone; took a stroll in the grounds, and returned about twilight.

It was just growing dark when Dr. Haworth, who had been riding out, came back and found Jean awaiting him.

"I have something for your excellency," said the boy.

"Very well," said Dr. Haworth, "bring it to my room. I am going to make my toilet."

He went up to his chamber, and ten minutes afterwards Jean entered and closed the door.

"Here is a letter I found in the mail-bag," he said, with quiet enjoyment. "I thought it would interest your excellency."

Dr. Haworth took the letter, which was unsealed, and opened it, muttering, "War is war."

It was not very long. Miss Burns had written in a large hand what follows:

"There is very little use in my staying here any longer. I am suspected and they are *watching me*. The boy suspects me—I can see him looking sideways at me at all times of the day; and *he* has begun to look at me, too, *in the same way*.

"I can't find any papers. I couldn't look in the day time, as all the doors are kept open, and I went *at night*. I was afraid at first, but I went—while they were both asleep. There was nothing there, and his trunk was locked, and I could not find the key. .

"I hate that boy; he is a *hateful little wretch*. And *he* is a *cruel* man. I as much as asked him to escort me to town, and he excused himself *on account of an engagement with that girl*, and I believe *made one* afterward with her. *Somebody* wants to know whether she cares anything for *him*. I rather think she does. She

is so *lovesick* about him that it makes *me* sick *at my stomach.* I
never knew it till lately—and he is just as bad about *her.* How I
hate her and *him.* I do believe they are engaged.

"I am going back home, as I am no use here. Why don't somebody write an *anonymous letter* telling them that he is an *escaped
convict,* or something? That would be nice. If they don't, he will
marry that simpering doll and *laugh at everybody.*

"P. S.—*Somebody* had better write that *anonymous letter.*

"P. S. again. I wish *Somebody* would have *that money* ready
for me, as I did not come here *to sew* for a trifle. You know why
I came here. Tell *Somebody* I want *that money.*"

This was not signed, but Miss Burns had the characteristics of
great writers—her productions reflected her individuality.

"What do you think of that, Excellency?" said Jean in high
good humor, "I took the liberty to read it."

"I think it very well written," said Dr. Haworth. "Take it
back."

"Back?"

"To your mail-bag of course; that is the proper proceeding.
Let us not try to surpass his French majesty. He always honestly
forwarded letters after discovering what they contained."

"You mean then—"

"To invite the anonymous letter? Yes. That will arrive in a
day or two. There is another point. Let us reap the reward, at
least, if we are to resort to underhand warfare. I prefer to have
Miss Burns remain here for two or three days."

"Your Excellency is right," said Jean in a low voice. "The
letter will be back there in fifteen minutes."

"Go at once; the mail-carrier may come."

Jean sauntered from the chamber, went down-stairs and out
through a side door. Once outside he began running, as it was now
dark and no one could see him. In ten minutes he was at the ash
tree and, depositing the letter, returned quietly to the house.

He had seen no indications that any one had visited the spot in
his absence.

XIV.

THE REWARD FOR HOLDING A LAMPSHADE.

DR. HAWORTH was quite correct in his surmise. Two days afterward the anonymous letter arrived.

It was a very mild evening, and the whole family had gone out to the veranda, when a servant, who had been sent to Abbeyville for the mail, returned with the bag.

Mr. Tim Maurice opened it and distributed two or three letters to the ladies. Then he extracted his newspaper and a letter addressed to himself, which he proceeded to open.

Dr. Haworth was conversing with Mrs. Maurice, but his eyes, passing beyond her, fixed themselves with interest on Mr. Tim Maurice's face. Suddenly that gentleman looked up with a singular expression and caught Dr. Haworth's eye.

"Here is something that will interest you, Doctor," he said. "I wonder who could have written it?"

"Interest *me?*" said Dr. Haworth, composedly.

"Read it."

Dr. Haworth took the letter and read this written in a bold hand:

"Sir: A friend takes the liberty of informing you that the Dr. Haworth now at your house is an impostor. He is not the person he pretends to be. He escaped from jail in Texas, and is traveling under a false name. You may not believe the writer of an anonymous letter, but there are reasons why this one is not signed. The only intention of the writer is to warn you against a crank and fraud."

Having read this letter Dr. Haworth handed it back to Mr. Tim Maurice, and said with a smile:

"Do you believe that?"

"Well," said Mr. Tim Maurice in a grave tone, "the writer seems to believe what he says."

"So he does."

"I am afraid appearances are against you, Doctor. Don't you think so, ladies? Just read this."

He bent over and gave it to Mrs. Maurice, who read it and said in a tone of surprise:

"That is really too outrageous! Who could have presumed to write it, and what was the object of it?"

Miss Cary had meanwhile snatched it and was reading it with flushed cheeks.

"Who dared to send this!" she exclaimed, raising her head with the air of a queen.

"I really don't know," said Uncle Tim. "There is no name to it, which I agree is a little suspicious; but then, there is the charge, my dear, and I need not say, even at the risk of hurting Dr. Haworth's feelings, that it is extremely serious."

Miss Cary Maurice looked into her uncle's face with the expression of a person who doubts if they have heard certain words aright.

"Serious!" she cried.

"Well, my dear little Cadie," said Uncle Tim sadly, "I would not wound you for the world. Dr. Haworth is your friend, and you know how much I esteemed him. I say *esteemed*—in the past tense, you observe—for really such charges demand refutation."

"Uncle! are you in earnest?"

"Of course I am in earnest, my dear. As the only gentleman of the family, I am under the painful necessity of requesting our guest, Dr. Haworth, to meet and refute these allegations. I have no doubt that he will be able to do so."

"Uncle," cried Miss Cary, with blazing eyes.

"An honest man should invite investigation—not endeavor to avoid it. If our friend, the doctor, is the person he professes to be, of course he will have no difficulty in establishing the fact. I do not say that he is an impostor, or has escaped from jail in Texas or anywhere else; but then mere sentiment will not answer."

Miss Cary gazed at the speaker as if she really believed that he was out of his mind. Her lips moved, but uttered no sound; the great blue eyes seemed to be the only living part of the white face.

"I will, therefore, take the liberty of addressing a few questions to Dr. Haworth," said Uncle Tim, who had not observed the girl's expression of anguish.

"I will answer them with pleasure, sir," said Dr. Haworth composedly.

"Be good enough then, Doctor," said Uncle Tim, "to state for my information and the information of the ladies of my family whether you did or did not escape from jail in Texas or elsewhere, and whether you are or are not an impostor?"

Miss Cary rose to her feet suddenly.

"You shall not even ask," she cried.

Uncle Tim started and looked at her.

" How can you—"

She burst into tears, and a moment afterward Uncle Tim had her in his arms, crying :

" Cadie ! Did you think I was in earnest ? Did you imagine I meant what I said ? I thought you would understand the joke ! I must be a wretched bungler—to hurt my dear Cadie's feelings—but no !" exclaimed Uncle Tim with pride, laughing and kissing the sobbing girl. " I must be a great histrionic genius !—an actor of the first order—for you thought I was in earnest ! "

" You were not in earnest, then ? " sobbed Miss Cadie.

" The very idea, my child, to suppose that my opinion of any-body, much less of *Dr. Haworth*, could be affected by the coward-ly sneak who wrote that thing. None but sneaks write anonymous letters, and I was only amusing myself at my little girl's expense."

" You ridiculous old thing ! " said Miss Cary, with candor ; after which she laughed and returned to her seat.

" I believe I have not replied to your question, my dear Mr. Maurice," said Dr. Haworth.

" My question ? Did I ask a question ? "

" You asked me if I had escaped from jail, or was an impostor—neither is the fact."

" I accept your apology—that is to say, your very satisfactory explanation, Doctor," said Mr. Tim Maurice laughing. " And now as this little family matter is settled, would you like to see the even-ing papers ? Light the lamps, Cadie—they are your charge."

Miss Cary rose and went into the drawing-room where the globe lamp was waiting on the center table.

" Will you hold this shade for me while I light the lamp, Dr. Haworth ? " she called.

He went in and held the shade, when Miss Cary scraped a match and lighted a wisp of paper. As it was flaming she held it up be-fore him—it was the anonymous letter.

A moment afterward the lamp was lit, and Dr. Haworth as he placed the shade upon it felt two warm lips touch his cheek.

" The lamps are ready, now," cried Miss Cary.

XV.

PRIVATE CORRESPONDENCE.

THE result of Miss Burns' advice had thus been very unfortunate. The anonymous letter had produced no effect. The Mauricewood family had simply laughed at it.

When they came in from the veranda to tea, every face was smiling, and Miss Burns, seated at the table with eyes modestly cast down, as usual, had the pleasure of hearing a number of jests uttered by Mr. Tim Maurice, to the effect that the newspapers were unutterably stupid now; there were no reports even of hair-breadth *escapes from jail,* and not a single clerical, medical or other *impostor* had been recently unmasked !

Miss Burns listened in modest silence. She was a very quick-witted young lady and had probably found the means of overhearing the conversation on the veranda. Something had certainly put her in a very bad humor—that was plain as she went up-stairs; and when she began the composition of a document late that night her handsome forehead was contracted into a frown.

As she slept in a small room by herself there was no chance of interruption. At about 11:30 o'clock she had finished her letter, which filled only a page or two of note paper, and having folded it and put it in the pocket of her apron, she went to her door and listened. The establishment was perfectly quiet, as the habit of the family was to retire about 10; and emerging from her room she saw no signs of light anywhere. She then arranged her shawl so as to protect her head, and went quietly down-stairs to the side door in rear of the hall, which she unbolted without noise and opened. She then listened again and satisfied herself that not a creature was stirring. There was no danger from the bark of a dog, as none were kept at Mauricewood, in deference to Mrs. Maurice's delicate nerves —she was easily awakened, and the barking disturbed her. Miss Burns therefore left the house without causing any stir whatever, and walked rapidly through the grounds in the direction of the ash tree. It was a superb moonlight night, and a little chill, which made her wrapping very comfortable. The lateness of the hour evidently did not disturb her. Mauricewood was a quiet place, where tramps or other intruders never came; and Miss Burns therefore went on confidently, and soon reached her ash tree.

It was a picturesque object in the moonlight which flooded the few remaining leaves, the gnarled boughs twisted into fantastic shapes, the huge roots, and the straight trunk with its fine bark. As the moon was sinking, the hollow under the root which she used as a postoffice was plain in the light—the trunk throwing a deep shadow on the rocky mass behind it.

Miss Burns stooped down and looked carefully in the crevice under the root where she evidently expected to find something. In this she seemed to be disappointed, as she rose up with empty hands.

She then drew from her pocket the letter which she had written, placed it carefully in the crevice and went back rapidly toward the house.

As soon as she was out of sight Jean Baptiste, who had been hidden in the black shadow behind the ash tree, came out, took the letter from its place, and going back to the shadow patiently waited.

He had not to wait more than half an hour. At the end of that time a man got over the inclosure of the grounds about fifty yards from the tree and walked quietly to it.

Jean had no difficulty in recognizing him—it was Mr. Job Wilkins.

Mr. Wilkins made a careful search in the hollow under the root, and having satisfied himself that there was nothing in the postoffice, drew a paper from his pocket and concealed it where Miss Burns had concealed her own note. He looked carefully around, listened for a moment, and, walking away, leaped over the inclosure and disappeared.

Jean then emerged from his friendly shadow, possessed himself of the second letter, and returned to the house. To effect an entrance he was obliged to use precaution. Miss Burns might be listening. Miss Burns was fast asleep by this time, however, and raising a window, which was not secured, Jean gained Dr. Haworth's room without attracting attention.

As he came in he drew a long breadth and said to Dr. Haworth, who was waiting for him:

"I hope this is my last night's work, Excellency! I don't like it; I might be taken for a burglar!"

"I like it no better than you, Jean," said Dr. Haworth. "It is wretched business. Every instinct of my character is opposed to it. I have made up my mind to fight this man openly hereafter, and not meet trick with trick."

"You have a right to fight him with his own weapons, Excellency! As you said to me, I remember: 'War is war.'"

"Yes. That is to say, a dirty and brutal business. I mean to have no more of this. What has happened?"

"*She* was there, and the *other*, too."

"Not—?"

"The Colonel? No, indeed!" said Jean, laughing. "He is much too prudent for that. He sent his go-between—or one of them—your friend, Mr. Wilkins."

"Ah!" said Dr. Haworth, in a tone which proved how much interest he took in Jean's statement.

"There was no mistaking him—the moon was too bright. He brought a letter and looked for *hers*. As I had found it before him, he left the one he had brought and went away. Here are both, Excellency."

Dr. Haworth took the letters with evident repugnance. Then as if he were disgusted with the whole affair, he threw them disdainfully on the table and said to Jean:

"Read them to me."

Jean who seemed to regard the whole affair as a pleasant comedy, opened the letter brought by Wilkins first and read it in a low tone. It contained only the lines:

"You may as well stop the watching, as it does no good. Get the papers and then come away. That anonymous letter was sent —was it received and what effect did it have? *Somebody* wants to know all about it at once.

"P. S.—Get the papers."

This was not signed in any manner and was in the handwriting of a woman. Jean laid it on the table and said:

"Some woman in the town wrote that, I suppose?"

"It seems so."

"Now for the communication from Miss B.," said Jean, laughing:

Miss Burns had written what follows:

"The *anonymous* letter came, and they only *laughed* at it. I was at the folding-doors in the parlor and heard what they said. Mr. Tim he pretended he believed it, and *she* was ready to *bite his head off*, and began to cry. Then he laughed at her and said he was *fooling*, and then she came in with *him* and she *kissed him*.

"That's all about *that*. I am coming home to-morrow, as I

don't mean to stay here any longer. If *somebody* wants *his papers* somebody will have to look himself. I am not going to try again. It is too *risky*, and it is no use, and I am not going out at night any more. I've *caught cold*. What is worse, I can see they suspect me, and I am sorry I ever had anything to do with *this business*. I wish you would tell *somebody* I must have *that money*.

" P. S. I thought I would write this note, which will be *the last*, as I am not certain I can get off to-morrow. I believe *that boy* is trying to find what takes me out walking *about dark*. I am going away from here. Tell *somebody* I must have *that money*."

" Well," said Dr. Haworth, drily, " everything is tolerably plain now. This comedy has reached the last act, and I wash my hands of the wretched business."

There was a small fire burning in the fire-place. He took the letters and threw them into it.

" Another person might have kept these papers to use against her," he muttered. " I will not! I am weary of tricks. I prefer real war. I will open it and try which is the strongest !"

He got up and stood before the fire, reflecting. At last he said, turning to the boy :

" Jean, have the horses ready after breakfast. I wish you to ride with me. As it is getting late and you are probably sleepy, we had better retire."

He went to the door and bolted it.

" It is not probable that our young friend will repeat her visit," he said, " but it is as well to make sure of it."

He had not observed that as soon as his back was turned Jean had snatched the notes from the fire and put them in his pocket.

About an hour after breakfast on the following morning Dr. Haworth came down stairs booted and spurred for a ride. The horses were ready at the rack—and Jean was seated on a root of the oak overshadowing it.

As Dr. Haworth came out the family carriage drove to the door ; and in reply to his question, who was going to ride, the dignified old coachman informed him that Miss Burns was going home.

Miss Burns came down a few moments afterward, followed by a servant carrying her small trunk, which was strapped behind the vehicle. Then Mrs. Maurice and Miss Cary appeared and shook hands in a friendly manner ; and Miss Burns got into the carriage and drove away.

She had not looked once at Dr. Haworth, but as the carriage passed by Jean, seated on his root, she shot a furious glance at him. Thereupon Jean rose suddenly, rushed to the vehicle and cried:

" You are not going, Miss Burns!"

In the ardor of his feelings he seized the young lady's hand which was hanging out of the window—when the youth found more than his match.

In a paroxysm of wrath Miss Burns administered a tingling slap on Jean's cheek.

"How dare you squeeze my hand, you hateful wretch!" cried indignant Miss Burns.

"Did I squeeze it?" said Jean, laughing and rubbing his cheek.

Miss Burns only replied with an exterminating frown, and the carriage then disappeared in the direction of Abbeyville.

As this scene occurred on the side of the vehicle opposite to the veranda it was not noticed. The group there were discussing Miss Burns.

"It sounds very inhospitable," said gentle Mrs. Maurice, "but I am glad Miss Burns is gone. There is something about her which I do not altogether like."

As nobody was more charitable than this kind woman, Miss Burns seemed to have made an unfortunate impression.

XVI.

THE WARRANTS.

AN hour afterward Dr. Haworth and Jean were at Prof. Lesner's. The morning was pleasant and the whole surroundings were as bright and homelike as ever; but the Professor seemed not to have been tempted out. He was not in the grounds, and leaving Jean with the horses Dr. Haworth went and knocked at the front door, half enveloped in creeping vines.

A feeble voice from the library on the right said, "Come in," and Dr. Haworth entered the room. Prof. Lesner was half-reclining in a large arm-chair with a book upon his knees. His eyes were dreamy, and there was an unmistakable odor of laudanum in the apartment.

"Good morning, sir," said Dr. Haworth in a tone of pity. W

was evident that the poor professor had been indulging in his fatal habit. But the indulgence did not seem to have been extreme. The pallor of his face and a slight trembling of his hands were the only indications that he had returned to his vice.

"Dr. Haworth," he said, rising politely, "I am truly happy to see you. I was by myself and moping. Sit down, Doctor, sit down."

He shook hands cordially, and pointed to a seat.

"Our friends at Mauricewood are well, I hope?"

"Quite well," replied Dr. Haworth.

"They are charming people, charming. I really envy you your good fortune as an inmate of the family. They are my old and cherished friends."

"Then you are even more fortunate than myself, Professor. I have only recently had the pleasure of becoming acquainted with them. You have known them a long time, you say?"

"Oh, yes," said Prof. Lesner, with a bright smile on his pale face; "all my life—or rather, all theirs, Doctor, for I am getting to be an old man, now."

"Yes, I recall our former conversation, which referred, you remember, to that unhappy affair at Mauricewood."

"I remember very well; we discussed, I think, the question of the real criminal," said Prof. Lesner.

"Yes; well, I think I have discovered something at last about the murder."

"Ah!" said Prof. Lesner, with an air of great interest.

"Your theory did not satisfy me—that Mr. Maurice had met his death by accidentally slipping and striking his head on a projection of his bedstead."

"It was only a conjecture, Doctor; it could scarcely be anything more."

"It is improbable, as I believe I said when we discussed it before. There was a bona fide murder, I am certain."

"It is, perhaps, more probable."

"And it was not committed with the hammer found on the floor."

"Not with the hammer?"

"You seem surprised, which is very natural!"

"You interest me deeply, Doctor. Then you have discovered something—some weapon which was employed, you think?"

"Yes, sir; I will explain," said Dr. Haworth. "Before going

any further, however, it is necessary to inform you that I have not called this morning on a merely friendly visit. My business is quite serious, and I beg you will regard what I say as addressed to you in your official capacity."

"My official capacity, Doctor?"

"As a magistrate. You informed me recently that you had been commissioned a Justice."

"That is true—a very poor one, I fear, but I was a sort of amateur lawyer once, and shall manage to stumble along, I hope."

"I have every confidence in your capacity, sir, and believe your friends have made an excellent selection. It is in your character of magistrate, therefore, that I shall say to you what I have to say."

"Certainly—it shall be strictly confidential. Do I understand you to say that it relates to the murder of Mr. Maurice?"

"Yes, sir."

"To the manner of his death, I think you said."

"Precisely. He was not struck on the head with the hammer or any other weapon—at first at least. He was garroted."

"Garroted! what is that? Oh, yes—I believe I understand you. Do you really think so? What induces you to believe it? Garroted!"

"The discovery of this cord in his bed," said Dr. Haworth, taking the garrote from his pocket.

"That very cord!" exclaimed Prof. Lesner, looking at the fatal object with an air of repugnance.

"This very cord. It had been dropped by the murderer or was broken in the struggle; here are marks of a fracture. Mr. Maurice was first strangled, and possibly finished by a blow."

"And that has lain there for twenty years? It is really horrible, Doctor!"

"The failure to discover it was very simple," said Dr. Haworth. "The hammer explained everything, and no one thought of searching the bed where the clothing was tossed about so that this cord was concealed. The room was then locked, and I only found this on a recent visit to it."

"Well, well!" said poor Prof. Lesner, looking with horror at the garrote; "who would have believed it? Why, Mr. Maurice must have been strangled, Doctor!"

"Unquestionably."

"Who could have been guilty of such a thing?"

"I think I have discovered who was guilty, or at least an accomplice in the crime."

"Who can you mean?"

"Col. Ross, of this neighborhood."

Prof. Lesner looked at the speaker with an expression of the profoundest astonishment.

"Col. Ross!" he exclaimed, "can you believe that?"

"Yes."

"It is impossible. Why, Col. Ross is one of the most respectable citizens of the county, Doctor!"

"That is his standing, I know. Men of wealth are almost always respected. The fact remains that Col. Ross is connected with the affair by circumstances which it will be necessary for him to explain."

"Col. Ross!" repeated the poor Professor, unable apparently to take in the idea; "could that be possible?"

"Yes. I understand your surprise. It is quite natural to doubt charges brought against rich and respectable people. I need not say that I would never have suspected such a thing of Col. Ross without grave grounds for doing so."

"You have grounds, then?"

"Certainly. I have come to state them, after which I shall request you to issue a warrant for his arrest on the charge of murder."

"A warrant!"

"Your magistrate's warrant. Having resolved to prosecute Col. Ross, and bring home to him if I can the guilt of that murder, I do so regularly by applying for a warrant to arrest him."

"Yes, certainly," said Prof. Lesner, sighing; "what you say is perfectly correct. It is my business to grant the warrant if I think your statement affords ground for it, Doctor. You must pardon me for being prudent in this very serious affair."

"It is proper that you should, Professor, or your Worship, as I ought now to call you."

"I prefer Professor, my dear Doctor! I fear I am a very inefficient worship. I will not hesitate to grant you the warrant for Col. Ross' arrest if you show me reasonable grounds for it. I am only a poor recluse and he is rich and powerful, but that will not deter me."

"I am sure it will not. I will therefore proceed to state the circumstances."

Dr. Haworth's statement consumed more than an hour. His theory of the murder of James Maurice was briefly this:

1. Mr. Ducis was entirely innocent and had been the victim of a plot.

2. The person who had conceived the plot was Col. Ross, who had quarreled and fought with Maurice the younger in South America about a woman. Maurice was the successful lover, and Ross had resolved to revenge himself.

3. They both returned to the United States, and John Maurice's marriage to his second wife, Miss Ellen Maurice, was the moment selected for his murder. This was arranged by Col. Ross—then Lieut. Ross, of the navy—his design being to put an end to his enemy on the very night of his wedding.

4. Col. Ross did not execute the design himself in all probability. The actual criminal was no doubt the man Wilkins who had been suborned by Ross to commit the murder. He had quarreled with the Maurice family and was known to have hated them.

5. The woman Pitts was an accomplice, and entered into the plot to secure the money paid by Mr. Ducis to Mr. James Maurice.

6. Ross supposed that the chamber of Mr. James Maurice was that of the bride and bridegroom, since the young lady's presents were displayed there. His accomplice entered through the window, strangled the person occupying the bed in the dim light of the night taper, and probably struck him afterward with the hammer; the woman Pitts carrying off the money.

7. The hammer and glove were or were not intended to criminate Mr. Ducis. If they were, the weapon was purchased for the purpose.

8. The whole affair was inspired by Ross, who had lived in South America and was familiar with the operation of the garrote. The aim in employing it was to insure the silence of the victim, who had, however, cried out and alarmed the house.

9. The proofs that Col. Ross had a thorough understanding with the persons engaged in the actual commission of the crime were his night visit to the man and woman in the hills; the words uttered by him on that occasion and overheard by Jean Baptiste; the visit of his paid agent, Miss Burns, to Mauricewood to watch Dr. Haworth; the employment of Wilkins to carry the letters; but above all the use of the Spanish garrote, which would never have entered the mind of a citizen of the United States as a weapon of murder.

"I have stated the case, sir," said Dr. Haworth. "Do you see fit to grant warrants for the arrest of all these people?"

"Yes!" said Prof. Lesner, with animation. "You have convinced me almost against my will, Doctor. What a black affair! Yes, I will make them out at once, returnable, shall I say, to-morrow at 10 o'clock in the morning?"

To this Dr. Haworth assented, declaring that he would take them in person to Abbeyville and place them in the hands of the constable. The blank warrants were then executed and handed to Dr. Haworth, and he and Prof. Lesner entered into a brief conversation on other topics. Dr. Haworth was struck by his host's power of mind and extensive information. The poor recluse had evidently cultivated his intellect to a very high degree. Unfortunately he had not trained his will to resist the insidious enemy, opium.

When Dr. Haworth went away they exchanged a cordial grasp of the hand, and Prof. Lesner said, shaking his head:

"This is a terrible affair, Doctor—charging so respectable a man as Colonel Ross with such a crime! But the law makes no distinctions. I am only a poor man and he is wealthy and influential, but you will not find me wanting. I will examine all of these people to-morrow, and unless they explain the suspicious circumstances, I will commit them to jail without bail."

"I see plainly that you will perform your official duty under all circumstances, sir," said Dr. Haworth.

He then bowed and rode away with Jean. An hour afterward he was at Abbeyville and the warrants were in the hands of a constable. Dr. Haworth then returned to Mauricewood.

XVII.

THE CONSTABLE'S RETURN.

ABOUT 9 o'clock on the following morning Dr. Haworth, accompanied by Jean Baptiste, set out on horseback for Prof. Lesner's.

His expression was animated, the look of the hunter who is on the track of his game. Now that the moment for action had come, his moody absorption had all disappeared. The soldier had replaced the dreamer, and he rode on rapidly with an air of almost joyous anticipation.

"I begin to think I have missed my vocation in life, Jean!" he said.

"Your vocation, Excellency? What pleases you so much?"

"I was born for a thieftaker—a policemen—to say 'I arrest you,' to people."

"I see. You are happy now at the idea of putting your hand, as you call it, on our friend the Colonel!"

"Yes. 'Happy' is not the word. Doing nothing in this business has rankled in me for years. I have been to the United States before on this errand, but could never see what was to be done. Now I see! In half an hour the game will open."

Having said this, Dr. Haworth spurred on and reached Prof. Lesner's, where he threw himself from his horse.

"Wait here until I call you," he said to Jean; "your testimony will be taken."

Jean sat down on the horse-block just outside the small gate smoking a cigarette, and Dr. Haworth went to the door and knocked.

"Come in," said the voice of Prof. Lesner, and Dr. Haworth entered the library.

The Professor had discarded his dressing-gown and was clad in a neat black coat in honor of the occasion. The table had been cleared of its litter of books and papers, an official-looking register was lying open upon it with pen and ink near, and a package of blank warrants, together with a Bible, lay beside them.

At Dr. Haworth's entrance Prof. Lesner rose courteously and shook hands. His face was friendly but grave. A night's reflection had no doubt shown him the full nature of the step he was about to take. Indeed, to issue a warrant for the arrest of so prominent a person in the county as Col. Ross was a very serious matter.

"I was expecting you, Doctor," he said. "Take a seat. It is past 10, I believe."

Dr. Haworth looked at his watch.

"We have still five minutes," he said, sitting down in one of two or three chairs which seemed to have been drawn forward for the occasion.

"My clock is a little fast, I am afraid," said Prof. Lesner, glancing at an old affair in the corner. "I was wondering why you had not arrived—and the constable with the prisoners."

" They will arrive soon now, I have no doubt, sir. They are not due for four minutes yet, as your warrant was made returnable at the hour of 10, I believe."

" Yes."

Prof. Lesner uttered the word after drawing a long breath. Dr. Haworth glanced at him, and he met the look.

" I see you think I regret having issued the warrants, Doctor," said Prof. Lesner. " I do not—it was my sworn duty; but you must make allowances for an old man who has lived so long in retirement. I almost wish now I had not been commissioned a magistrate—I am not born for these agitating affairs. Col. Ross is a man of good standing—I have never heard anything against him since he was a young man, and then he was only a little wild. Are you certain there is just ground for arresting him on this fearful charge ? "

" Yes ! " said Dr. Haworth briefly. " His good character has nothing to do with the matter, sir. It is a legal investigation. When there is a question of that no man's apparent good character should exempt him from inquiry—from arrest, if necessary."

Prof. Lesner sighed and said :

" You are no doubt right. I agree that the circumstances you mentioned are very suspicious."

" They are much more than suspicious, sir ! "

" And if the question had only been the arrest of the man Wilkins and that woman—"

" I understand your distinction, but the law applies to all, high and low alike. An honest man ought to invite investigation if any one brings a charge against him. If Col. Ross is innocent you are acting as his friend."

" Do you really think so ? " said Prof. Lesner, brightening up a little.

" Certainly."

" I am glad you mentioned it. I will tell him that such was my view—it will at least smooth matters a little I think."

" There is no objection to your doing so of course. You are about to have the opportunity. I hear the sound of hoofs. Our friends are coming."

Prof. Lesner listened, and hearing the sound from the road arranged his papers with a rather tremulous hand—due to agitation at the approaching ceremony or his unfortunate habit.

"Here is some one," said Dr. Haworth, hearing a footstep on the porch. "Where are the rest?"

A man came in, and took off his hat. He was a rough looking personage, in a suit of soiled brown and horseman's boots.

"Well?" said Prof. Lesner, with a rather ludicrous assumption of official dignity.

"The return on the warrants, your Worship," said the man, ducking his head and coming forward with some papers in his hand.

"Where are the persons I desired to be arrested?" said Prof. Lesner.

"Non est inwentus, sir?" returned the man in a gruff voice.

"Not found!"

"That's jest it, your Worship. Mr. Briggs he was took sick and give me the warrants to serve. Well, Wilkins and his wife ain't at home and Col. Ross is gone to Washington."

Dr. Haworth sat still, looking fixedly at the man.

"Is that true?" he said, in a hard voice.

The constable turned round and looked at him rather insolently. He said nothing, but his look said: "Who are you?"

Dr. Haworth was about to reply to the look, but Prof. Lesner forestalled him. The poor Professor was evidently not ill pleased. Indeed he seemed scarcely able to suppress his satisfaction. He made an effort, however, and said, with grave dignity:

"Do I understand you to say that Mr. Briggs intrusted the warrants to you?"

"I'm his deputy—yes, he give 'em to me to serve, your Worship."

"And Wilkins and his wife, you say, were not to be found?"

"House locked up and not a livin' soul on the premises," said the deputy.

"You went to Col. Ross' of course?"

"In course, your Worship. He had left by the morning train—6:30."

Prof. Lesner looked at Dr. Haworth, whose brows were contracted until his eyebrows nearly met.

"With your Worship's permission I will ask the constable a question," he said.

"Certainly, Doctor, certainly."

Dr. Haworth turned to the man and said:

" Are you acquainted with Wilkins or Mrs. Wilkins ? "

" Well, I've seen 'em," said the deputy shortly.

" Are they related to you ? "

" You mean kin ? No, they are not."

" Are they friends or relatives of Mr. Briggs ? "

The man hesitated.

" Answer," said Dr. Haworth.

" I've heard tell that Wilkins' wife was a Briggs afore she married her first husband."

" Well," said Dr. Haworth, in the same hard voice, " I have no further questions to ask you."

The response was a rather sullen look, and the deputy then said to Prof. Lesner :

" Done with me, sir ? "

" I—I really am in a maze," said Prof. Lesner feebly. " What would you advise, Doctor ? But I ought to decide for myself, I suppose. These warrants are returned indorsed ' not found.' I had better issue new ones and direct a search to be made for the parties. Those people must be found, and Col. Ross must have a new warrant served on him. Would you advise me to issue it now ? "

" No, sir," said Dr. Haworth, after a moment spent in gloomy reflection ; " it is useless. Some accident might happen. Mr. Briggs might be taken ill again. I will apply to you when I think it is necessary."

" But the other parties ? "

" They will not be found—unless I find them. The whole matter is perfectly plain. You may issue the warrant I requested against them, however, if you think best."

" I think it would be better," Prof. Lesner said, in some agitation. " I really feel quite unwell, but I will make out the new warrants."

With a shaking hand he then took a blank warrant and made it out for the arrest of Wilkins and his wife.

" Use every exertion to find these people," he said to the deputy constable. " It is unnecessary to trouble Mr. Briggs. As soon as you arrest them bring them here at once, and I will send for the Doctor to be present at the examination."

The deputy took the papers and said :

" That's all, your Worship ? "

" Yes—use due diligence, my friend."

And much relieved either by this legal phrase, or the result of the whole affair, Prof. Lesner bowed formally to the deputy, who ducked his head in response and went away.

As he left the room Dr. Haworth rose.

"You are not going so soon, my dear Doctor?" said Prof. Lesner.

"It is quite useless for me to remain longer, sir," was Dr. Haworth's reply in his hard, calm voice; "the farce is over and I have business to attend to."

"The farce?"

"The matter is perfectly plain. This man Briggs is a relative of that woman, and notified her last night that she was about to be arrested. To prevent suspicion he is taken sick, and the warrant served by his deputy—or not served. The reason why the parties were not found is easy to understand. The woman having been warned, warned her husband, and he warned a friend of his—Col. Ross. Hence the sudden necessity of Col. Ross' presence in Washington."

Prof. Lesner looked at Dr. Haworth with a helpless expression. He then said a little indignantly:

"Is that possible? But you must be right. It is an insult to my authority! I will have this man Briggs removed."

"You have no proof against him—it is a mere surmise. I will take the necessary steps. On Col. Ross' return I will call again on your Worship. If Wilkins and the woman are arrested, I shall be glad to hear from you."

"Promptly—you will be notified promptly, Doctor! And I will issue a new warrant for the arrest of Col. Ross whenever you request me to do so. I shall then be better prepared to conduct the examination. I am a little unwell to-day, and cannot say that I regret the delay. But I will not be wanting, Doctor—I will not be wanting!"

It was unnecessary for poor Prof. Lesner to say that he was not as much disappointed as his guest. Nothing was plainer than his air of relief. Like most persons who have spent their lives in seclusion he evidently shrunk from resolute action; and his nerves were doubtless unstrung from other causes.

He accompanied Dr. Haworth to the door, and shook hands with a friendly smile.

"Come again and see me unofficially," he said. "Your visits are a great luxury, as I have no company but my birds and bees!"

Dr. Haworth bowed and then rode away with Jean. The boy had asked no questions, but his look did so.

"You are anxious to know what has happened, I suppose, Jean?" said Dr. Haworth.

"Yes, Excellency."

"Well, Col. Ross was notified last night that he would be arrested this morning and took the train at daylight for Washington."

"What effect will that have on your Excellency's plans?"

"It will have none."

PART III.

CONVERGING.

I.

DR. HAWORTH ENGAGES THE WIRE TO LIMA.

THE journals which came to Mauricewood and afforded entertainment if not instruction to Mr. Tim Maurice and the ladies, all at once began to be filled with the details of a scandal.

Col. Ross was the hero of it, and loomed up suddenly as the great South American Colossus who managed affairs social, political, industrial and international in that quarter of the globe.

He was alternately exalted as the flower and climax of modern civilization, and denounced as the incarnation of all that was corrupt. His enemies laughed at him, styling him Col. Sellers Ross, and said that he bribed people. His friends defended him and declared that he was a model of a good citizen. Having been summoned before a committee he was badgered unmercifully; and as his Russian Majesty had not been shot at for a fortnight, and there was nothing new from the East, the newspapers in the dearth of news filled their columns with Col. Sellers Ross and his private affairs.

As Mr. Tim Maurice was a great reader of the newspapers, and took a number, he became familiar with the proceedings, and seemed to derive great pleasure from the daily reports of the badgering to which Col. Ross was subjected. He made pleasant comments in the bosom of his family, and one morning said to Dr. Haworth, rubbing his hands with evident enjoyment:

"Our friend, the Colonel, seems to have gotten into difficulties!"

"It seems so," said Dr. Haworth.

"The fate of public men! Now I have always considered my-

self lucky in occupying a ' private station.' Let a man once get out
of it and all is over with him."

" That is very true."

" It really is a debasing business ! " said Uncle Tim in a disgusted tone. " What makes people ambitious ? Take the case of
a human being who has health, competence, and lives happily—well,
one day he is suddenly bit by a morbid longing to be somebody —
a Senator or President. What good will it do him ? As soon as
he becomes a candidate everybody opposed to him swears he is a
scoundrel. The morning papers take away his appetite. The
evening edition keeps him from sleeping. Gall and wormwood are
his bill of fare for breakfast, dinner and supper. Is it worth it ? "

" It is far from being worth it."

" Why do they play the losing game, then—losing whether they
win or not ? They are apt to be gray, for ambition generally attacks
that sort of people. They have twenty years to live say—why do
they prefer living it in hot water ? "

" They seem to like it," said Dr. Haworth philosophically.

" Well, every man to his taste. I would rather eat and sleep and
laugh and enjoy my life a little than be Senator or President if my
liver is to be out of order and I am to breakfast on the opposition
newspapers ! "

Uncle Tim thereupon laughed heartily, and refolding his paper
said :

" Friend Ross is having a hard time of it. They are charging
him with all sorts of rascalities. I suppose it is the penalty for becoming a rich man."

" The committee, I believe, is still engaged in examining him, and
he will no doubt be detained in Washington," said Dr. Haworth.

" I don't know. I have not seen him since his last visit, and he
has not mentioned the subject."

Uncle Tim smiled when he said " since his last visit." The
Colonel's mishap was now no secret.

Dr. Haworth made no further allusion to him, and an hour
afterward rode in the direction of Abbeyville. As he went along
he said :

" There will be time enough. He will be obliged to return, and
then—war ! The main point is to be ready."

He rode on, and soon reached Abbeyville, where he dismounted
in front of the telegraph office. This was attached to the railway

recently built through the town, and the operator was a polite young man, who bowed with an utter absence of "official dignity."

"Do you connect by telegraph at Lima, sir?" said Dr. Haworth.

The agent looked at his book and said :

"Yes, sir; by cable or the City of Mexico and Panama."

"I wished to ascertain. I shall probably have a dispatch to send to-day or to-morrow. Is it possible to control the wires for an hour, say—I mean, to monopolize them?"

The agent looked a little dubious.

"It might be done, sir—except public dispatches—on government business—but it would be costly."

"I should expect it to be. My object is to send and receive a number of messages to a person stationed in the office at Lima."

"I understand—to have a talk," said the young man, smiling.

"Yes."

"It might be easy or the opposite to keep the wires clear."

"I will probably call then and try. My business is private."

"It will be so regarded under all circumstances, sir—as far as this office is concerned."

"You mean that messages not in cipher are not private in the fullest sense, since they are repeated by the instruments in every office?"

"Yes, sir."

"It is of no importance, since your rules of privacy apply, I suppose, to all."

Dr. Haworth then bowed, remounted his horse, and instead of returning to Mauricewood, rode in the direction of Dr. Seabright's. As he reached the outer gate he saw the gray-haired physician approaching from the opposite direction and waited for him.

"Good morning, Dr. Seabright," he said; "have you a moment's leisure?"

"No," said Dr. Seabright, shaking hands with what he meant for cordiality. "Never have any—don't know what the word means. But that's no matter, I take it! Come in—glad to see you."

II.

DR. SEABRIGHT.

THEY rode in and dismounted, Dr. Seabright leading the way into his small home, where, being a widower and childless, he led a life which must have been a dreary one if it had not been so busy.

"Sit down, Brother Sawbones," he said, with grim jocularity. "You know that's a pet name with the vulgar crowd who don't appreciate the dignity of intellect."

He drew forward a split-bottomed chair for Dr. Haworth and added :

" I have not smoked to-day."

He then lit a long-stemmed clay pipe, offering another to Dr. Haworth, who, however, declined.

" Tim Maurice and the ladies are well to-day ? " he said.

" Perfectly well."

" He is a friend of mine—a genuine man. I have known him since he was a boy."

" You are no doubt acquainted with every one in the neighborhood ? "

" Every living soul, and a number of people who are dead."

" You remind me," said Dr. Haworth, " that we were speaking the other day of that unfortunate affair at Mauricewood. You knew Mr. James Maurice and Mr. Ducis, who was charged with that murder ? "

" Certainly."

" I think you said Mr. Ducis was a friend of yours ? "

" The best friend I ever had—one of nature's noblemen ! " said Dr. Seabright, smoking like a steamboat funnel.

Dr. Haworth made no reply. He fixed his eyes upon Dr. Seabright, and for about a minute continued to look straight at him. This fixed gaze evidently attracted his companion's attention, for he returned it with one from beneath his bushy gray brows which seemed keen enough to bore a hole.

" Dr. Seabright," said Dr. Haworth, " I have come to this country to find who murdered Mr. James Maurice of Mauricewood, on the night of the 7th of May, 1860, and require your assistance."

At these words Dr. Seabright rose slowly in his chair, knocked the ashes from his pipe, and said :

" Who are you, and what is your object ? "

" It is unnecessary to reply to either question. I will reply to both when the time comes, and that will be very soon. I repeat what I said. I mean to discover who murdered James Maurice—and the first step is to discover who did not."

Dr. Seabright had never taken his eyes from the face of his companion.

" Explain what you mean by the words ' who did not,' " he said.

" It is not necessary, since you already understand. Mr. Ducis, you say, was innocent ? "

" Yes—I'll swear to that."

" It has never been proved."

" No, it has not been proved in a court of justice."

" Do you wish to have the fact established there ? "

" The innocence of my friend Henry Ducis? Dr. Haworth, if you will furnish me with evidence to wipe off the stain on his name I will sit down there at that table and make you a deed for this home, my farm, and all outstanding accounts due me for ten years back."

" I will furnish the evidence—or make the attempt—without the deed ; but I require your help. Do you mean to give it ? "

" Yes ! " said Dr. Seabright with a flush in his wintry cheeks. " And now talk plainly. I don't care to know why you are interested in this matter, or anything about it. If you think you can clear the memory of Henry Ducis from this charge, you can count on Robert Seabright."

Dr. Haworth extended his hand and said:

" It is agreed then that from this time we will act together, is it ? "

" It is agreed ! " said Dr. Seabright, grasping the hand with the wrench of a vice.

" Well, now that this is understood I will ask you some questions."

" I will answer any and all I can."

" Are we alone ? "

Dr. Seabright went and shut the doors.

" There is not a soul in the house but my old house-keeper, who is as deaf as a post," he said.

He then sat down again.

III.

THE APPOINTMENT.

DURING this conversation Dr. Haworth's expression had gradually grown animated. It is possible that he had anticipated difficulties which had not presented themselves.

"What I shall now say, Dr. Seabright," he began, "is said to you with absolute confidence—to the friend of Henry Ducis."

"Understood! I am not a gossip ; what you say to me is said to no one else."

"I am sure of you—I am not sure of many people. I will now come to the point."

"Nothing I like better ! "

"Who was the keeper of the warehouse where Mr. Ducis purchased the fertilizers on the 7th or the 8th of May, 1860? "

"His name was Thomas Williams."

"Is he living? "

"Yes."

"You are, perhaps, acquainted with him? "

"I ought to be. I have practiced in his family for twenty-five years."

"Is he still in business? "

"No ; his nephew is, however."

"At Sinclair Station? "

"They call it Sinkler's—yes."

"Do you ever ride in that direction? "

"Frequently."

"Will it be agreeable to you to do so to-morrow? "

"Yes. I think I understand what your ride is for, but—"

"I will come back to this point in a moment. On the trial of Mr. Ducis the hammer and glove found at Mauricewood were produced I suppose."

"Of course."

"Where are they now? "

"Don't know. The Sheriff or jailer may have them."

"Are the same people living? "

"They are both dead."

"You are acquainted with those serving at present? "

"I know them both."

"It is possible that the hammer and glove may be found. These pieces of evidence are sometimes kept—or they are thrust into some closet when they are not given away to curiosity-hunters."

"Yes."

"It is desirable to secure them both if they can be secured."

Dr. Seabright had re-filled his pipe, and was smoking and reflecting.

"Well, I think I understand what you are after," he said at length. "You are curious to have a look at the hammer which was said to be the weapon that murdered James Maurice—though it never did; the glove that was found outside the window; and the leaf of the ledger with the entry of the purchase of the fertilizers by Henry Ducis."

"Precisely."

"It is doubtful whether the glove and hammer can be found," said Dr. Seabright, "but there will be no trouble about the ledger. Old Tom Williams was a methodical man and never destroyed papers. His ledgers for thirty years are piled up somewhere—but it will be useless to look at the entry."

"Why?"

"I examined it myself at the time of the trial. The date was May 8, which was the day after the murder, and the alibi fell to the ground."

"Was Mr. Williams sworn?"

"Certainly. He testified that he had no means of fixing the exact day besides the entry; he only remembered that Mr. Ducis had been at the warehouse about sunset, and after finishing his business rode further on to spend the night at his friend's, Mr. Russell's, he said."

"Mr. Russell, I understand, could not swear positively whether this was the night of the 7th or 8th?"

"He said he could not swear—he believed it was the 7th."

"So the entry in the ledger was corroborated?"

"To that extent—that Russell could not positively contradict it."

"The entry has been tampered with," said Dr. Haworth, "to destroy Mr. Ducis."

"Well," said Dr. Seabright, coolly, "that theory was set up, but there was no erasure."

"That is the question."

"I examined it myself."

" I wish to examine it in my turn."

Dr. Seabright shook his head.

"Can you arrange with Mr. Williams to afford the opportunity?"

"Easily—there will be no trouble. The ledgers are apt to be at Williams' house—but it is time lost."

" I will lose the time. Are you willing to lose yours, too?"

" Yes."

"To-morrow?"

"Yes."

" Well, I will be here at 9 in the morning if that is not too early."

" At 7 if you like better."

"Nine will answer. Meanwhile, there is the hammer and glove. It might be better for me not to appear too prominently in this business."

"You are right. I will go this very evening and see whether they are about the jail or the sheriff's. I can make up a pretext without lying, which I don't like."

"Then all is understood, Doctor?"

"Yes—understood as thoroughly as if you told me that you had your own reasons, outside of mere curiosity, to clear up this affair. I don't care a baubee what they are, Dr. Haworth. I don't mean to ask you a single question. I don't like strangers, as a general thing, and I have never had any very extraordinary confidence in human nature, which, according to my thinking, is rather a slippery affair. Some men are genuine, but the majority are sneaks. I like your face and I will trust you. I never saw a man with your look out of the eyes who was a rascal! That's the way I caught the expert asses on the trial—every eye was the eye of a sneak! The trash knew nothing of what they were talking about, and they knew they knew! I'll help you up to the handle in this affair, Dr. Haworth! You are not going to make anything of that ledger entry, but I'll see that you have a look at it all the same. Are you going? Grog? No? Well, good day. I'll be ready."

7

IV.

THE ENTRY IN THE LEDGER.

WHEN Dr. Haworth made his appearance at Dr. Seabright's on the following morning he found him seated smoking a pipe in the sunshine of his small porch.

"You are punctual," he said, taking out a huge silver watch; "it is one minute before 9."

As he was speaking an ancient clock within slowly struck the hour.

"Confound this watch! It is never right!" exclaimed Dr. Seabright. "That clock keeps perfect time and this watch never will run with it two days in succession!"

"The difference is slight—your horse is ready, Doctor?"

"I was indulging in a smoke. I could not find the hammer and glove."

"Then you searched for them?"

"Everywhere. I have no doubt they were taken by curiosity-lovers. That is a queer phase of human nature."

"Strange, indeed."

"It is a perfect passion with some people. They will pay dear for a piece of the rope that hangs a murderer. I suppose a chip of the nitro-glycerine shell that blew up Czar Alexander would bring $1,000."

"Yes—"

"To come to business. I went to the jail and the Sheriff's and talked of this and that and found they knew nothing about the hammer and glove. They are non est inventus, if that's Latin."

"I attached no importance to them."

"I understand you agree with me that the murder was committed with that cord you showed me—or garrote, as you call it."

"Yes."

"There's your real curiosity! Why don't you put it up for sale —it would bring its weight in gold! But here I am getting away again. As the cord was the cause of all, the hammer amounted to little—and it never was identified as Henry Ducis' property; nor the glove, which was a common riding gauntlet. I examined it, and there were no marks upon it. There was nothing to show that it belonged or didn't belong to Mr. Ducis."

"It is of little importance. It is the entry in the ledger that I am curious about."

Dr. Seabright shook his head, and said in a discouraged tone:

"That amounts to no more than the rest."

"I have not satisfied myself that you are right."

"You think there is—"

"Time to talk on our side," said Dr. Haworth, quietly. "We can be certain of nothing without a sight of the entry."

"You will be no more certain after seeing it."

"Let me judge."

"You can," said Dr. Seabright, drawing a folded sheet of paper from his breast pocket; "here it is."

"The entry!"

"The leaf from my friend Williams' ledger which you wanted to look at," said Dr. Seabright, unfolding the paper in a deliberate manner. "After you left I thought it would be better for you not to appear in the business, as you said—it might create remark. So I rode to Sinkler's yesterday evening and found old Tom Williams on his porch. He was glad to see me and showed me the ledger at the first word without asking why I wanted to see it even. It was waste paper only now, he said, and to make a long story short, I cut out the leaf before his eyes. He neither knew nor cared why I did—and here it is."

Dr. Haworth had been looking fixedly at the paper which Dr. Seabright had handed him.

"This is the actual entry, then!" he said, with a glow on his face. "May 8, 1860—the day *after* the murder! The alibi was disproved, unless this date was falsified!"

Dr. Haworth drew from his pocket a small but very powerful microscope, which he applied to the spot on the paper. For some minutes he examined it closely.

"Well?" said Dr. Seabright.

"There has been no erasure," he said, with a gloomy expression. "There is a difference in the strokes of this figure and the same figure elsewhere—but that may have arisen from the fact that different persons made the entries."

"Yes."

"And the same persons form letters and figures differently in writing at different times."

Dr. Haworth was looking at the paper, moodily, his brows knit together.

"There is absolutely no erasure," he muttered; "the surface of the paper is not frayed in the least degree, but—"

"That proves it was a clerical error."

Dr. Seabright stopped, looking with some curiosity at the movements of his companion. In fact, Dr. Haworth had raised the leaf to his mouth and touched the date of the entry with the tip of his tongue.

"What do you mean by that?" said Dr. Seabright.

"I mean that I was right, after all," was the reply in a low voice, accompanied by a threatening flash of the eye, "the entry has been changed."

"How was that possible?"

"By a very simple means—oxalic acid or the oxolate of potash are cheap and accessible chemicals. The real date has been obliterated from this paper by a solution of one or the other and the false date substituted."

"Are you sure of that!" exclaimed Dr. Seabright.

"Judge for yourself. Touch this spot upon the paper with your tongue."

Dr. Seabright did so.

"Sour!" he said.

"Salt of sorrel is sour enough! A salt of potassium and the oxide resulted from the application of the solution—the real date disappeared, and the false date was written above it."

"Is it possible?" said Dr. Seabright gruffly. "Yes, it is!—Who was the scoundrel?"

"You use a plain word. Do you wish me to speak as plainly?"

"Yes!"

"Is Col. Ross, of this neighborhood, a friend of yours?"

"Col. Ross!—a friend of mine?—no, he is only an acquaintance."

"Well, Col. Ross can inform you who falsified this date and destroyed Mr. Ducis!"

At this announcement Dr. Seabright rose erect in his seat, looking at his companion with unmistakable astonishment.

"Col. Ross!" he exclaimed.

"We agreed to speak to each other plainly—I keep the agreement,"

"You are right. But do you really believe that Col. Ross could—?"

"I counted on your surprise. I don't believe in half-confidences with men like yourself. You have been frank with me—I am frank with you. You were the friend of Mr. Ducis, who died in jail, convicted of a crime which he never committed. I tell you the name of the man who either committed the murder or was the prime mover in the whole black affair. If you wish to know why I bring this charge against Col. Ross I will tell you."

"Tell me—leave out nothing," said the old physician in his gruff and resolute voice. "If that man was the real murderer he shall be brought to justice, or my name's not Robert Seabright!"

<hr>

V.

THE PSYCHOLOGY OF OPIUM.

ONE morning, a few days after the interview with Dr. Seabright, Mr. Tim Maurice locked his arm in the arm of his guest, Dr. Haworth, as they rose from breakfast, and said, as they went into the drawing-room:

"Do you know, my dear fellow, I think you have something on your mind? That locked-up chamber must have made you gloomy. Even Cadie can't make you smile, sometimes!"

Mr. Tim Maurice laughed. The engagement was, of course, no secret from him.

"It is only your fancy that I am gloomy, my dear Mr. Maurice," said Dr. Haworth; "I am not. I am naturally quiet."

"You ought to be happy."

"I am."

"Well, you seem—I say again—to have something on your mind! or you are too idle here—a man of action rusts when he has nothing to do. The great mistake you have made in life was not becoming a guano and nitrate agent."

"Like Col. Ross?"

"Precisely, and then you would pass time in a lively manner."

"His examination still continues, I see, there before the House Committee."

"Yes, and I fancy our friend is bothering the worthy people—I doubt if they are a match for him."

"I have not seen the morning papers. Is there a prospect of Col. Ross' return?"

"He is not apt to be detained much longer, I fancy; but you know we never see him now, and it makes no difference as far as the people at Mauricewood are concerned."

Whether Dr. Haworth acquiesced in this view or not did not appear. He said no more, and, sitting down, took up a book which was lying on the center-table in the drawing-room—with the air of a man who does something merely to employ his hands.

The title of the volume was the "Psychology of Opium," and Dr. Haworth knew at once that it was Prof. Lesner's work, which had just appeared.

"A new book," he said to Mr. Tim Maurice.

"Yes, I picked it up in the book store at Abbeyville yesterday."

"The name of the author is not on the title-page, I see."

"Well, the work is rather peculiar and very personal, and so I suppose he suppresses his name."

"Personal?"

"The author gives his *experience*, as the Salvation Army people say. I have been looking into the book, and see he describes his own sensations."

"Under the influence of opium?"

"Yes."

"What is his conclusion? That the sensations are pleasant or otherwise?"

"Paradisical, I think he says—it is all mere rhapsody."

"And he says nothing of the Inferno under the Paradise?"

"Not a word. The fact is, I rather suppose Mr. what's his name don't believe in any Inferno. As far as I can make out he believes in nothing—but opium."

"He believes, I suppose, in a soul, since he employs the term psychology."

"Not at all—in nothing of the sort. He incidentally mentions as a fact accepted by all intelligent minds that death is the end of life in every sense and that there is no hereafter. I don't trouble myself much about these materialist people and their cranky ideas—I'm much too busy seeing the wheat seeded and straightening up the fences. But now and then I amuse myself with these whim-whams—when they are amusing."

"I understand you; they are frequently dull?"

"Well, yes—awfully dull. This writer on opium psychology puts me to sleep. I had a delightful snooze with his book on my knees. But some passages are rather striking—had a good supply of opium on board when they were written, I suppose."

He took the volume and read a paragraph aloud to Dr. Haworth. It was a rapturous eulogy of the effects of the drug. Existence was sublimated—the real horizon of the world disappeared—then two pages of rhapsody set off with exclamation points.

"You are right," said Dr. Haworth; "that smells of opium at a league's distance. The man is a slave, and is bent on making others slaves, too. I prefer being a free man."

"Well, so do I," said Uncle Tim cheerfully. "As you say, the author of this book says nothing of the hell under his opium heaven. I am willing to bet that he is a miserable creature after his spells with his poison, and don't enjoy his breakfast, dinner, or supper."

With which decisive commentary on the opium habit, Uncle Tim put on his gloves, mounted his horse and went to look after farm matters.

Dr. Haworth took up the "Psychology of Opium," and read here and there in it for about half an hour. It was a curious performance. There were rapturous descriptions, evidently inspired by those of De Quincey, and the author plainly aimed to show only the bright side. But the miseries of opium here and there came out in somber flashes—chance phrases which reveal gulfs unfathomable and full of darkness.

"It is really pitiful," said Dr. Haworth, laying down the book. "This man was fitted to be a useful and even admirable member of society. His intellect is clear and vigorous. He is a person of extended information. His nature seems to be amiable to the last degree and his instincts all excellent, but this cursed drug has ruined him! He believes in nothing—but opium. He cares for nothing— but opium. He juggles with words, and speaks of *psychologies*, and has no faith whatever in any *psyche!* It is the most curious demonstration that a human being may be morally irreproachable, and intellectually a monstrosity."

He had been sitting with his back to the folding doors between the drawing- and dining-rooms. All at once a soft touch came to his shoulder, and looking up he saw Cary.

She was rather an attractive figure, though not romantic-looking in a very high degree at the moment. She had on a calico work-

apron extending from her chin to her boots, confined at the waist
by a belt, and she was busily wiping a saucer.

In fact, Miss Cary Maurice was washing up the "breakfast
things" like a dutiful young woman who would not have her mamma
do it, or allow careless servants to smash the best china. As her
sleeves were rolled up, one could see a very white pair of arms, and
Miss Cary was laughing quietly, both with her red lips and her blue
eyes, which were bewildering under the brown bangs.

She had heard Mr. Tim Maurice depart, and then Dr. Haworth's
muttered words. Curiosity compelling, she softly opened a fold in
the door, without attracting attention, stole behind the occupant of
the arm-chair, touched his shoulder, and when he looked up into her
eyes looked down into his.

Then Miss Cary went through a ceremony which is always
charming in her sex in case one is fond of them. She pushed the
hair back with a caressing movement from his forehead—after
which she laughed.

What followed this agreeable pantomime ought perhaps to be
regarded as confidential, but then there is perhaps no impropriety
in briefly alluding to the circumstance.

Dr. Haworth took the hand smoothing his hair and kissed it
with almost passionate tenderness. Then he pressed his lips to the
white arm also in the vicinity of the elbow and drew it toward him,
looking up at her.

Miss Cary's person naturally followed the arm, and then something took place.

She hesitated, resisted a little, looked behind her and blushed.

Then she stooped and touched his forehead quickly with her
lips and disappeared with a low laugh.

The rattle of cups and saucers a moment afterward, from the
dining-room, clearly indicated that business had supplanted romance.

VI.

JEAN RETURNS WITH GOOD NEWS.

DURING the whole day Dr. Haworth seemed to be absorbed in
thought and anxiously expecting something or the appearance of
some one.

He walked to and fro on the veranda, turned his head from moment to moment and even during an afternoon interview with Cary in the drawing-room exhibited every indication that something occupied his thoughts. Cary's smiles drove away his moody spell for a time, but when she went to her household duties he got up and began to pace to and fro again.

As the sun was sinking he put on his hat and walked out in the grounds, taking the path toward the oak-tree which had served as Miss Burns' post-office. He looked absently at it—he was evidently not thinking of it. All at once he heard the foot-falls of a horse from the country road beyond the inclosure.

He went and leaned on the fence, which was of substantial plank set in locust posts. A line of shubbery followed the line of the inclosure, and through an opening in it he caught sight of the horseman—Jean Baptiste.

A word stopped him. He turned his head, saw Dr. Haworth and pushing through the opening in the shrubbery, dismounted quietly and threw his bridle over one of the posts.

"Good news, Excellency!" he said. "I have found them!"

"Found them?"

Dr. Haworth's face indicated the profoundest satisfaction, and he exclaimed :

"I knew you would never stop if you were once on their track, Jean!"

"Well, the trouble was to get on the track," said the young man with his bright smile. "There's no great merit in running down a fox if you can only start him—it is a mere question of speed and bottom. I have found our two foxes—male and female—at last!"

"Tell me everything! How did you find them?"

"Well, your Excellency gave me an old hound to lead. After you told me everything I went straight to Dr. Seabright. He is the hound!"

"Dr. Seabright?"

"You have set him on fire in this business. He thinks of nothing else. I can't explain it."

"Mr. Ducis was his dearest friend!"

"Well, now I understand everything. I did not understand before. I knew enough though, from what you told me of your talk with him, that he was with us heart and soul."

"You went straight to him, you say?"

"As soon as I left you. You know I had worked by myself without finding out anything. I suppose I have been at that house in the hills twenty times if I have been once. Nothing there. Every door and window shut, not even that cur dog in the kennel. There were no foot-prints, no wheel tracks, and I could see through a chink in the shutter that everything was just as it always was— the tub and stool, and even the frying-pan. They had got off between sundown and sunrise, as the country people say, and had not had time to take the least thing with them."

"They were warned during the night probably. But Dr. Sea-bright—?"

"I am coming to the Doctor, Excellency. He's a curious old fellow. When I walked in he growled out, 'Who are *you* ?' I said, 'I am Jean Baptiste.' He growled again, 'Don't know you! Who are you, I say, and what do you want ?' I looked at him and took his measure—mangrove fruit with sharp prickles but sweet and full of juice that makes good wine! So I said, 'I am Dr. Haworth's secretary, though he is so good to me that I am more like his son, and I have come to ask you to help me to find Job Wilkins and his wife.'"

"To the point !"

"Yes—it is the best way I think with men like the Doctor."

"You are right. Well ?"

"The words made him look around quickly, for he was about to turn his back on me. Then he bored me through with his eyes. 'Come in here,' he said, and then he went and shut the door and put me through a course of questions. I could see that he meant to satisfy himself that I was what I said I was—and in ten minutes he had no doubt about it. Then he leaned back in his arm-chair, knit his brows and said nothing. At last he got up and said : 'I am going to ride—you might be going in the same direction.' You see he had made up his mind to hunt in the pack, Excellency."

"Yes."

"Well, we rode to the hill country south of this, and Dr. Seabright stopped at about a dozen houses. I held his horse, and he did not stay long. Nothing—. I could see that by the expression of his face when he came out. At last we came to a cabin, about twenty miles from here, and Dr. Seabright staid there longer. All the people he had met knew him, I could see, and you know doctors are always welcome with that sort—they bring the news, may be,"

" Yes !—well ? "

" I saw as soon as he had come out of the cabin that he had heard something. I was right. What he heard was that Job Wilkins and that woman were at a house ten miles west of the hills— hired there to do farm work and cook. There was no doubt about it."

" You went on ? "

" Without a word, Excellency, and came at last in sight of the house. I then went into the woods and the Doctor rode on. I could see him stop at a field and talk with a man who was working. They then rode up to the house, and after half an hour Dr. Seabright came back. ' Are you thirsty ? ' he said to me, looking at me from under his gray eyebrows. ' No, sir,' I said. ' Well, if you are you can get a drink of water yonder—I did.' I looked at him— he was like a bear who has heard good news. ' I saw *the woman* cooking,' he said, ' and Wilkins is not far off. Come on home.' I understood without another word. The Doctor was coming back for the warrants of arrest."

" Yes, yes ! " said Dr. Haworth with a flush on his face.

" There was no trouble at all about it. We went straight to the Sheriff at Abbeyville, who summoned Briggs and directed him to produce the warrants you got from Prof. Lesner. He could not find them—they had been intrusted to his deputy who was absent, he said ; but new warrants were at once made out by another magistrate, and Briggs was obliged to go and serve them, whether he liked the business or not."

" And—! "

" We all rode together—Dr. Seabright, the constable and myself—and took Wilkins and his wife by surprise. There was nothing for them to do but to come with us, and they are now in jail, Excellency."

Dr. Haworth listened with an expression of the deepest satisfaction.

" You are an invaluable ally, Jean ! " he exclaimed, " and worth more than all of us. The arrest of these people was a vital necessity. They were either the murderers or the murderer's accomplices. A thorough examination of them must result in a discovery of the real criminal, whoever he is. If one turns State's evidence the case is ended."

" I knew that—so I meant to find them."

Dr. Haworth grasped the boy's hand and said :

"If you had been my son you could not have done more for me."

"You know that all I can do to serve your Excellency seems little to me," Jean said, simply.

"I know your devotion to me—I swear I will prove mine to you," said Dr. Haworth.

"So the man and woman are in the Abbeyville Jail ?"

"I never left them till I heard the bolts shut on them."

Dr. Haworth drew a long breath, and muttered :

"Something tangible at last !"

He then looked intently at Jean.

"You are tired," he said. "Go home and rest now. You have rendered me an invaluable service, Jean. I repeat that I will not forget it."

He then walked back to the house, and Jean returning on horseback by the front entrance rode to the stables in rear. He had been absent for three days, but as he frequently rode on business for his master his absence had attracted no attention.

VII.

THE BOMBSHELL.

THE arrest of Job Wilkins and his wife created a great sensation in Abbeyville. The little town was in commotion, and a thousand surmises were indulged in. The details were not yet known, but it was said that they had been arrested on the charge of complicity in the murder of Mr. James Maurice of Mauricewood, twenty years before. When the magistrate of the town, who had issued the warrants, examined and committed them, this rumor took definite shape.

Then animated discussion ensued. There are always people to advocate both sides of a question, for the sake of argument. If there is no difference of opinion talk loses its savor. What is wanted is controversy, which affords an opportunity for intellectual gymnastics.

Had not Mr. James Maurice been murdered by Mr. Henry Ducis ? A jury, after hearing all the evidence, had so declared. Mr. Ducis had been a gentleman of the highest character and

could never have murdered anybody? Well, men of high character had been known to kill their fellow-creatures, and the jury had
said that Mr. Ducis killed Mr. Maurice.

Then there was the question whether the arrest of Mr. and Mrs.
Wilkins was not illegal. Had they not been tried once for the
same offense and discharged? They had not been *tried?* Well,
they had been examined and committed for trial, at least, and that
was the next thing to being indicted. And, moreover, the present
arrest was a hardship. There was a thing called the statute of limi-
tations which barred the recovery of money after the lapse of a certain time. The theory was that the claim could not be disproved
in all cases. Why not apply that to so serious a question as a
man's life?

There was a great deal of excitement and discussion in the bor-
ough, and then another vague report began to creep about—how,
no one could tell. Another person, much higher in the social scale
than Wilkins and his wife, was said to be mixed up with this mysterious affair. It was not known who he was—but he was a citizen
of the county. Beyond this there was not even a rumor—but the
nameless person was the topic of conversation everywhere under the
convenient designation of Mr. Whoever He Is.

The County Court was to meet in about ten days, when Wilkins
and his wife were to be indicted and tried for complicity in the
Mauricewood murder. Dr. Haworth had formally identified himself
with the case as the informant. Having been closeted for three
hours with the attorney for the Commonwealth, he came out,
mounted his horse, and rode back to Mauricewood, where he remained quietly waiting.

What Dr. Haworth was probably waiting for was the next move
of his real adversary. It was impossible that Col. Ross had remained ignorant of the arrest of Wilkins and the woman, since it
had been announced in the " Abbeyville Gazette." At the end of
the paragraph recording the arrest the editor had added :

" There was a report yesterday that other persons will be arrested as accomplices in the murder of Mr. James Maurice. Among
them there is said to be a prominent citizen of this county, though
no person to whom we have applied for information can even suggest his name. The matter is mentioned only as a rumor, and for
no more than it is worth."

So mysterious an intimation necessarily excited curiosity, and when the curiosity of a community is aroused it is apt to be soon gratified. If not legitimately, then illegitimately. The name of some one will be found to fill the hiatus in the record—the aching void which tortures. It was therefore probable that the name of Col. Ross would sooner or later be uttered by somebody—that he would be driven to bay. Then he would strike and strike heavily, if he could—perhaps he would strike in advance. Dr. Haworth said this to himself, and the event proved that he had accurately estimated his dangerous adversary.

Suddenly a bombshell exploded at Mauricewood.

One evening the family were assembled in the drawing-room, and Dr. Haworth and Mr. Tim Maurice were engaged in a game of chess. Miss Cary and her mother were seated in front of a cheerful blaze, as the nights were growing a little cool—the young lady crocheting and Mrs. Maurice tranquilly knitting and smiling sweetly, as was her habit. It was difficult to say which of these two charming persons was the more attractive—the girl just budding into womanhood with her rosy cheeks and artless lips, or the still beautiful mother, a little pale, but smiling with her air of exquisite sweetness and tranquillity.

All were thus engaged when a servant brought in the mail-bag. The trains had become tardy of late, and Mr. Tim Maurice often maligned the railroad and threatened to denounce it in the " Abbeyville Gazette."

" Well, here is the mail at last," he exclaimed, "and we can finish our game, Doctor, after looking at it."

He took the bag and emptied it on the table. It contained a magazine, two or three newspapers and a single letter—for Mrs. Maurice.

" For you, my dear," said Uncle Tim, looking at it. " I think I recognize Col. Ross' hand."

He gave her the letter, and she took it, saying as she opened it :

" A letter from Col. Ross—to me ? "

" It certainly is not to me, as my name is Timothy and not Ellen," said Uncle Tim, " and now, Doctor, as the papers can wait, suppose we finish our game—I am going to check-mate you."

Mrs Maurice had in the meanwhile opened the letter and was reading it.

" What on earth has he to say, mamma ? " said Miss Cary, laughing quietly.

Mrs. Maurice did not reply. Her face had suddenly changed color.

" Mamma !—you are not well ! What is the matter ? "

" I—I—a slight giddiness," said Mrs. Maurice, rising. " I will soon recover from it. A glass of water—"

" Let me get it, mamma ! " Cary said, rising quickly.

" It is not necessary," said Mrs. Maurice quietly. " Keep your seat, my dear. My giddiness is over already. This note is on a matter of business which I will tell you of—I will go up-stairs and lie down for a few minutes."

" Let me come with you, mamma ! "

" No, dear—I will be back in a few moments."

Cary and the gentlemen looked at the speaker inquiringly, but her face was quite tranquil now and the smile had returned to it.

" Keep your seat, dear," she said to Cary. " I will soon return."

She then went up-stairs to her chamber. A cheerful fire was burning on the brass andirons, sending flashes through the lace window curtains and lighting up the portrait of Mr. John Maurice. Cary's bed was near her mother's, and as it was lower than her own Mrs. Maurice lay down upon it, covering her face and trembling slightly.

She then rose, lit the candle in the silver candlestick on the small center-table, and seating herself in an arm-chair, finished the perusal of her letter.

The letter was from Col. Ross, and in the following words :

" WASHINGTON, *November* 20, 1880.

" My dear Mrs. Maurice :

" There are some duties so painful that we are apt to wonder why an evil fate should impose them upon us. Something has recently come to my knowledge which has occasioned me the utmost concern, and I find myself under the distressing necessity of communicating it to you. Believe me I do so with the very greatest reluctance. I shrink from writing what I am about to write, but I am very sincerely your friend under all circumstances, and it is absolutely necessary that you should be notified of a matter of painful personal interest to yourself and your family.

" You will perceive that I approach the subject with reluctance. I am aware how much pain you will feel. I wish some one else had the duty imposed upon him of informing you. It is imposed on *me* by the circumstances, and I am obliged to tell you with the

sincerest regret that your marriage to your late husband, Mr. John
Maurice, took place *before the death of his first wife in South
America.*

"This distressing fact only recently came to my knowledge, and
I at once resolved to return home and communicate everything to
you in a private interview. I am, however, detained here for a few
days longer as a witness before the Foreign Committee, and am
compelled to write. The circumstance alluded to was discovered
by a commissioner at ·Lima who has been engaged in auditing the
accounts of the Peruvian Guano and Nitrate Association. It appears that Mr. John Maurice during his residence at Lima purchased an interest in the nitrate stock, and upon his marriage with
a French lady settled the stock upon her as her separate property.
As no claimant for the stock or dividends had appeared for many
years, the commissioner, it seems, investigated the matter, and found
that Mrs. Maurice had died a few months after her marriage. The
date of her death was ascertained from the mortuary register in the
Desemparados Church and Parish, and is given in the report as
October 10, 1860. As your own marriage, I believe, took place in
May of the same year, the painful question arises whether or not it
was valid.

"Do not, I beg, understand me to intimate for a single moment
that Mr. John Maurice was aware that his first wife was living at
the date of his second marriage. I am satisfied that he was not.
There had been a misunderstanding between them, I believe, and
they had separated. He returned to the United States, and must
have been convinced of her death, on what grounds I am unable to
state, but I am sure that he *was* convinced of it.

"I have to add, my dear Mrs. Maurice, the disheartening circumstance that the fact I have stated is included in the commissioner's public report now before the Foreign Committee. I can only
say, as a personal friend, that I am by no means certain that the
date is correctly stated. I sincerely trust that it is an error—that
the first Mrs. Maurice died in October *preceding* not *following* your
own marriage. The question is very painful, since if the commissioner is correct you were never married to Mr. Maurice.

"I terminate this long letter by saying that on seeing the commissioner's report I promptly telegraphed to Lima to test the accu-
racy of the date by an examination of the mortuary register. As
my telegram was sent two or three weeks since I expect to receive

the necessary documents at any moment by mail. The reply to my cable telegram was undecipherable.

"I shall return home in a few days, and as soon as I arrive shall do myself the honor of calling upon you, and trust it will then be in my power to furnish you with conclusive documentary proof that the first Mrs. Maurice died *before* your marriage.

"With high respect,
"Your faithful servant,
"FERDINAND ROSS."

Mrs. Maurice read this letter carefully through with a heaving bosom.

When she had finished reading it she rested her forehead on her hand, and a tear rolled down her cheek.

"It is a falsehood!" she said, in a stifled voice. "That man has invented it!"

She looked at the letter once more. The italicised line caught her eye—"*before the death of his first wife in South America.*"

"It is false! false!" she exclaimed, raising her head with a quick flash of the eye.

Then she looked up at the portrait of her husband, which was smiling at her, and said, sobbing:

"I *know* it is false, John!"

VIII.

MR. TIM MAURICE IS OUTRAGED, BUT RESIGNED.

MR. TIMOTHY MAURICE was walking up and down the veranda on the morning after the reception of Col. Ross' letter—the victim of curiosity and apparently, also, of jealousy.

For the first time his niece, Mrs. Maurice, was concealing something from him, and what made the fact more aggravating was at that very moment in private conversation with another person.

This person was Dr. Haworth. Mrs. Maurice had made her appearance at breakfast with a composed if not serene expression of countenance, and had not referred to the letter. Nothing, therefore, was said in regard to it by any member of the little circle, since

all understood that the gentle and dignified lady had her own reasons for not discussing it at the time.

Uncle Tim had waited and deferred his ride to be informed on
the subject. Mrs. Maurice had not, however, signified any desire
to have a private interview with him—on the contrary she had
quietly requested *Dr. Haworth* to come into the drawing-room for
a moment.

He had followed her thither and the door had closed on them in
the very face of Mr. Tim Maurice. What did it mean?

The worthy Mr. Maurice was very far from being a jealous or
suspicious individual, but then some things will mortify the best of
us. He was extremely fond of Dr. Haworth and adored his niece
—but why had not he been consulted instead of the Doctor, who
was nearly a stranger!

He could catch glimpses of them through the window in earnest
conversation. The matter was evidently important. What could
it be?

It had been quite plain to Mr. Tim Maurice for some time that
his niece and Dr. Haworth "understood each other." Something
had probably passed between them on the day following Cary's fall
from horseback, involving more than the simple demand of the young
lady's hand in marriage. This something was unknown to the male
head of the household, but it had plainly established confidential relations between the lady and their guest.

Was the present business connected with that, and was Mrs.
Maurice consulting Dr. Haworth in reference to the letter from Col.
Ross?

Having scowled with the air of a conspirator at this unheard of
preference of a stranger's advice, Uncle Tim burst out laughing,
mounted his horse, and went to take his morning ride.

When he came back he found Dr. Haworth seated on the veranda, as the day was pleasant, reading the " Psychology of Opium."
He sat down opposite with a cheery smile on his face and said :

" Well, what were you and the madam consulting about, Doctor ? "

" About the letter received last night. Mrs. Maurice will inform
you of its contents herself," said Dr. Haworth.

" Hum ! She tells *you* about it first, and I have been bitterly
jealous all the morning. Nothing disagreeable, I hope."

" I hope not," said Dr. Haworth, in a matter-of-fact manner,

"Something about Cary, I suppose. He had better give up that matter, don't you think so, Doctor?"

And Uncle Tim laughed in a significant manner.

"He is distanced in the race!" he added, "and I don't mind saying I am glad of it. The Colonel is a gentleman, of course, as his father was before him, but his manners are—well, too *varnished.*"

"He is a man of the world, no doubt."

"I have known many, and the best company is not varnished, as I call it; it is simple and natural. I know a gentleman when I see him. His origin is not so important. To be a gentleman is the main thing. The stupid pretense of this age is that the sneak and the hero are alike—one as good as the other, and, faith! a great deal better!"

Having thus unburdened his mind, Uncle Tim said:

"You were reading that curious book, I see."

"Yes."

"Do you like it?"

"I cannot say that I fancy it much. The author is a gross materialist, and yet he professes to have a religion."

"What is it? I have only read a few pages."

"He calls it *The Religion of Humanity.*"

"A handsome phrase, at least. What does it mean?"

"It means anything you choose. What it does not mean is *faith*, as you and I understand the term. Hatred of Christianity is about the sum of it, but as the writer thinks by the aid of opium, his ideas are a little mystified. It is rather an unpleasant book, but may convey an unjust impression of the real character of the writer."

Dr. Haworth laid the "Psychology of Opium" on the seat beside him and rose.

"I am going to Abbeyville for an hour," he said. "I see my horse is ready. I will return before dinner."

"Something more to be done in that affair?"

"Nothing."

"No new developments?"

"I believe not."

"And you still think you will be able to fix the guilt of my poor brother's murder upon the man or woman?"

"I think so."

Uncle Tim sighed.

"We have said so much on the subject, Doctor, that it is useless to say more. These people may or may not be guilty. But I suppose you have heard the rumor. It is said now that some other person was concerned in the affair—a man of prominence. Who on earth can be meant?"

"I will answer that question, my dear Mr. Maurice, on my return from Abbeyville, where I think I will find a letter," said Dr. Haworth.

————

IX.

DR. HAWORTH HEARS FROM COL. ROSS.

WHEN Dr. Haworth said that he expected to find a letter awaiting him at Abbeyville, he meant a letter from Col. Ross.

He had no difficulty whatever in reading between the lines of Col. Ross' letter to Mrs. Maurice. What it meant was simply this:

"I am about to be prosecuted as principal or accomplice in the murder of James Maurice. If the prosecution is not arrested, I will proclaim to the world that you were never married to John Maurice, since he had a wife at the time in South America. You were not, therefore, his wife, and your daughter is not his lawful offspring. If the prosecution is promptly stopped evidence will be produced to show that John Maurice's first wife died *before* your marriage. If it is not stopped the evidence will show that she died *after* your marriage. Choose!"

This had been quite plain to Dr. Haworth when he had read the letter. Mrs. Maurice had laid it before him in the drawing-room and said: "What shall I do? It is a falsehood and a gross outrage." And Dr. Haworth had simply said at the end of the interview, "Let us wait."

Whether Col. Ross had or had not ulterior views involving a more daring scheme would soon be known. Meanwhile, as it must now be obvious that he, Dr. Haworth, was the mainspring of all, it was nearly certain that Col. Ross would open a correspondence also with him.

He was not at all mistaken. There was a letter for him at the Abbeyville office. He put it in his pocket without opening it; stopped at the telegraph office and conversed in a friendly manner with the young operator, inquiring if there was a dispatch from

Lima; ascertained that there was none, and returned in the direction of Mauricewood.

On the way he opened the letter. It was from Col. Ross, as he had seen from the direction, and contained these words, written in the same bold hand as the letter to Mrs. Maurice:

WASHINGTON, *November* 21, 1880.

GEN. HAWORTH—SIR: I am informed that an outrageous imputation has been made upon my character, namely, that I was cognizant of the intent to murder Mr. James Maurice, of Mauricewood, and that *you* are the author of this gross charge. The object of this communication is to notify you that I shall hold you personally responsible. I shall return immediately to meet this secret attempt of a personal enemy to destroy my character. I confess myself ignorant what object you have in view, and what motive prompts you. That is your affair, sir. You have presumed to circulate or authorize the circulation of these monstrous imputations on my good name, and I know in what manner to seek for redress.

Your obedient servant,

FERDINAND ROSS.

Having read this letter, Dr. Haworth folded it up, put it in his pocket and rode on slowly, with a grim smile on his lips.

"A cool hand," he muttered, "and the master of a flowing style. The only trouble is he is a knave; he may have been a gentleman once, but that was some time ago. Well, I am glad he is going to make fight. It suits me a great deal better than to have him abscond, which would be unfortunate."

For more than a quarter of an hour Dr. Haworth rode on slowly in deep reflection. Then he said:

"I wonder if he is really daring enough for *that?*—to demand *Cary* as the price of his silence, as well as the suppression of the prosecution. If he tries that—well, I should lose my patience, I think! I wonder if he has the nerve?"

Three days afterward this question was answered. The "Abbeyville Gazette" of that morning contained the following item of personal intelligence:

"Our popular countyman, Col. Ross, returned last night from Washington. He has been absent some time as a witness before a committee to examine Peruvian claims."

Mr. Tim Maurice had noticed this item, and looked around for some member of the family to communicate it to—but none were to be seen. Mrs. Maurice and Cary were up-stairs, and Dr. Haworth had ridden out. Therefore Mr. Tim Maurice put the paper in his pocket, mounted his horse, and went to make his tour of inspection on the estate.

X.

COL. ROSS VISITS MRS. MAURICE.

MRS. MAURICE was in her chamber with Cary, who was reading to her, when a maid servant came and informed her that Col. Ross was in the drawing-room.

At this information Mrs. Maurice betrayed a little agitation, and said to the maid:

"Say that I will be down in a moment."

"What does he want, mamma?" said Cary, looking at her mother and feeling vaguely that something more than a morning call was meant by Col. Ross' visit.

"He wishes to see me on business," replied Mrs. Maurice, with a slight tremor in her voice. "It will not take very long, my dear."

"Let me go down with you, mamma?"

But Mrs. Maurice shook her head.

"That would not be proper," she said. "Col. Ross has not asked for you. I had rather you would remain here."

Mrs. Maurice was an exceedingly gentle person, but when she spoke in a certain tone the members of her family never replied Cary resumed her seat, wondering what Col. Ross' letter and visit meant; and Mrs. Maurice, glancing in the mirror to assure herself that her toilet was proper for the reception of a visitor, went downstairs.

Col. Ross was seated in the drawing-room. At her entrance he rose and bowed with an air of the deepest respect—his face was a little flushed. Mrs. Maurice, slightly inclining her head, sat down opposite to him. She was somewhat pale, but otherwise exhibited no emotion.

"You received my letter, I trust, madam?" said Col. Ross, resuming his seat and speaking with some emotion.

"Yes, sir," was the reply of Mrs. Maurice in a low voice.

"It was exceedingly painful to me to be obliged to write it. The intelligence conveyed in it was a complete surprise to me. I had never imagined˙ such a thing before looking at the commissioner's report."

Mrs. Maurice made no reply. She was leaning back in her arm-chair, with her head bent forward a little and looking at him.

"I knew Mr. John Maurice in South America, as you are probably aware, madam," continued Col. Ross in the same˙ tone of respect.

"I was aware of it, sir," said Mrs. Maurice.

"I also knew, of course, that he had married in Lima, but understood that his wife had died soon after his return to the United States. It was only the other day that the painful fact came to my knowledge that this was altogether a mistake; that the lady was still living when—it is really *too* painful for me to finish my sentence, madam."

"When we were married, you mean, sir?" Mrs. Maurice spoke in a very low tone.

"Unfortunately, the commissioner's report seems to establish that fact, madam. I am afraid there is no ground to discredit it. The official who prepared it had, of course, no object in falsifying the statement. His authority was the mortuary register of the church parish in which Mrs. Maurice died."

"At Lima, sir?" murmured Mrs. Maurice.

"Yes, madam. Mr. Maurice met his wife there, and they continued to live in the city after his marriage. I can state this of my personal knowledge, though I am sorry to say I had but a limited intercourse with him. I was an officer of the navy, and my ship was stationed at Callao; and another circumstance was an obstacle to our familiar intercourse."

"Another circumstance, sir?"

"I am sorry to say that Mr. Maurice and myself had become unfriendly. A very few words will explain the origin of this interruption of our friendly relations. Mrs. Maurice was a young lady of the opera—a troupe had visited Lima—and was much admired. After her marriage with Mr. Maurice he objected to the attentions still paid to her by some of her old friends, myself among the rest—attentions perfectly respectful on my part—and I regret to say I had a personal rencounter with him. He may have mentioned it to you."

"Yes, sir."

" I trust his statement and my own on the subject do not con-
flict. I have endeavored to make my own strictly accurate. As my
ship was sent on a cruise I remained ignorant of his subsequent
movements. When I came back I heard that he had returned to
the United States."

Col. Ross looked respectfully and with some feeling at Mrs.
Maurice.

"This is absolutely all I knew, madam, until the other day," he
continued. " I was at home, you may probably remember, just
before his marriage to yourself—I was absent, however, at the precise time, as I was forced to join my ship—and it certainly never
entered my head that the first Mrs. Maurice was living. She could
not be divorced, with her own consent, at least, as she was a Ro-
man Catholic; and I of course adopted the natural supposition that
she was dead."

" Yes, sir," said Mrs. Maurice in a very low voice.

" As soon as I made the painful discovery mentioned in my letter, madam, I telegraphed to Lima. I was utterly incredulous. I
was quite certain that it was a mere clerical error—the mistake of a
copyist. Mr. John Maurice I knew was a man of honor; if he paid
you his addresses it was because he had proof, I said to myself, that
his first wife was dead. Unhappily he was mistaken, madam—fa-
tally deceived in some manner. She was living."

" Living!" repeated Mrs. Maurice, not asking the question by
the tone of her voice, but uttering the fearful word as if unconsciously.

" Unhappily I have proof that the first Mrs. Maurice was living
at Lima after the month of May, 1860, when your marriage to Mr.
John Maurice took place in this house."

Mrs. Maurice drew a long breath, and her bosom heaved.

" Proof ? " she said.

" I will explain everything, my dear Mrs. Maurice," said Col.
Ross, bending forward and speaking in a tone of some emotion.
" The statement in the commissioner's report amounts to nothing—
it will pass as a clerical error. The important, the fatal proof, is
the mortuary register."

" Yes."

" I see you are somewhat agitated. I beg you will dismiss any
apprehension," said Col. Ross. " I alone know of this, for I repeat

that the official report is nothing. A stroke of the pen will correct it as a clerical error—in the printed copies it will pass as a mere misprint. That is absolutely the only means; it is a little irregular, but I promise you that I will see that it is done."

Mrs. Maurice betrayed slight agitation, but made no reply.

"The report of the commissioner is not the important point— the official record at Lima from which it was taken was the vital matter. Right or wrong, I directed my agent there to obtain possession of the paper at any risk or expense, and to promptly transmit it to me. He obeyed my order, and on the pretext of examining the church register cut out the leaf containing the record of the first Mrs. Maurice's death. I deeply regret to say that the record supports the commissioner's statement. Mrs. Antoinette Maurice died at Lima in the month of October succeeding your marriage with her husband. The entry was the proof of the fact. Here is the leaf."

Col. Ross then took from the breast pocket of his coat a faded sheet of paper, yellow at the edges except upon the left side, where an uneven edge proved that it had been hastily cut.

"This is the proof," he said; "the only proof in existence that you were not the lawful wife of John Maurice and your daughter his lawful daughter."

Mrs. Maurice extended her hand to take the paper and examine it. But Col. Ross did not seem to observe the gesture. She looked at him and withdrew her hand, but said nothing.

"I am a very unhappy man, madam!" exclaimed Col. Ross in his deep voice. "I loved a young lady who was beginning to have some regard for me in her turn. I was dreaming of a long life of happiness with her, when an unknown stranger, a person she does not know, put a sudden end to all my hopes! The young lady rejected my suit, and is reported to encourage his; and not content with his triumph over me, this same unknown stranger has set on foot a criminal prosecution to destroy me. You are aware whom I refer to, madam, to this General or Dr. Haworth—a man of doubtful antecedents, of whom no one knows anything with certainty— and you may have been informed of his last outrage. He has not only supplanted me with Miss Maurice—he has circulated the vile slander that I was cognizant of the design to murder your father!"

Col. Ross spoke in a deep, even hoarse, tone. He seemed to

8

become aware of the fact and made an effort to soften his voice, but without effect.

"I am to be crushed, you see, madam—I who have wronged no one! Well, I will not be crushed! I am innocent as the babe unborn of this vile charge, and repel it with indignation. I have come this morning to say this, among other things, though I hope it is unnecessary. The real object of my visit, I need not say, was to bring you the leaf from the mortuary register."

His eyes were fixed upon the lady with an intense expression now.

"Need I say that I came to deliver into your hands this sole proof that you were not the wife of your husband?" he said. "That was my object."

Mrs. Maurice looked up.

"It is yours—at the moment when it is destroyed there will no longer be the least proof that you were not the lawful wife of John Maurice."

Mrs. Maurice made the least possible movement with her head.

"There is the fire. You have only to reach out your hand and you will still be Mrs. John Maurice, of Mauricewood, your daughter the heiress of the Maurice estate."

Mrs. Maurice raised her hand as if she were about to take the paper.

"I attach only one condition—it is not so much since I save the honor of your family."

"One condition?"

"That the outrageous imputations upon my character will be publicly disclaimed by the Maurice family—that the person calling himself Dr. Haworth shall be requested to terminate his visit to this house, and that—shall I end, madam?"

"Yes."

"That Miss Maurice will permit me to resume my visits to Mauricewood."

Mrs. Maurice shrunk back in her chair.

"The price of your silence then is—Cary's hand?"

Col. Ross leaned forward with a glow on his face.

"Pardon my presumption," he exclaimed. "I knew that a person of your exquisite refinement would shrink from my proposition. But I have made it in spite of myself, madam! I love Miss Maurice with all the strength of my being. You may say I am bargaining for her hand—I am not. I am simply begging the poor boon of not seeing it wrested away from me! I might have come to you like a highwayman, if I had been a person of that character, and said to you: 'You were never the lawful wife of your husband—your daughter was not born in wedlock—give me her hand—here is the only proof of your misfortune—if you consent, take it and destroy it!' I have not meant to say that, madam. I am not bargaining with you—I am only pleading! What I say is, 'Give me the simple hope that I *may* some day obtain your daughter's hand.' As to this paper—there is the fire—burn it!'"

He placed the paper on the table.

"Only a word, madam! It is not even a condition! There is the paper—it is yours!'"

Mrs. Maurice made no reply, and did not offer to take the paper.

"Only a word—one word—that this prosecution shall be stopped, and the author of it informed that his presence in your house is no longer agreeable to you."

Col. Ross spoke in a voice full of emotion, which probably accounted for the fact that the sound of footsteps on the veranda did not attract his attention.

Mrs. Maurice turned her head. He followed the direction of her eyes and at last distinguished the steps. The door of the drawing-room then opened, and Dr. Haworth came in.

PART IV

THE CRIMINAL TRIAL AT ABBEYVILLE,

I.

THE PAPERS FROM LIMA.

AT the appearance of Dr. Haworth, Col. Ross wheeled and confronted him. His expression was what is called black and his eyes flashed.

"I have the pleasure of meeting *you*, sir, at last!" he exclaimed.

"Yes," said Dr. Haworth, looking grimly at the speaker. "You will judge for yourself whether it is a pleasure or not."

"I returned from Washington with that object!"

"Well, you have accomplished it."

Dr. Haworth had been looking around him. He was apparently searching for something. He saw the paper upon the table.

"Col. Ross has no doubt called on business, madam," he said to Mrs. Maurice. "In the absence of your uncle, may I ask as a friend what the business is? Is it connected with this paper?"

He went to the table and took up the sheet from the register.

Col. Ross made a movement to prevent him, but he had the paper in his hand.

"That is a matter of private business between Mrs. Maurice and myself! You have no concern with it whatever, sir!" he cried.

"I venture to concern myself with it, unless Mrs. Maurice objects to my doing so," replied Dr. Haworth.

"I do not object at all," said Mrs. Maurice.

Col. Ross measured his adversary from head to foot, and seemed about to attempt to tear the paper from his hand. The prospect of success did not seem encouraging, and turning suddenly to Mrs. Maurice, he said:

" Is it possible, madam, that you will permit a stranger, a person unknown to you, to meddle with your family affairs ? "

" Dr. Haworth is a friend—he is not a stranger," said Mrs. Maurice.

· " He is my personal enemy—an intruder on this interview ! I demand possession of that paper, sir ! "

" And I refuse to put you in possession of it ! " said Dr. Haworth, placing the hand holding the paper behind his back and confronting Col. Ross.

For a moment the two men stood facing each other, one flushing with suppressed rage, the other cold and collected. Col. Ross then said :

" So be it, sir ! Since I am to choose between a disgraceful scene in the presence of a lady, or submission to your insolence, I make my choice. Read the paper ! You may then understand why I objected to your doing so without Mrs. Maurice's permission."

" It is not necessary to read it—I know its contents," said Dr. Haworth. " It is the leaf of the register at Lima containing the entry of the death of Mrs. John Maurice."

" Yes ! "

" My agent reported to me that it had been abstracted from the register. That circumstance is now accounted for."

" Well ! Say that it was abstracted ! Say that I am responsible for that trifling offense. If you are aware of the contents of that paper without reading it, as you say you are, you are probably aware also of my object in securing possession of it."

" I think I am," said Dr. Haworth.

" The honor of the Maurice family was involved—of this lady and her daughter ! As long as that paper was in existence—you know the consequence, sir. You profess to be a friend of this family—a friend of somewhat recent date ! If you are really such, you will understand why, as a real friend and an old one—not one of yesterday—I ventured on a step for which I am liable to a heavy penalty, to save the honor of the Mauricewood household ! "

Dr. Haworth had not paid much attention to these passionate words. He was looking at the paper.

" Let us leave this general discussion, sir," he said, " and come to business. This is the leaf from the Desemparados death register, I see. Here is the record of the death of Marie Antoinette

Maurice, wife of Senor John Maurice, citizen of the United States, and *attaché* of the North American Legation, formerly residing at Lima.   The date is October 10, 1860."

Dr. Haworth held up the paper between himself and the window.

" Mrs. Maurice did not die in the year 1860," he said.

" Do you mean, sir—? "

" That the date has been altered?   Yes, and in a bungling manner.   You may see for yourself, madam," he said, turning to Mrs. Maurice and holding the paper up before her.   " An erasure is always dangerous.   It produces unevenness in the thickness of the paper, and the result is greater transparency.   It is easy to see that this document has been—*improved*, let us say.   The actual date of Mrs. Maurice's death was October, 1859, and not 1860.   As you were married in May, 1860, I need not call your attention to the importance of the difference."

Mrs. Maurice had taken the paper and was looking at it against the light.

" The date has certainly been changed! " she said.

" Beyond any doubt."

Col. Ross had been standing still.   As he spoke now the intonation of his voice indicated that his teeth were set together.

" Am I to understand," he said to Dr. Haworth, " that you charge me with forgery—with falsifying that register? "

" It is falsified, and in your possession."

" Sir!—this outrage !   There are limits—! "

" Registers have been falsified in other instances—the circumstance occurs. . The entry in another caused the conviction of Mr. Henry Ducis for the murder of Mr. James Maurice."

Col. Ross had blushed with rage ; at these words his face grew a little white.

" The fate of Mr. Ducis hinged upon the proof of an alibi," said Dr. Haworth, " and that depended upon the entry in a ledger. Well, the entry was *improved*, as this one has been; that is no secret to you, sir.   Remember, we spoke of it one day.   The question then was a man's life ; at present it is the honor of a lady."

It was plain that Col. Ross required all his powers of self-control to reply.

" Yes, we spoke of that," he said with a suppressed fire in his eyes, " but it has nothing to do with this question.   You are more familiar, no doubt, with forgeries than I am.   Say that this paper has been falsified. Do you charge *me* with that? It is a gross calumny, for which I will compel you to give me personal satisfaction. I have explained to Mrs. Maurice the manner in which this paper came into my possession, and precisely as she now sees it. I was actuated by friendship, the desire to protect her family—herself personally—from a great misfortune. She had no knowledge when she married her husband that he was already married. She was innocent—she had a daughter—it was to guard the good name of mother and daughter that I sent to Lima for this record—subjected myself to prosecution. If the record is falsified, it was falsified by others."

"That is your explanation, then—your entire explanation, sir."

"It is. I indignantly repel your gross insult—you shall answer for it!"

"Well, one business at a time," said Dr. Haworth; "we can talk of that afterward. The question at present is more serious. You have said so yourself—it is the good name of a mother and her daughter. Let us come, then, to the vital question. Mr. John Maurice marries in South America, his wife dies, and he marries a second time. The natural supposition is that a man of honor like Mr. Maurice would not have committed bigamy—but twenty years afterward, when he has been dead a long time, the question arises whether he was *not* guilty of that. The decision depends upon a burial register recording the date of the first wife's death. The register is produced by a third person, and it establishes the charge of bigamy. There is only one flaw, and that is serious—the register has been falsified. The obvious question is—who falsified it? and the first step in the inquiry is to ascertain the motive of the forgery."

"Do you mean, sir—!" exclaimed Col. Ross with his head lowered and looking at the speaker sidewise.

"I will tell you what I mean if you will allow me to do so without interruption. We have come to the production of the paper by the third person, but there was also a fourth person. This fourth person had his own reasons for ascertaining the real facts connected with the first Mrs. Maurice. He accordingly wrote to Lima and ascertained what he wished to know."

"You ascertained!"—

"I see you identify me with person number 4," said Dr. Haworth; "well, you are not wrong: I not only wrote, but growing a little impatient communicated with Lima by cable. The reply of my agent was that the papers had been sent."

"The papers, sir—!"

"Not by mail. The mails are unsafe. By private hand. A friend visiting South America was about to return to the United States. He was acquainted with my agent at Lima, and hearing my name pronounced informed him that I was a friend of his. The result was that the papers were entrusted to him for delivery to me on his return. He has delivered them."

"The papers, sir—!" repeated Col. Ross.

"Here they are," said Dr. Haworth, taking some folded sheets from his pocket. "This is the certificate of Fray Antonio Guarrez, canon of the church of Desemparados, that Marie Antoinette Maurice, wife of Senor John Maurice, was interred in his parish on October 10, 1859, as appeared from the mortuary register—not then abstracted. That may be called the ecclesiastical proof, here is the civil—the certificate of Alguazil Perez that the death of Marie Antoinette Maurice was reported to him officially at the same date, as appeared by the civil record."

Dr. Haworth presented the papers to Mrs. Maurice.

"These facts were known to me before the arrival of the papers," he said. "My agent telegraphed them in cipher. Accidents happen."

Col. Ross said nothing. His expression was that of an animal driven to bay and dangerous.

"The whole matter is now perfectly plain, I suppose," said Dr. Haworth. "That leaf from the register is of no importance whatever. It is not worth destroying. It was not abstracted in time, and the change made in it was deferred too long. It is therefore waste paper."

Col. Ross advanced a step and said in a cold and resolute voice :

"Am I to understand, sir, that you formally charge me with the forgery of that date ? "

"You acknowledge that you obtained it—you or your agent—from the register."

"Answer my question, sir ? "

"Well, I think your agent was the actual forger—in obedience to an order or an intimation of your wishes in the matter. Since you question me I reply."

" That is enough, sir," said Col. Ross, white with anger. " Will a friend of mine find you here to-morrow ? "

" Here or at Abbeyville. But these personal matters must wait."

" They shall not wait ! I will send you a message here, or force *you* to send *me* one—at my house, where it will find me."

" A message will find you to-morrow at the jail in Abbeyville," said Dr. Haworth in his cold voice.

He went to the door and called a person standing on the veranda, who came in.

" You will serve the warrant of arrest on Col. Ross for complicity in the murder of Mr. James Maurice," he said to the constable.

" My arrest—for murder !" exclaimed Col. Ross with an outburst.

" You did not expect it so soon then," said Dr. Haworth. " You must have heard from your confidential friends that I once before procured a warrant for the same purpose from another magistrate."

The constable produced the warrant and said :

" Sorry, Colonel, but needs must."

Col. Ross, shaking with wrath, turned and fixed his eyes upon Dr. Haworth.

" Well, sir, the matter is in shape now," he said. " This is war to the knife and the knife to the hilt. I accept it—look to yourself ! "

Dr. Haworth inclined his head and said :

" I will do so."

And this was the end of the interview.

Col. Ross rode back to Abbeyville with the constable, and was supplied with a comfortable apartment in the town jail to await his examination the next morning.

The examination was prolonged and attracted a great crowd, who evidently sympathized with the prisoner. But the testimony of Jean Baptiste and others was serious. Col. Ross was refused bail and committed for trial at the County Court, which would sit in a few days.

He therefore returned to his apartment in jail, where he was surrounded with every comfort, and was reported to view his approaching trial with disdainful composure.

II.

AN OUTRAGED COMMUNITY.

I**F** the arrest of the two obscure "hill people" surprised the inhabitants of Abbeyville and the vicinity, the arrest of Col. Ross astounded them.

He was one of the richest and most prominent gentlemen of the county. His good name was unstained, and his friendly manners had made him popular. If old people recalled that he had been a wild youth, too fond of the tavern bar, the young generation knew nothing of that and no one was disposed to regard it as the unpardonable sin. It was wrong to get tipsy, of course, but there were some things that were even worse. There was hating your neighbor or backbiting him—being self-righteous and loving "filthy lucre." Some people who went regularly to church and held up their heads were often guilty of that; and nothing pleased them better than to point at the victim of drink and say: "I thank thee, O Lord, I am not as that man."

But that was in the Colonel's youth; people who disliked him had no longer the satisfaction of shaking their heads. His life was irreproachable—and who was this unknown man, this Dr. Haworth, who had charged him with the worst offense known to the law?

It was an outrage, and the magistrate who had refused him bail and committed him to jail would probably be sent into retirement at the next election.

Thus Abbeyville was outraged—also the county of which it was the county seat. Crowds flocked to offer the expressions of their sympathy. The fair sex manifested a desire to storm the prison bounds and clasp the interesting accused to their bosoms. It was said that a party had visited him, and that two of their number who were young and pretty, had cheered his solitude with a kiss. His photograph was in demand, and an enterprising artist having secured one, made his profit from the circumstance. If he had chosen, Col. Ross might have affixed his autograph to them and driven a brisk trade with them. But that was unnecessary. He was a man of wealth. What was better, he was eminently respectable. To charge so rich and respectable a man with murder was an absurdity—even an outrage!

Meanwhile the unknown stranger, Dr. Haworth, who had aroused all this storm, remained portentously quiet. He was even more cheerful than he had been for a long time. Somebody with blue eyes, who had remonstrated with him now and then in a low voice for his moody silence, no longer had any occasion to do so. He looked into the blue eyes under the brown bangs with a new expression of happiness; and the eyes filled with happy light in response to the light in his own.

An acute observer in fact, subjecting Dr. Haworth's face to thoughtful inspection, would have said : "This man has succeeded or is about to succeed in some darling object."

One morning Dr. Haworth said to Miss Cary Maurice :

"Would you like to take a ride on horseback to-day ? The weather is really too superb to remain in the house."

"I should like it very much," said Cary, with a glance which meant, "since I am to ride with *you*."

"I will order the horses, then," said Dr. Haworth.

And half an hour afterward they were riding through the splendid woods, in the direction of Prof. Lesner's. The road leading by his house was winding and picturesque, and Miss Cary Maurice preferred it.

"We might call and inquire if the poor Professor is well," she said, with a happy laugh.

And Dr. Haworth replied, looking at her with great tenderness :

"I meant to propose that. A friend is visiting the Professor whom I promised to call and see."

"A friend of yours ? "

"Yes, and a very fine fellow, as you say in the South. He brought some papers for me from Lima—but that is not very interesting."

"Who is he ? "

"You shall know him soon, as I am going to give him the pleasure of making your acquaintance."

"Is he fond of you ? "

"It is possible—I am fond of him."

"Then I shall like him," said Miss Cary, with a side glance and a charming smile.

She raised a small ungloved hand as she spoke to push back her brown hair ; and as the hand was not far from him her riding companion took it and pressed it to his lips,

" I never thought I could love a woman as I love *you*," he said.
And Miss Cary, casting down her eyes, replied in a whisper :
" That makes me *very* happy."

III.

DR. HAWORTH'S FRIEND.

THEY had soon passed over the distance between Mauricewood
and Prof. Lesner's, and found themselves in front of the small home-
stead.

The place was much changed. The end of autumn had come
and the flowers had disappeared. The birds, also, which had made
the vicinity vocal with their gay carollings, were silent ; and there
was a general air of sadness and solitude about the attractive little
establishment.

Prof. Lesner was not visible in the grounds ; he was probably
afraid of the rheumatism. They would undoubtedly find him, however, in his study, and having assisted Miss Cary to dismount and
tethered the horses, Dr. Haworth walked up to the house.

He knocked, but no one replied, though voices were distinguished
in the library on the right.

" I am afraid the poor Professor is unwell, he is always so
prompt," said Cary, " but I think I hear some one. He is the friend
you spoke of, no doubt."

" No doubt, and he is probably conversing with his traveling
companion, a young lady."

" A young lady ? "

" From South America."

You have not told me who they are ? "

" Well, you will know now. Here is my friend."

Steps were heard, the door opened, and Mr. Burdette, of New
York, made his appearance. He was the same jovial and attractive
personage, with his ruddy cheeks, his bright smile, his hair parted in
the middle and curling, and his eye-glasses secured by a guard to
his button-hole.

" Why, Haworth, old fellow," he cried, " I thought a good wind
would blow you in this direction to-day ! "

" Well, you see it has blown me—"

" For fear *I* would blow you up for not coming, mio amigo."

Mr. Burdette saw his friend's companion and made her a bow full of grace and high breeding.

" Miss Maurice," said Dr. Haworth, " permit me to present my friend Mr. Burdette."

Mr. Burdette and Miss Maurice exchanged friendly bows, and then the former exclaimed, laughing :

" This is delightful ! I thought I was to sustain the infliction of your society *solus*—and lo ! you lift the weight from my mind."

" I am glad you are relieved," said Dr. Haworth—the very sight of his laughing friend seemed to put him in good humor.

" I am ! immensely ! And then my little friend, Miss Giorgione, will be delighted. She's rather tired of *me*, I suppose, by this time."

" Miss Giorgione ? "

" Otherwise, Miss Carrie Fenton. She is a little lady from the North who has been living with an aunt of hers in Lima. As I was going down that way her friends asked me to escort her home. I call her Giorgione from her splendid hair—like the painter Giorgione's pictures, you know—the real bronze gold—Titianesque and that sort of thing."

The gay voice of Mr. Burdette made the lonely house a different place.

" I shall be very glad, indeed, to become acquainted with Miss Giorgione," said Cary, smiling, " but where is Prof. Lesner ? "

Mr. Burdette shook his head.

" He is quite unwell. I called by to see him, as he invited me to spend a few days—we have had some business relations. But I find him confined to his chamber."

" Poor dear Prof. Lesner ! " said Cary. " I am so sorry."

" It quite changes my plans. My arrangements are all made to spend a week here—but I am detaining you, Miss Maurice. Allow me the pleasure of presenting Miss Giorgione."

They went into the library, and were met by a very pretty young girl of 18, with a bright face and superb hair of a rich-shaded gold. She wore a fawn-colored traveling dress, which defined a slight and graceful figure.

When Mr. Burdette presented his friend she came forward quietly and held out her hand smiling. All were friends in a moment, and while Miss Cary and Miss Giorgione chatted in one corner Mr. Burdette and Dr. Haworth strolled out to the porch.

"What is the matter with the Professor?" said Dr. Haworth.

Mr. Burdette shook his head as before. "The old business," he said in a low voice. "The Mott street complaint."

"You have seen him?"

"Yes, but he scarcely recognized me. He is in a sort of stupor. I thought he had made up his mind to let that poison alone."

"I am afraid he is too much under its control. So you are disappointed in your visit?"

"It seems so. It won't do to stay—nobody but an old negro woman to do the honors of the establishment!" laughed Mr. Burdette.

Dr. Haworth was evidently disappointed at the idea of having his friend depart so quickly.

"We will see about this," he said, "and I will send up my name to the poor old fellow; he may see me. Let me first thank you for bringing these papers and delivering them as you got out of the train. You are not aware what a service you have done me."

"Glad to hear it. Espartero said they were important, and he didn't like to trust them to the mail. I made his acquaintance in Lima, and incidentally mentioned that I knew you—so he sent them along by me."

"They came just in time. I will tell you about it when we have more leisure."

Animated voices were heard in the library, and the voice of Miss Cary cried:

"But I insist upon it."

"I should like it so much—but you must ask Mr. Burdette!" replied the voice of Miss Giorgione.

"It is not necessary to ask him. The masculine sex were made to submit to the weaker vessels," said Miss Cary. "You and he positively shall come! Dr. Haworth is—a very dear friend; and his friends are ours."

"But—"

"Poor Prof. Lesner is too unwell to make your visit agreeable—so you see—now do!"

Mr. Burdette, overhearing this colloquy, laughed.

"Your friend Miss Maurice is trying to persuade Miss Giorgione to make her a visit," he said.

"Why not? I thought of that. You would come!"

" Come ? Why, certainly I would come. I am on the wing, and ready to light anywhere."

" Light at Mauricewood, then—Miss Maurice's mother's. It is a pleasant perch."

" With pleasure. Do you think they will take care of us for four or five days ? "

" Not for any specified term—that is not the fashion in the South. The people are precise ; they insist upon their visitors remaining— indefinitely. The longer the better."

" Well, I believe that's the fact," said Mr. Burdette, in a jovial manner. " I'll come—but I positively must be in New York in one week."

They went in. Miss Cary urged her invitation ; it was at length cordially accepted, and the carriage was to be sent for them on the same evening.

Dr. Haworth then summoned the old black servant woman and sent her up to ask Prof. Lesner if he was able to see him.

In a few moments the old woman hobbled down stairs and brought the reply that Prof. Lesner was so unwell that he could not see his friends. He had the asthma, but would soon be better. Company excited him, but he hoped Dr. Haworth would call again.

From this it was plain at least that his *asthma* had not wholly deprived him of his faculties, and musing sadly for a moment at the melancholy weakness of the good old scholar, Dr. Haworth looked at Miss Cary, who thereupon rose.

" You will come this evening!" she said, holding out her hand and beaming on Miss Giorgione.

" But you have not told your mamma."

" Mamma is my subordinate—I rule her with a rod of iron," said Miss Cary.

" Then you are spoiled," laughed Miss Giorgione.

" I believe I am ! Everybody does spoil me."

She glanced sidewise at Dr. Haworth.

" But don't be afraid ! We'll all be delighted. You must cer- tainly come, Mr. Burdette, and bring—Giorgione ! "

Thereupon Miss Cary Maurice went through the formula which is the feminine indication of mild regard—she kissed Miss Giorgione.

Once in the saddle again and going at full speed through the beautiful woods, Dr. Haworth said to his companion :

" Do you like my friends ? "

"They are charming."

"Burdette is a fine fellow."

"And so is Giorgione! What hair! How I envy her."

"You need not," said Dr. Haworth.

And as Miss Cary's brown curls had fallen on her shoulders he took one of them and touched it with his lips. It was the second time on the ride that he had performed a romantic ceremony.

On the same afternoon the Mauricewood carriage was sent to Prof. Lesner's, and returned with Mr. Burdette and Miss Giorgione.

IV.

JEAN'S FRIEND.

DR. HAWORTH had gone up-stairs to make his toilet for tea when Jean came into the chamber with his face full of blushes. Chancing to glance at him Dr. Haworth noticed the deep color in his cheeks and said:

"What is the matter, Jean?"

"The matter is, Excellency," stammered the boy, "that—that—"

He stopped, attempting to laugh, but exhibiting the greatest confusion.

"Tell me what you mean. Has anything disturbed you, Jean?"

"Yes, Excellency."

"Speak plainly; tell me what it is."

"I never expected—what could have brought her here—the young lady—Miss Carrie Fenton!"

"Do you know her?"

"Know her! She is the one—the one—I knew so well in Lima!"

Dr. Haworth looked at Jean with surprise and then smiled.

"Well, that is curious indeed—that you and she should be thrown together in this manner! I understand—she is *inamorata!* Well, you have an excellent opportunity to renew your suit."

Jean colored more than ever and then began to laugh.

"I'm afraid there's no hope, Excellency. She is prettier and more mischievous than ever! When she got out of the carriage I could scarcely believe my eyes, I was up here looking out of the window. How did she come to be here?"

Dr. Haworth explained and then proceeded in a direct manner

to catechise Jean. He had known that the boy had suffered a love disappointment at Lima. Now he asked all about it, and Jean with some confusion and a good deal of laughter confessed everything. He had made Miss Fenton's acquaintance at Lima, and became a regular visitor at her aunt's, where she had lived for some years, as her mother and father were both dead. The result had been the common one when two impulsive young people of different sexes meet as familiar friends. Miss Fenton and Mr. Baptiste, Gen. Haworth's private secretary, had become more than friends—the youth had "told his love," and she had replied with a laugh that she was too young, had insisted upon the same reply, and the youth finally construing this into a polite form of the phrase, "No, I thank you," had gone off in despair to travel and forget his woes.

"Well, that is very simple," said Dr. Haworth, much interested and amused. "It is a good omen that you should meet again in this odd manner; and I shall assist your suit in every manner possible, as you have it so much at heart. Am I wrong?"

"Very far from it, but—" Jean stopped, blushing.

"You think Miss Fenton has finally made up her mind? One is never certain of that as to women, the philosophers say. You can satisfy yourself at least, and I am glad a friend has arrived to induce you to emerge from your room and mingle more with the household. Your modesty is intense, Jean, but remember you owe it to Miss Fenton to show your pleasure at seeing her again. After tea, therefore, you must not go up-stairs, but come into the drawing-room, and do your part to make this pretty little South American at home. Common courtesy requires that."

The boy laughed and blushed; at the same moment the tea-bell rang and Dr. Haworth said:

"Come, Jean!"

V.

A MAN OF BUSINESS RESTING.

PRETTY Miss Giorgione and jovial Mr. Burdette were thus domiciled for the time at Mauricewood.

It was a very great pleasure to two persons—Dr. Haworth and Jean. The first had many things to talk about with Mr. Burdette, and Jean had even more to say to Miss Giorgione.

She had met him, when he appeared at tea, with a stare of astonishment.   Then her face filled with laughter, and she held out her hand, which Jean hastened to take.   The broken intimacy of Lima seemed to have been cemented in a moment ; and any one glancing at the face of Miss Giorgione during her interview with Jean would have said, " There is a little beauty who is shut up in a quiet country house, and hails with delight the opportunity of teasing an old lover for her amusement."

Every member of the Mauricewood family was charmed with the gay traveler, Mr. Burdette.   He was full of fun, and had the tact of becoming quickly acquainted with people—also that of making friends of them.   He adapted himself to his surroundings with the ease of an old voyager, acting up to his favorite maxim—" When you are in Turkey do as the turkeys do, and if you are in Caracas do as the Crackers do ! "

Mr. Tim Maurice was delighted and found only one fault with him—he was too easy to beat at chess.   Otherwise he was an immense acquisition, and host and guest had long and animated talks.

"You have a fine old place here," said Mr. Burdette, smoking his mild cigar on the veranda with the assistance of a newspaper. " This is the way to live."

"You like it because it is quiet, I suppose ? " said Uncle Tim.

"Precisely.   We are driven to death in New York one way or another.   I went off for a little rest."

" Did you find it ? "

" Oh, yes.   I forgot all about business, and lounged along, laughing and enjoying everything."

"You went to South America—Lima—by Panama, I suppose ? "

"No, by Buenos Ayres, stopping at Cuba and Rio Janeiro.   I had something to attend to there—and, by-the-by, I ran over to Florida."

" To see some friends in the country ? "

" Well, a little business."

"I thought you said you left business behind you when you turned your back on New York ? "

"What took me to Florida did not amount to much.   I merely went there to buy a villa and an orange plantation for Mrs. B. and my brunettes.   I then went back to Havana, where I had a little matter to arrange, since I have come to think of it."

"Business again ? "

"Well, not much. I had an interest in a sugar manufactory, and one of those Spanish dons you meet in New York had persuaded me to invest in a cigar *fabrico*. I thought I would straighten things, as I was on the spot. So I sold out my sugar interest, pocketed half the amount of the insurance on the cigar factory, which had just burned down, and went on to Rio Janeiro."

"Where I do trust you had no business!"

"Well," said Mr. Burdette, laughing at his companion's tone, "it amounted to nothing at all—a mere share in a coffee plantation. I was compelled to go there, however, to look after some stock I hold in Dom Pedro's street rail-car company. My idea was to talk the senors into adopting the compressed air motor—but that's a long way ahead of South American progress; so I went on to Buenos Ayres and crossed over to Lima."

"Don't tell me, I beg, that you had business there! You left home to rest!" exclaimed Uncle Tim, in a state of outrage.

"I am sorry to say I had a trifle, both in Buenos Ayres and Lima. Don't be uneasy; it was not connected with guano or nitrates. To tell you a secret, I have invented a new electric brake for railway cars—to get ahead of my friend Edison—and as I am one of the directors of the Lima & Quito Trunk line—"

"Good, Heavens! Not more business!"

Mr. Burdette laughed with an air of enjoyment.

"I didn't mind it," he said. "In fact, I am used to it. But I see I am boring you. I soon picked up little Miss Giorgione and set out for home."

"You didn't stop, I hope?"

"For a day or two only, on the Isthmus and at New Orleans."

"Not—"

"Well, it did not signify. De Lesseps is a friend of mine, and —the ship canal, you know—I had to audit some claim—as a member of the board; but I was soon in New Orleans. A charming place."

"You enjoyed it, I hope, without—"

"Well, my business there was really a mere bagatelle. As Vice-President of the Ashtabula Line of steamboats—but I see I am growing tedious. I never enjoyed a trip more—it was such a complete rest! I am growing positively idle, and will find it a hard struggle to get back to business!"

With which foreboding Mr. Burdette sighed, and then laughed in response to the laughter of his delighted companion, Uncle Tim.

VI.

MR. BURDETTE WHISTLES.

DR. HAWORTH had not ceased to manifest from the first moment of his friend's arrival the real pleasure he experienced from that event.   It is a great satisfaction sometimes to have one call one " old fellow "—which, wanting in distinguished consideration, has a much greater charm.

So they rode and walked together, and had long talks.   Dr. Haworth, without reserve, told his friend everything connected with the approaching trial at Abbeyville ; and having listened in deep astonishment, Mr. Burdette uttered a prolonged whistle.

He then turned around and said, fixing his eyes upon Dr. Haworth :

" Are you literary ? "

" Literary ?   I am not sure I understand."

" Are you engaged on a romance ? "

" Writing one ?   Certainly not."

" Well, I thought you were, and that you were giving me an outline of your plot ! "

Thereupon Mr. Burdette whistled again and exclaimed :

" Write it up !   There's millions in it !—fifty thousand copies ordered in advance !—presses working night and day and unable to supply the demand !   Write it up, Haworth, write it up ! "

" You forget there is no denouement, my dear Burdette," said Dr. Haworth grimly, " but that is not far off now.   You have come just in time to be present."

" I must get back—business calls me.   I have rested too long. When does it come off ? "

" Next week."

Mr. Burdette inspected his note-book, muttering :

" Meeting of the board—Tuesday the—appointment with Billin to—well, I may be able to stay, perhaps."

" You will see something worth seeing," said Dr. Haworth in his grave voice.   " This man is going to show fight—it is a matter of life and death with him."

" Do you think you can bring that horrible affair home to him ? " asked Mr. Burdette in an earnest tone.

"I mean to make the attempt, at least. You can judge for your-self, as I have told you everything."

"And I never was more flattered, Haworth. A man like your-self rarely talks as plainly as you have talked to me."

"Take the fact, if you choose, as an evidence of my estimate of your character. Yes, the issue is now joined between myself and Col. Ross. Whether he strangled James Maurice with his own hands or not, he was concerned in it!"

"A man of his high position!—and I think I heard some one say that the whole country sympathized with him and thought the charge an outrage?"

"You heard the truth," said Dr. Haworth coolly. "Col. Ross is a man of position, and what is more serious, of wealth and influence. He has engaged the ablest counsel and insists upon a prompt trial. His friends are manufacturing public sentiment—here and in the prominent journals. At this moment I am an object of positive de-testation to the good people of this country. I, an unknown stranger, am presssing a gross and fatal charge—the charge of secret murder —against one of the first gentlemen of this community!"

"Well," said Mr. Burdette, with the same earnestness, "I know you too well not to be sure that you know what you are doing."

"I know perfectly well! I have him in my hand, Burdette! If he is guilty I swear he shall not escape—as long as I am alive I will not let him rest!"

"There is no possibility of mistake then? His character—"

"Of mistake? His character?" exclaimed Dr. Haworth; "what would you say of a man who forged a paper reflecting dishonor on a lady to force her to give him the hand of her daughter?"

"I should say he was a scoundrel!"

"Then you have the proof that this man is such—since he did so."

They had walked out in the grounds and were coming back toward the house now.

"Well, I'll stay—whether I can or not," said Mr. Burdette sud-denly. "One doesn't meet with such a drama every day. Yes, I'll stay over to the trial."

"I am glad to hear it; and now let us come to something more agreeable. I see your young friend, Miss Giorgione, as you call her, yonder—walking out with Jean."

"It looks like a case," said Mr. Burdette, resuming his cheerfulness, "and I am glad I brought the young thing away from Prof. Lesner's. Poor old fellow—how sorry I am for him."

"It is really melancholy. I have seen his book—the 'Psychology of Opium.' It is a strange performance."

"Yes—I hesitated about publishing it; but he was so pressing that I sent it to *press !* "

"Then publishers are accessible to human feeling?" said Dr. Haworth, evidently striving to throw off his gloomy mood.

"Publishers?" said Mr. Burdette, "accessible to feeling? My dear fellow, they are babes—babes! No author ever appeals to them in vain, and they live up to their lofty ideal and grand mission."

"What is that?"

"To lend a hand to struggling genius—and make money!"

Mr. Burdette had evidently regained his good spirits, and said kindly:

"Poor old Lesner! He is a scholar and a gentleman—and he has become the slave of opium. I sympathize with him deeply, and would do anything in my power to assist him—as I know you would, Haworth."

"Anything whatever — but these slaveries are discouraging. There is but one course for a man of feeling—to treat them gently and endeavor to touch the *morale.* That is the only hope; and this poor old gentleman, I fear, has weakened his will too much."

"It looks like it. Well, I'll hope for the best. What a jolly old place," said Mr. Burdette, looking up at the Mauricewood house as they drew near.

"A good example of a Southern country home."

"Yes, cheerful with the door wide open. But just think of that terrible business! Which is the room?"

"That to the left yonder."

"With the closed blinds?"

"Yes."

"Well, I've often stopped to look at the house where the Nathan murder took place—on Twenty-third street—but this seems stranger. It is hard to connect the idea of *murder* with a place like this. Which window did the murderer enter at?"

"That one," said Dr. Haworth, pointing.

"You think he was really Ross?"

"We will know next week," said Dr. Haworth.

VII.

THE OPENING OF THE TRIAL.

THE day for the trial came, and a great crowd filled the court-house at Abbeyville.

It was an old brick building, discolored by age, standing in the middle of a grassy yard, and the court-room was spacious, with a raised platform for the Judge, seats for the jury to the left, and a long desk for the bar in front.

The Prosecuting Attorney occupied an arm-chair near the Clerk, who sat just beneath the Judge. In one corner was a small elevated dais surrounded by a railing—the dock. But this was rarely used.

By 9 o'clock in the morning all the avenues to the court-house had been thronged, so great was the public curiosity; and by 11, when court opened, a dense mass packed the court-room. It was difficult to move an inch, and when the Sheriff was compelled in the exercise of his official functions to make his way through the crowd he did so at the imminent risk of his apparel.

The accused, Col. Ross, Job. Wilkins, and Mrs. Wilkins, were seated behind the long desk facing the Judge and near their counsel, two in number, one of them the most eminent criminal lawyer in a circuit of fifty miles, and the other a rising young advocate who had already developed an original knack for working upon juries.

The jury was chosen with difficulty, and only after long and hot discussion. There had been, apparently, very few persons who had not formed an opinion, namely, that the charge against Col. Ross, at least, was an outrage, and securing a panel consumed nearly two hours. At last that was effected, however, and the trial began.

At this moment the large apartment presented a striking spectacle. The autumn sunshine streaming through the lofty windows, covered with dust and cobwebs, lit up the contrasted figures of the dense crowd—the well-dressed gentlemen, the roughly-clad, and at the door some dusky Africans, who, like their white fellow-citizens, recently their masters, had caught the general contagion. A stray beam fell on the ancient clerk seated behind his table, upon the silent jury, and the face of Col. Ross, with its expression of unalterable composure. He was scrupulously neat in his toilet, and wore fawn-colored kid gloves, according to his habit. His black coat and spotless bosom gave him the air of a person attending a fête, and

Mr. Burdette, who was standing in the crowd immediately behind him, looked at him with philosophic interest.

The Wilkins people were a great contrast—they were dirty and sullen. On the man's face there was seen a sort of ferocity as of an animal driven to bay; on the woman's a stolid and cunning look, which defied the penetration of the crowd staring intently at her.

His Honor the Judge and the counsel have not received their due amount of attention, in this rapid *coup d'œil* of the court-room. Judge Gideon Bootlack was a little man with a red nose, and a pair of watery eyes, who had supplanted his gray haired predecessor, a Judge of the old *régime*—the result of his ardent support of the powers that were. He had enemies—every great man has—and these foes went so far as to declare that the orthography of his name was defective, that in reality it was "Bootlick," and derived from "bootlicking the boss," whatever that might mean. This was probably a mere slander, however, as the Judge, according to his own statement, was a man of expanded views. He aspired to Congress, the Cabinet, and the Presidency, on the ground that in this great country the humblest, etc., etc. Meanwhile, and previous to being obliged to give dinners at the White House with bouquets at the plates, he was little Gideon Bootlack, with smirking lips stained with tobacco, a weazen face like a winter apple, small red eyes, an obsequious manner, a complete ignorance of law, and a pleasing habit when appealed to for his judicial decision of clearing his throat, saying, "Ah, well," and proceeding to flounder in mud and incomprehensibility.

Mr. Dunn, Prosecuting Attorney, was a gentleman of about 40 —tall, thoroughbred, good-looking, with a lazy smile, quiet manners, very friendly, but a rough wrestler and fond of philippic. He was an excellent lawyer, an admirable public speaker, and universally popular, though he took no pains to wheedle anybody. The Judge was rather afraid of him, and also of Mr. Shirley, the senior counsel for the defense, a man of imposing manners, piercing eyes under bushy brows, and a way of taking snuff which awed people. As to Mr. Sparrow, the junior counsel, he hopped and chirped, and while speaking shook his fist, appealed to the bystanders, executed gymnastics, and seemed to have taken a contract to remove the roof of the court-house with his circular-saw voice, whose terrible rasping had been known to make women in the audience faint.

The trial began. The three accused persons had been joined in one indictment—Wilkins and his wife as principals, and Col. Ross as accessory before the fact.

The familiar preliminary proceedings of a criminal trial having come to an end, the Commonwealth introduced its witnesses.

The first witness called was Jean Baptiste.

The young man at once went and was sworn. He then took his stand facing the Commonwealth's Attorney, with the jury on the left, and the prisoners and their counsel on his right behind the long desk.

"Turn so as to address the jury in giving your evidence," said Mr. Dunn. "What is your name?"

"Jean Baptiste Maurice," said the young man in a respectful voice.

"Maurice? Then the name Jean Baptiste is not your full name?"

"It is not. My full name is Jean Baptiste Maurice, as I have said."

A movement had passed through the dense crowd at the utterance of the name Maurice. It plainly produced a sensation.

"Where were you born?" said Mr. Dunn.

"In the City of Lima."

"How old are you?"

"I am just 21 years of age, as I was born in the month of October, 1859—the precise day I do not know."

"You call yourself Maurice. The name has an intimate connection with this trial. Who were your father and your mother?"

"My mother was Marie Antoinette Lascelles Maurice and my father was John Maurice, *attaché* to the American Legation at Lima."

At the name of John Maurice the sensation in the crowd was greater than before. Every eye was fixed upon the witness, and Col. Ross was seen to lean forward and look at him with an astonishment which he made no effort to conceal. Dr. Haworth, who was not far from him, had never ceased to watch his adversary, and understood his expression without difficulty. That expression meant "The son of *John Maurice and Antoinette Lascelles!*"

"Do you mean to state," the attorney continued, "that your father was John Maurice of Mauricewood?"

"Yes."

9

" What evidence have you to offer in support of your statement? "

" The certificates from the civil and church records at Lima of the marriage of my parents, and my mother's wedding-ring."

Jean drew from his breast a folded paper.

" There are the certificates and the ring," he said, holding them out.

Mr. Dunn, the attorney, took them and examined the ring. It was a plain gold band, on the inner surface of which were engraved the letters J. M. and M. A. L., in the form of a monogram.

" These are the initials of the names you mention—John Maurice and Marie Antoinette Lascelles? " he said.

" Cost of engraving—ten cents a letter? " interpolated Mr. Sparrow, junior counsel for the defense, with a gay chirp.

Jean turned his head.

" The genuineness of the ring is another question," said Mr. Sparrow, hopping about.

" It is my mother's wedding-ring! " said Jean haughtily ; " what right have you to question my character? "

" Or to interrupt the witness—it must be stopped," said Mr. Dunn curtly.

"I am not a forger! " exclaimed Jean, looking over Mr. Sparrow's head straight at Col. Ross.

At this apostrophe Col. Ross' color changed, but he said nothing and continued to look intently at the witness.

" Well, now," said Mr. Dunn, leaning back with his arms behind his head, " as this little matter is settled to the satisfaction of the learned counsel, I will come to the certificates."

He unfolded the papers and said to Jean :

" These are the certificates, you say, of the marriage of your parents. They are in Spanish, I see. Is there any one in the court-room who understands Spanish? "

He looked around in the midst of a deep silence.

Jean raised his finger and pointed straight at Col. Ross.

" *He* understands Spanish," he said.

" That might have occurred to me, as Col. Ross has resided in South America."

Mr. Sparrow laughed gleefully, and hopped about, rubbing his hands.

" Not a bad joke—to apply to the Colonel," he said. " He is slightly interested in this cause, or I would propose to you to put him on the witness stand."

"I don't want him on the stand: I want him where he is," said Mr. Dunn, with his lazy smile.

At Mr. Sparrow's joke the crowd had laughed aloud. It was plain that scarcely a person in the whole assembly believed in Col. Ross' guilt.

"Will Col. Ross," said Mr. Dunn, "be good enough to tell the court, in the character of expert, if these papers certify to what the witness has testified, and whether they are in form?"

"With pleasure, sir," said Col. Ross, and the papers were handed across to him. As he took them a close observer might have noticed a slight tremor in his habitually firm hand, but this at once disappeared.

"These papers are in Spanish, as you say," he said coolly, after examining them, "and are civil and ecclesiastical certificates of the lawful marriage of the parties."

"Of John Maurice and Marie Antoinette Lascelles?"

"Yes."

"Have they marks of being genuine?"

"My client is not on the stand!" shouted Mr. Sparrow in overpowering wrath. "I object! I object! I—"

"Well, the matter is of no material importance," said Mr. Dunn. "As the papers are stamped with the official seals I suppose they are all right. It is not material. I am not going to ask the court for a commission to South America. They manage that sort of business better in Washington!"

He resumed the direct examination and said:

"Your father married your mother then in South America—I have heard something of that—and she died, I suppose?"

"She died soon after my birth, in October, 1859."

"But your father was left to you?"

"He was absent from the country at the time."

"Poor fellow!" said Mr. Dunn, "you must have had a hard time of it. But your friends cared for you?"

"I had none—my mother was a stranger. I was taken care of by an old half-breed woman named Juanna Panza, who lives near Lima, and had waited on my mother, I believe. She was very ignorant and could scarcely speak intelligibly. I never knew my father's name until recently."

" Very well—that is a straightforward story, and I for one believe it."

" Your belief," cried the irrepressible Sparrow, " is not—"

" Well, as I was saying," continued Mr. Dunn negligently, " you
are then closely related, it seems, to the estimable family so painfully
connected with the prosecution. You no doubt came from South
America to visit your relatives ? "

" No, sir, I knew nothing of the relationship until a few days
since. The old woman had told me nothing, and left me to run
wild, and I afterward became a street boy. I was taken and educated by a kind friend, who made me his private secretary, and I
came to this neighborhood as his traveling companion."

" A kind friend, you say ? "

" Dr. Haworth."

" Who is Dr. Haworth ? "

" He is a gentleman who lives near Lima. He was a general in
the Peruvian army, but resigned after the war, and travels under the
title of doctor, which he received from a foreign university."

" He is very much interested in the trial of this cause, I believe ? "

" Yes."

Mr. Dunn nodded. He then said :

" I will now ask a question which will probably save my friends
on the other side some trouble."

Mr. Shirley raised his head quietly—Mr. Sparrow hopped up
and sat down.

" Has there been any previous acquaintance between Dr. Haworth and Col. Ross ? "

" Yes."

" State anything you know on the subject."

" Yes, state the circumstances," cried Mr. Sparrow.

" Col. Ross and Dr. Haworth, who was at that time Gen. Haworth, had a personal encounter with cutlasses in Callao harbor,"
said he. " A market boat armed with a torpedo was turned adrift
and hauled in by a Peruvian steamer. The Chilian ship then came
to close quarters and a fight followed, in which, I think, Col. Ross
and Gen. Haworth slightly wounded each other."

" They are not friends, then ? "

" They are not."

" Why ? I was a soldier once and never felt any spite. Why
did Gen. Haworth ? "

" He probably had other causes for disliking Col. Ross."

" What were they ? "

" I suppose he will tell you."

" Well, they may come out in the progress of the trial. I will come now to another point. Was your father, John Maurice, acquainted with Col. Ross ? "·

Mr. Sparrow bounded to his feet and shook his fist at the ceiling. His excitement was overpowering.

" I object ! " he shrilled. " Are we to go into the history of the world and all its inhabitants ! Are we to have lugged into this cause every— ! "

" Well, let's go to dinner," said Mr. Dunn, laughing and looking at his watch. " I'm hungry."

This was a cruel extinguisher on Mr. Sparrow's eloquence, but as Judge Gideon Bootlack had been kept from his dear tavern bar for many hours, he also consulted his watch, said " Hum !—ah !— later than I supposed. I will adjourn court until to-morrow, gentle-*men ;*" and the court accordingly adjourned.

The crowd then dispersed, and the accused were reconducted to jail. Col. Ross received on his route many evidences of popular sympathy, and bowed with his habitual courtesy; but it was afterward remembered that he looked a little pale. This was singular, as he had preserved his composure up to the last question asked by Mr. Dunn. The long exercise had probably fatigued him.

VIII.

THE TESTIMONY OF JEAN BAPTISTE.

THE court-room on the next morning presented nearly the same spectacle. The crowd was as dense, the curiosity as absorbing, and Judge Bootlack, fortified by a stiff constitutional, was ready to expound the law and, if necessary, the Constitution.

As soon as court was opened Mr. Sparrow hopped to his feet. He had before him a pile of law books and a quire of foolscap containing the heads of his intended discourse—he had, in fact, remained up all night preparing a few impromptu remarks.

" May it please your Honor," said Mr. Sparrow, drawing down his waistcoat and clearing his throat—

"I withdraw the question," said Mr. Dunn, yawning; "it is of no importance."

Mr. Sparrow looked thunderstruck.

"My friend ought to be obliged to me—it saves him trouble," said Mr. Dunn, laughing lazily.

Mr. Sparrow looked daggers, which Mr. Dunn responded to by an amiable smile. He then said:

"I suppose documentary evidence is admissible in a court of law, your Honor?"

"Documentary evidence, sir?" said Judge Bootlack. "Certainly, sir—it is, of course, the best of all evidence, sir."

"To save time, then, and before resuming the direct examination, I will read a deposition concerning the point referred to in my question asked yesterday."

"A deposition? Certainly, sir."

Then, fortified by the approval of the court, Mr. Dunn unfolded a document and said:

"I am obliged to apply to some one in the audience again to read this. It is Spanish or some foreign lingo. I am only acquainted with English, Greek, Latin, and Hebrew—my education was neglected."

This was appreciated by the crowd, who laughed, and Mr. Dunn added:

"It is really giving Col. Ross too much trouble; perhaps the witness Baptiste, or rather Maurice, who has lived in South America, might interpret for us, and Col. Ross might say if he translates correctly. Call Jean Baptiste Maurice."

Jean came forward.

"You understand Spanish?"

"Yes, sir."

"Well, translate this paper into English for the court."

Jean took the paper and said:

"It is headed, 'Deposition of Pedro Nunez, formerly master-of-arms, now retired."

At the name of Pedro Nunez, Col. Ross visibly changed color, but said nothing.

"Proceed," said Mr. Dunn; "the object is to show that Col. Ross and John Maurice were personal enemies in South America."

"That has nothing to do with this case!" cried Mr. Sparrow. "Nobody murdered John Maurice!"

" What I mean to show is that a man supposed to be John Maurice was murdered at Mauricewood on the night of May 7, 1860," said Mr. Dunn, coolly. " Translate the deposition."

Jean did so. What Pedro Nunez deposed to was that some time in the year 1858 or 1859 Senor John Maurice and Senor Ferdinand Ross had fought with swords obtained from his fencing gallery. From an altercation between the parties, which took place in his presence, he became aware that the cause of the quarrel was the marked attention paid to Mrs. Maurice by Senor Ross, who had been acquainted with her before her marriage. Mr. Maurice had ended by slapping Senor Ross' face, and in the encounter which followed ran him through the shoulder, which put an end to the affair —soon after which Senor Maurice left the country.

" Is that all ? " said Mr. Dunn.

" There is the signature of the notary Espartero before whom the deposition was taken, and a certificate of the authorities to the official character of Espartero and the credibility of the deponent."

" Very well," said Mr. Dunn. " I will now resume the direct examination of the witness, Jean Baptiste Maurice."

He looked as he spoke at Col. Ross, whose face was as black as night.

" We will proceed to the testimony connecting the principals and accessory in the guilt of the murder of James Maurice," said Mr. Dunn.

He turned to Jean and said :

" Have you been present on any occasion when the accused in this case, principal and accessory, had any conversation together ? "

" Yes."

" State the occasion and the circumstances according to the best of your recollection."

Jean thereupon described the night interview between Col. Ross and the woman in the hills. The subject of their conversation, he said, was Dr. Haworth's visit to the house a short time before, and Col. Ross had warned the woman that he was *tracking her*, and to take care. They then went into the house where Wilkins himself then was, and whispered together, after which Col. Ross came out and rode away.

At this direct testimony to a private understanding between the Wilkins people and Col. Ross the crowd moved to and fro, and a buzz rose from it. Mr. Dunn reflected for a moment and then said :

"I understand you to say that there was a direct reference made by Col. Ross in this night interview to the presence of Dr. Haworth in the neighborhood?"

"Yes."

"With the view of *tracking* some one?"

"Yes; tracking the woman."

"Was Dr. Haworth's name mentioned?"

"It was not, but the person was described by Col. Ross in his first question to the woman."

"Well, it seems that there is no love lost between the parties. Has any other fact come to your knowledge going to show that Col. Ross was—well, let us say *tracking* Dr. Haworth?"

"A spy was employed to watch his movements."

"A spy?"

"A young woman of this town—Miss Burns."

"Ah! State what you know about that."

"Miss Burns was engaged as a seamstress at Mauricewood, and watched Dr. Haworth, writing regular reports to some one here and receiving replies. She also came into Dr. Haworth's room one night and tried to open his traveling valise."

"Well, that is interesting. Do I understand that you saw her?"

"Yes."

"You must have taken her for a ghost; an attractive feminine article as she must have appeared in her—well, her night raiment?"

The crowd, holding its breath, had the immense relief of a laugh.

"She was dressed. I saw her, as I was wide awake."

"What was she looking for?"

"Papers, I suppose."

"To show the object of Dr. Haworth's presence here?"

"I suppose that was her object."

"Well—you spoke of letters written by Miss Burns, and of her replies?"

"Yes."

"How did you ascertain the facts you state?"

"I found the correspondence."

"Where?"

"In a spot in the Mauricewood grounds. The messenger who came for them and brought answers was the man Wilkins."

"Ah! Well, that is an interesting fact. You say you *found* the correspondence. Did you destroy it?"

"Dr. Haworth meant to burn it and threw it in the fire, but I snatched it out. Here it is."

Jean produced the letter written by Miss Burns and the response.

"I see mention of an anonymous letter," said Mr. Dunn, coolly. "Was that sent?"

"Yes."

"What was the result?"

"Everybody laughed at it, and Dr. Haworth seemed to despise it."

"I suppose he did. I have not heard of many respectable anonymous correspondents in my time. I will read this interesting literature aloud now for the benefit of all the world and his wife."

"This gentleman seems fond of his joke and his forged letters!" said Mr. Sparrow furiously.

"Well," said Mr. Dunn, lazily, "I don't enjoy these forensic struggles as much as I used to do when I was young. They bore me, generally speaking, and I like to get in a laugh whenever it is possible."

He then read the letters, and laying them on the table, said:

"One thing seems plain—that *somebody*, whoever he or she was, was deeply interested in Dr. Haworth. Perhaps it was some fair admirer, but I think the letters show that he was of the male sex. Job Wilkins at all events seems to have been a mutual friend."

Col. Ross was leaning back in his chair with an expression of scorn and defiance. He said nothing, but his face seemed to indicate that he regarded the whole affair with contempt.

"Well," said Mr. Dunn, "let this point pass for the moment. We will have Miss Burns in court, and perhaps her town friend. You can take the witness, gentlemen."

For three hours Jean was subjected to an exhausting cross-examination, and all the points brought out in the examination-in-chief were touched upon by the unerring acumen of Mr. Shirley. Mr. Sparrow seemed to have vanished for the time from the case—was actually silenced.

The cross-examination resulted in nothing. Jean repeated his testimony and the attempt to shake it in any manner entirely failed. If he was perjuring himself he was doing so too skillfully to be detected. As to the effect of his evidence on the jury, nothing was known; and the audience made no demonstrations. Col. Ross preserved a grim silence; and when the proceedings ended for the day, and the court adjourned to the next, it was impossible to say what people thought, or what was coming next.

IX.

DR. SEABRIGHT AND OTHERS ARE EXAMINED.

WHEN court opened on the next day the crowd was if possible greater than on the days preceding. The room was a sea of heads, and at the doors and windows swarming black faces served as a background.

Looking at these friends of his unjustly banished from their proper sphere—the front—Judge Bootlack sighed. It was a violation of civil rights. Did not the American Constitution recognize the equality of all citizens? One prominent gentleman of color was so well dressed and looked so influential that the Judge meditated the propriety of inviting him to come up and take a seat beside him on the bench. It would tell, in a political point of view, and make him popular with the dusky "allies," but Mr. Dunn was there to laugh in his terrible way, and perhaps say something sarcastic, so the Judge refrained.

Mr. Dunn seemed in high spirits, and spent a few minutes joking with his friend Sparrow. With Mr. Shirley he was quiet and courteous—looking at and addressing him with the respect felt by a swordsman for an adversary worthy of his steel.

Then the court was opened and there was a profound silence.

Mr. Dunn looked over his memorandum lying on the table, rubbing his hands negligently.

"Miss Burns is next on my list—the handsome young mail carrieress, or postmistress," he said; "shall we call her? I don't want her, but we may as well ask her what she knows about the private postal service. Call Miss Burns."

Miss Burns was called and came forward. She was in gorgeous array and giggled behind her handkerchief as she was sworn.

A farce followed, to the great delight of the crowd. Miss Burns represented her performances at Mauricewood as a mere jest. Her friend, Miss Larkins, of the town, had a friend who—here Miss Burns giggled—well, who took an interest in Dr. Haworth. This friend was a Miss Somebody—that was all she knew about her. She was jealous, it seemed, as there was a nice young lady at Mauricewood of whom the Doctor was fond ; and when Miss Larkins, acting for Miss Somebody, proposed to her, Miss Burns, to discover what was going on, she agreed—it was a good joke—and put her letters under a tree. Had she gone into Dr. Haworth's room at night ? What an idea ? She *did* walk in her sleep sometimes—it was a bad habit—she wished she could get over it. But—go into a gentleman's room ? She would cheerfully expire before committing such an impropriety ! and Miss Burns giggled.

Mr. Dunn laughed in response—that jocose Mr. Dunn.

" Well, that's rather interesting," he said, "and sounds like a dime-novel. Jealousy—mystery—nocturnal somnambulists — and unknown ' somebodies.' Perhaps Miss Larkins might tell us something."

Miss Burns regretted that Miss Larkins had been called away to a distant part of the country by the illness of one of her sisters.

" I thought her sister would be unwell, or some other member of her family," said Mr. Dunn, nodding his head. " I have no further questions to ask Miss Burns."

And as the defense had none, Miss Burns retired, with a last giggle.

" Call Mr. Timothy Maurice," said Mr. Dunn.

And Mr. Tim Maurice came forward, was sworn, and took the stand.

" Mr. Maurice," said Mr. Dunn, resuming his seriousness, "will you state all that you know of the circumstances attending the murder of your brother, Mr. James Maurice ? "

Uncle Tim did so in a clear and succinct manner. The murder cry in the night, his alarm, the scene in the apartment, his hastening to procure the brandy, and his meeting with the woman Pitts, with her hands under her apron. The whole scene was painted in the simplest but most effective manner ; and Uncle Tim's pain at the recital evidently affected the crowd.

" Mr. James Maurice, you say, was dead when you returned ? " said Mr. Dunn. " What theory did you form—the question is proper—of the cause of his death ? "

Mr. Sparrow was about to hop up, but Mr. Shirley restrained him.

"I naturally concluded that some one had murdered him," said Uncle Tim.

"Did you see any weapon?"

"Yes, a hammer, lying beside the bed. A glove was also found which belonged to no one in the establishment."

"Which hammer and glove, I understand, were supposed to be the property of Mr. Henry Ducis, who was convicted of the murder."

"I never supposed so; I don't believe Mr. Ducis was guilty."

"It is important about the woman. I think you said her name was Pitts, and that she was a servant or housekeeper."

"Something of both."

"She had her hands under her apron, and the sum of money you mentioned had disappeared?"

"Yes, sir."

"When you reached the apartment was the window open?"

"Yes."

"It is natural to suppose, as you believed Mr. Maurice had been murdered, that you connected the open window with the murderer."

"I certainly did."

"With any person in particular? With—?"

Mr. Dunn caught the fixed eye of Mr. Shirley.

"I am not going to ask the witness if he suspected Col. Ross or any person, by name," said Mr. Dunn. "I have the right to ask the witness what impression was made upon him at the time."

"Yes," said Mr. Shirley.

"I suspected Wilkins, who had been my brother's manager and had quarreled with him, and also the woman Pitts, now his wife. I believe that he murdered my brother and that the woman was his accomplice."

"Well," said Mr. Dunn, "there is no statute, I believe, against putting two and two together. The friends of Wilkins are known. They pay him visits at night and Wilkins himself carries letters for 'somebody' to put in trees. Now a word on one or two other points. Mr. Maurice, will you describe the chamber in which your brother was murdered?"

"It was on the first floor, opening on the veranda."

"Was it his habit to sleep there?"

"Yes, but as it was the best chamber in the house it had been arranged as the bridal chamber of my niece, Mrs. John Maurice.

The change was made on the night of the wedding, and my niece's bridal presents which had been exposed on the bed were taken up stairs."

"For some days, then, before the night of Mrs. Maurice's marriage this room was supposed to be designed for her bridal apartment ? "

"Yes."

"Is it not possible, therefore, that the murderer supposed he was striking at *Mr. John Maurice!*"

"At my nephew? He had not an enemy in the world."

"Was the room well lit ? "

"There was only a taper swimming on oil—the candle had been put out."

"The result of which was half darkness ? "

"More than half darkness."

"More than half darkness," repeated Mr. Dunn. "You say that all this occurred late on the night of the wedding. Do you remember what guests were present ? "

"Nearly all the neighborhood."

"Were there exceptions ? "

"I remember none of our friends except Col. Ross, who was then a young man. I think I heard that he was absent from the country.

"He was at the time an officer in the navy, I believe ? "

"Yes, but was frequently at home."

"Were he and your brother James Maurice friendly toward each other ? "

"Well, they had at one time a misunderstanding, but I do not believe it amounted to anything."

"They were not what you would call enemies ? "

"I should not call them enemies."

"Your nephew, Mr. John Maurice, had no enemies either, you say ? "

"I never heard that he had one in the world. He was most amiable, though a high-tempered man when he was aroused; an affair in South America with Col. Ross, which has been deposed to, is the only quarrel of his I have ever heard of."

"I understand you to say that you never thought that Mr. Ducis was guilty ? "

"I have never thought so for a moment."

" Take the witness, gentlemen," said Mr. Dunn.

The cross-examination brought out no new facts, and Mr. Tim Maurice retired, when the Prosecuting Attorney called Dr. Seabright.

" You were the family physician of the Maurices at the time of the murder of Mr. Maurice, I believe, Doctor ? " said Mr. Dunn.

" Yes," growled Dr. Seabright.

" Were you sent for on the occasion of the murder ? "

" Of course—people say we doctors kill, so we are expected to bring the dead to life."

" Mr. Maurice was dead when you arrived ? "

" Stone dead."

" What was the cause of his death—a blow with a hammer or other weapon ? "

" No."

" What then ? "

" He was strangled."

A murmur rose from the crowd.

"Strangled!" said Mr. Dunn, quietly. "What grounds have you for such an opinion ? "

"I saw the marks on his neck. He was strangled, I say—*garroted*, as the Spanish people call it."

" The experts on the former trial declared, I am told, that he died from a blow."

Dr. Seabright flamed out :

" The expert asses may have said so ! I am not responsible for what that cattle say ! "

" Well—the deceased came to his death, then, by strangling, or the *garrote*, to use your expression. That is a curious idea. American murderers generally resort to a knife or revolver."

" I did not say the murderer was an American—I know nothing about it."

"Not an American ? Oh ! I understand. You mean that he was a foreigner or a person who had lived abroad—in Spain or Spanish countries."

" I know nothing about it ! I only know that James Maurice was strangled ! garroted ! There was no knife or revolver about it."

" And yet no better weapons could be found for putting a man out of the way."

" They make noise—if you want my idea."

" Noise ? "

" Certainly ! People hear a pistol shot, and a man who is stabbed cries out if he is not dumb."

" I understand, then, that your opinion is that the murder was committed by a skillful person—one who meant to do his work quietly, without noise, and go away as he came."

" Yes."

" There were no indications of a blow with a hammer or other heavy instrument ? "

" There were none—to account for his death. A slight abrasure was visible under the hair, but it amounted to nothing. He may have been struck afterward. The real cause of his death was the *garrote.*"

Mr. Dunn arranged his papers and reflected.

" I am curious about this garrote business," he said. " It is the Spanish method of execution, I am told, and breaks a man's neck better than a rope. How does it work ? Can anybody tell me— any one familiar with the operation ? "

He looked round and incidentally glanced at Col. Ross, who had grown rather pale. He was seated behind Mr. Shirley, paring the nails of one of his white hands. The hand shook a little ; then, as Mr. Dunn resumed his examination of the witness, the tremor disappeared.

" Well, Doctor," said Mr. Dunn, " I believe I have no further questions to ask you. Mr. Maurice was strangled, you say—you saw the marks of the garrote on his neck. But he was not dead when his brother came in ? "

" He died from syncope—he was a man of feeble health."

" The hammer found was not the death weapon, then—the one said to have been the property of Mr. Ducis ? "

" Mr. Ducis had nothing to do with the affair. He was as innocent as the babe unborn ! The expert asses and the donkeys that tried him were the cause of his conviction ! "

" You seem to have been a friend of Mr. Ducis ? "

" I was ; he was the noblest man on earth, and as innocent as you are."

Mr. Dunn nodded.

" I understand, then, your agency in arresting two of the accused parties."

" That was it. As soon as I had information I never rested until I had them in jail."

"Who gave you the information ? "

"Dr. Haworth."

"Who is Dr. Haworth ? "

"He is Dr. Haworth, of South America."

"How is he interested in this affair ? "

"You can ask him."

"That's true.   You have met him frequently, I suppose ? " ·

"A number of times—I was at Mauricewood and saw him yesterday."

"He is on a visit to the family ? "

"Yes."

"And a suitor, I understand, of Miss Maurice ? "

"I understand so."

Mr. Shirley listened with profound astonishment, looking at Mr. Dunn.

"Can you inform the jury whether Col. Ross has been a frequent visitor to Mauricewood this autumn ? "

"I believe he has."

"He is also a suitor for the hand of Miss Maurice, I think ? " said Mr. Dunn carelessly.

Mr. Shirley elevated his eyebrows and looked fixedly at Mr. Dunn.

"I think I have heard so."

"So that it is reasonable to conclude that Dr. Haworth is not friendly to Col. Ross ? "

Mr. Shirley looked inexpressibly puzzled.

"Probably he is not," said Dr. Seabright.

"Well, that perhaps explains Dr. Haworth's interest in this trial, so far as one person is concerned," said Mr. Dunn, picking his teeth. "You can take the witness, gentlemen."

But the counsel for the defense were in consultation.   Mr. Shirley had become composed, but Mr. Sparrow with difficulty suppressed his agitation.   He gesticulated, whispered hoarsely, and then, rising, said :

"We have no questions to ask the witness."

"Well, I'm glad of it," said Mr. Dunn, with his lazy smile.   "I attended a Readjuster gathering last night, and feel rather exhausted. I should like to procure a toddy or julep and a little dinner.   I move an adjournment to this evening—say at 6."

The court promptly acquiesced.   The mention of toddy probably acted on its nerves. Proclamation was therefore ordered by Judge Bootlack that the court would adjourn to meet in the evening at 6 o'clock.

" Is Dr. Haworth here ? " said Mr. Dunn.

" Yes, sir," said Dr. Haworth, coming out of the crowd.

" I will call you next, Doctor," said Mr. Dunn ; " and now I'll go and look up that toddy. Are you going my way, Judge ? "

X.

DR. HAWORTH'S TESTIMONY.

IF the court-room was a striking spectacle during the morning session it was much more striking at night.

When Judge Bootlack, in a thoroughly comfortable state of mind and body, took his seat on the bench it was already dark, and candles had been lit. One had been placed in front of his Honor, lighting up his ruby nose ; another beside the clerk, and two or three on the desk in front of the counsel for the accused. In the great room they made only a feeble glimmer, however, and outside the circle of light there was half darkness.

In this half darkness moved to and fro the densely packed crowd. From time to time a murmur rose from it. The dusky faces were full of expectation. The officers of the court could scarcely make their way. From this mass, undulating to and fro, no one could have been dragged out it seemed if he or she had fainted and was in danger of suffocation.

The court was opened, and Mr. Dunn with a cheerful countenance called Dr. Haworth.

Dr. Haworth at once came forward and was sworn, after which he took up a position facing the jury. His expression was composed, and he was clad as usual in a neat and unassuming manner. He glanced around him naturally and was observed to fix his eyes for a moment intently upon Col. Ross, who, seated behind his counsel, returned the look with the same intentness.

" Your name is Dr. Haworth ? " said Mr. Dunn, leaning back in his arm-chair.

" It is the name I call myself by," was the reply.

" What is your real name ? "

"Henry Haworth Ducis," said Dr. Haworth in his composed voice.

"Ah! Ducis!—Henry Haworth *Ducis?*"

"Yes; I am the only son of Henry Ducis, who was convicted of the murder of James Maurice and died of misery and despair in consequence of that conviction."

The crowd moved to and fro, and a vague sound rose from it— then there was silence again.

As Dr. Haworth replied to the question he turned his head slowly, fixed his eyes upon Col. Ross, who had grown suddenly pale, and said:

"My name will probably explain the interest I take in this case, and why I have used every exertion to bring the real murderers of James Maurice to trial and punishment."

"Yes," said Mr. Dunn quietly, "but your statement is an extraordinary one, to say the least of it."

"I was aware that it would surprise the jury."

"If your name is really Ducis, why do you call yourself Haworth?"

"It was the family name of my mother."

"Well, that partially explains the fact of its adoption; but why not bear your own name, Ducis? It is an honorable name—there are very few people who believe that it is not."

"I have a good reason."

"What is it?"

"My father's command—as he was dying."

A profound silence followed the words. The vast audience did not move a muscle.

"As he was dying—your father, Mr. Henry Ducis?"

"Yes: it was his last injunction to me."

Mr. Dunn seemed to reflect for a moment on this singular response of the witness. He then said:

"This is all rather strange, Doctor—tell us about it. It would be better, I suppose, to leave you to tell your story in your own way, and not to worry you with questions. My learned brother—or brethren, as there are two—on the other side will take care of that part of the business. I will ask you, therefore, to tell the jury all the circumstances, as I need not say they will affect the value of your testimony."

"I will do so if the jury wish."

It was not doubtful what the jury wished. They were looking at him with the deepest interest and curiosity, like the whole audience. Even the counsel for the defense exhibited unmistakable surprise. Col. Ross was behind them in the deep shadow and his face was thus hidden.

"I think the jury will like to hear all about it," said Mr. Dunn, in a matter-of-fact manner. "So go ahead, Doctor. You are the son, you say, of Henry Ducis, convicted twenty years ago of the murder of Mr. Maurice?"

"Yes, sir. He had no other children," said Dr. Haworth, "and as my mother was dead I was his only companion. I was at the time about fourteen years of age, and the natural result of intimate association with a person of my father's character was a very great devotion to him."

"Everybody will understand that," said Mr. Dunn. "I was not acquainted with Mr. Ducis, but I have heard the highest opinion of him expressed by all who knew him."

"Including the Maurice family," said Uncle Tim in a distinct tone from his place in the crowd.

Mr. Sparrow hopped to his feet.

"I protest against these interruptions!" he cried, looking indignant.

"Well," said Mr. Dunn lazily, "they are rather irregular, but I, for one, in my character of a citizen of this county am glad to hear that the family of the murdered man scout the idea that he was put to death by a man like Henry Ducis."

"Hem!" said Judge Bootlack, with dignity; "the witness will continue his testimony."

"Unless my friend over the way would prefer to have him muzzled," said Mr. Dunn with a sarcastic smile. "You can go on, Doctor."

Dr. Haworth had quietly waited and now resumed his testimony.

"I have been asked to explain," he said, "the grounds for my adoption of the name of Haworth instead of my proper name, and I understand the jury to wish information on that subject, as the fact affects my testimony."

The jurymen nodded, and Mr. Sparrow subsided in great disgust.

"I will continue then," said Dr. Haworth composedly. "I was fourteen years old and living with my father on his estate in the lower end of this county when the murder of Mr. Maurice took place. I first heard of it from the servants—if there is any startling news they discover it quickly. What I heard was that, on the night before, Mr. Maurice had been murdered in his bed—by some unknown person, with the design of robbing him it was supposed."

"What you heard is not testimony," cried the irrepressible Sparrow.

"Good heavens!" said Mr. Dunn, "are we in a court of law or a Readjuster meeting? I *have* heard of a debating society in which the rule was that only *four* people should talk at once, but—"

Thus extinguished, Mr. Sparrow subsided, with muttered protests, and Dr. Haworth continued:

"As I informed the jury, the intelligence of the murder reached me through the servants on the following morning. My father was absent. On the day before he had ridden to Sinclair Station to purchase some fertilizers, and, as the place was distant, had remained all night—the night of the murder—at the house of a friend. He only returned on the following evening, too late to ride to Mauricewood, which he expressed a strong desire to do. And I remember his expressions of horror. He was deeply depressed at having quarreled with Mr. Maurice a few days before. They had been friends, and his old friend's death moved him deeply. On the next day he ordered his horse to go to Mauricewood, but gave up the design; his presence there might not be welcome; and he shut himself up in his library. In the evening he was arrested for the murder.

"A constable came and showed him the warrant, issued by a magistrate who had always been unfriendly to him. At sight of the paper my father exclaimed: 'Good God! to charge *me* with the murder of James Maurice! It is monstrous!' But there was nothing to say—there was the warrant of arrest and the constable was waiting. From horror my father passed to composure—he was a man of great gentleness and sweetness of temper, but of the utmost resolution of character. He therefore said no more, and was driven to Abbeyville, where he was examined—the quarrel between himself and Mr. James Maurice, together with the expressions used by himself were testified to—and he was committed for trial at the next court by the magistrate who had issued the warrant. Of the trial it is unnecessary for me to speak. He was convicted upon evidence purely circumstantial, and though the jury were unanimous, it was said, in the opinion that he ought to be pardoned—were even ready to sign a petition to that effect—he was not pardoned—he died of shame at the stain on his good name."

Dr. Haworth stopped. His voice had not faltered for a moment in telling his painful story, or his eyes lost their expression of somber composure.

"And that stain on your father's name accounts for your dropping it ? " said Mr. Dunn.

"No ; I should never have called myself by any other name than his own if he had not laid his command upon me. I saw him every day in jail, and he discussed without reserve every feature of the case. He cared nothing for the Governor's pardon, he said ; his name would remain dishonored. He had been the victim of some unknown enemy who hated him and meant to destroy him— who was skillful, daring, unrelenting and probably rich, since he had not struck, himself, it seemed, but by the hands of others. This conviction became rooted in my father's mind, and he never lost sight of it. He had the presentiment of his own death, and said to me one day in a low tone: 'You are my only hope. The name of Ducis will remain dishonored unless you remove the stain from it.' He then explained his wishes. The real murderer or murderers of Mr. Maurice would never be discovered if the search for them was pursued publicly. It was necessary to do so privately. His injunction, therefore, was that I should dispose of the family estate, leave the neighborhood, assume the name of my mother and acquire a complete education as a preparation for the work before me. Thus trained I was to return and quietly pursue the investigation. The name Haworth was unfamiliar here, since my mother's family was from a distant state—it was, therefore, probable that no one would suspect the object of my coming. I promised my father that I would obey his command—he gave me his blessing—and three days afterward he was dead."

Dr. Haworth looked composedly at Col. Ross, but behind the pupils of his eyes, so to say, there was a latent fire which contradicted his calm tones.

"I have explained why I call myself Haworth and not Ducis," he added coldly. "It will remove the impression that I am a nameless impostor. I was denounced as one 'in an anonymous letter sent by the person who corresponds through hollow trees."

All eyes were turned toward Col. Ross, but he bore the ordeal without changing color—he even looked a little defiant.

"Well, to end this explanation," said Dr. Haworth, coolly, "I went away and grew up, and became an engineer in South America. Some years afterward I returned to this place, and endeavored to discover who had really murdered James Maurice. I completely failed—there were no traces whatever—and the name of Ducis remained dishonored. Then I went back to South America, where I had succeeded in amassing some money, risked it in speculation and found myself rich. That was what I wanted. I had satisfied myself that the man I was looking for was rich and powerful. And at last I had discovered what I thought a clew—shall I explain that to the jury, sir?"

"Certainly. Let all the facts come out," said Mr. Dunn. "I defy my friends over the way to stop you. If they attempt to do so I am ready to meet them."

Mr. Sparrow gesticulated defiance and was about to bound up, but Mr. Shirley stopped him."

"It is always a sign of a bad case," said Mr. Dunn in a philosophic tone, "when there is an objection to have all the facts stated. The Commonwealth does not object on this or any other occasion. I am myself much interested in Dr. Haworth's testimony, and would like to know about that clew. What do you mean, Doctor?"

"I mean," said Dr. Haworth, "that I found a boy running about in the streets of Lima and discovered that he was the son of John Maurice of Mauricewood."

"The youth Baptiste—or Maurice?"

"Yes; I was falling into a sort of apathy, and had nearly despaired of ever discovering anything. I had thrown myself into affairs—fought, speculated and then retired, in disgust with all things, to a hacienda near Lima. The discovery of John Maurice's son again put me on the scent of the murder. I will explain why. I had taken him into my service because I was struck by his face—it was the face of a gentleman, not a vagabond; and hearing him mention, one day, the name of a half-breed woman, who had been his nurse, I went and visited her near Callao. She told me everything—he was the son of John Maurice and a Mademoiselle Lascelles, whom he had married. There had been trouble between husband and wife and Mr. Maurice left the country—and some months afterward the boy was born. Soon afterward his mother died, directing that he should be called Jean after his father. The priest who baptized him had added Baptiste, and the woman, whose name was Panza, had taken charge of him and brought him up, concealing his name from him for fear he would be taken away from her, as she had grown fond of him. As an evidence of his birth she had his mother's wedding-ring, which I secured by appealing to her avarice—it has been produced."

"Yes," said Mr. Dunn.

"To finish. I thus found that I had taken into my service the son of John Maurice, who was married a second time at Maurice-wood on the very night of James Maurice's murder. Why had his father quarreled with his mother? I discovered. A fencing master named Pedro Nunez, whom I knew informed me—Mr. Maurice was jealous. Col. Ross had been an admirer of Mrs. Maurice before her marriage, and continued his attentions. Mr. Maurice thereupon insulted him, wounded him in a duel with swords, and subsequently left the country. His wife had died soon afterward—the fact had, no doubt, been reported to him—and he had remarried."

Dr. Haworth paused and said:

"I am compelled to enter into these details to make myself understood."

"Continue," said Mr. Dunn.

"I wished to show how I came to connect Col. Ross with the affairs of the Maurice family."

"Yes."

"The fact was established that he and John Maurice had been enemies. He had been in this neighborhood just before the murder, as I afterward discovered—there was the material to work upon. The difficulty was to reconcile the apparently honorable character of Col. Ross with secret murder. An incident occurred which changed my views. He invented or connived at a discreditable trick to blow up a Peruvian steamer—a ruse scarcely defensible—and we met personally in a fight which followed. After that I began to think that probably Col. Ross knew something about other ruses—among them that which ended in the conviction and death of my father. Am I to go on?"

"Yes—let the whole come out. The jury wants to know the facts."

"Very well," said Dr. Haworth, coolly. "I came to the United States this autumn to resume my search for the murderer or murderers of James Maurice."

The jury and audience had listened with profound attention to this long statement, looking now and then curiously toward Col. Ross—scarcely at the other accused persons. The testimony of Dr. Haworth seemed to have no effect upon him. He neither lowered his eyes now, nor exhibited any emotion. And yet the testimony going to convict him seemed to be approaching its climax.

In the midst of a deep silence Dr. Haworth resumed his testimony.

XI.

DR. HAWORTH CONCLUDES HIS TESTIMONY.

"I ARRIVED in New York this autumn," continued Dr. Haworth, "and chanced to observe Col. Ross in a theater with the ladies from Mauricewood. I was then sure of his presence in the United States, of which I had been informed. Jean Baptiste Maurice, who had preceded me to New York, also recognized him, and a few days afterward I left the city with the youth and came to this neighborhood—under the name I had always borne, of Dr. Haworth."

"You did not go to Mauricewood?"

"No—to a house in the hills, ostensibly for the purpose of hunting. My real object, of course, was to make inquiries without exciting suspicion, and to ascertain as much as possible about Col. Ross and the Wilkins people, who I was now nearly certain, were connected with the murder."

"A natural idea," said Mr. Dunn, "as they had been arrested on the charge once before."

"I accordingly visited the house in the hills where these people resided, and was satisfied of their guilt. The woman became agitated when I spoke of a case in which a murderer had been convicted by the numbers on some stolen bank notes—and the look on the face of the man was the *hunted* look. The evidence of Jean Baptiste Maurice in reference to Col Ross' visit, and the allusions to my object in coming to the neighborhood, is before the jury."

"Yes."

"I soon had a proof," continued Dr. Haworth, "that I was regarded as a suspicious character. I think I can state that I was fired upon."

And he related the incident in the hills, with his visit to the cabin afterwards.

"That was a little hazardous," he continued, "and I moved my quarters. I had become acquainted with Mr. Timothy Maurice, and accepted his invitation to visit Mauricewood, where it seems I was made the object of special attention on the part of Miss Burns. I do not wish to detain the jury with that comedy—with the "some-bodies," the anonymous letters, and night searches for papers—let that pass. I had a much more important subject to occupy my thoughts—the question who had murdered Mr. Maurice and suf-fered my father to die dishonored, as the author of the crime. For some time before I had convinced myself that I had made the dis-covery."

Dr. Haworth paused for a moment. In the midst of a profound silence he resumed his testimony.

"One day I requested Mr. Timothy Maurice to show me the room at Mauricewood in which his brother had been murdered. Col. Ross was present and entered the room with me. As he ex-hibited little emotion I was fortified in my previous opinion that he had not committed the murder."

At these words a buzz of astonishment ran through the crowd. As Dr. Haworth's testimony had seemed to lead straight to the theory that Col. Ross was the guilty person the words he had just uttered were a profound surprise.

"My inspection of the apartment had an important result, how-ever," said Dr. Haworth. "I found concealed in the bed this gar-rote, with which, I have no doubt, the murder was committed."

He drew from his pocket the cord and placed it upon the table before Mr. Dunn, who looked at it with interest.

"The next step," Dr. Haworth continued, "was to ascertain whether there were marks on Mr. Maurice's neck which supported my theory. I paid a visit to Dr. Seabright, the family physician, and nearly the first words he uttered were that James Maurice had been *strangled*—there were marks on his neck which could not otherwise be accounted for."

"Dr. Seabright's testimony is to the same effect," said Mr. Dunn.

"He rendered me important assistance in other ways," said Dr. Haworth, "since he enabled me to secure possession of the leaf of the ledger at Sinclair's, recording my father's purchase of fertilizers. Here it is."

He drew it from his breast and unfolded it.

"The apparent date of the purchase is May 8, the day after the
10

murder. The original entry has been falsified—the ink discharged from the paper by an infusion of oxalic acid. That may be tested by the tongue, as oxalic acid is extremely sour."

One of the jury took the paper and touched it with his tongue.

"It's sour enough," he said, "but I don't believe there was anything else written there."

"So be it," said Dr. Haworth. "Unfortunately the question was not raised on the trial of Mr. Ducis. This sheet of paper destroyed him."

"You think that date is forged," said Mr. Dunn. "Well, who is the forger? If you know, tell the jury."

"I do not know the name of the forger, but I am certain I know *who* he was."

"Who was he?"

"He was the man who murdered James Maurice, whether he was present on the night of the 7th of May or not; who conceived the design, brought about the result, and took the steps that brought the crime home to an innocent person."

"A curious affair altogether," said Mr. Dunn. "Then you think that the alteration in this entry—the hammer and glove found near the spot of the murder—all was a conspiracy to destroy an innocent man, as you say?"

"Yes; to my own mind, at least, the circumstances exclude every other hypothesis, as you say in your profession, sir."

Mr. Dunn reflected.

"I should like to get at your precise idea," he said, "and I think the jury would like to hear it. As the late Mr. Seward said to Mr. Stephens, it seems to have a philosophic basis."

Mr. Shirley rose and objected. His point was that the private opinions of a witness had nothing to do with a legal investigation, and he urged the view with great force.

Mr. Dunn's reply was equally forcible. The impressions produced on the mind of a witness by the facts coming to his knowledge are a legitimate subject of inquiry. What the jury wanted was all the facts and circumstances connected with this case. The rules of evidence were intended to guard the accused—to afford him a fair trial—not to cover up the facts. The witness was intimately acquainted with the details of the case now before the jury, and might legitimately be asked his convictions resulting from that intimate knowledge. The jury were at liberty to agree with them or to disagree with them—to accept them, or to laugh at them as absurd.

Judge Bootlack thought the question was improper—but was not certain that it was not entirely proper. In his opinion it ought not to be asked—but on the whole, and as the result of reflection, he would permit the inquiry to be propounded.

Whereupon Mr. Shirley, much disgusted, said he would except, and sat down.

"Well, now," said Mr. Dunn, "give the jury your idea of the murder, Doctor. It will not take long, I suppose?"

"I can do so, briefly. Here is my conviction. The person intended to be murdered was not James Maurice, but his nephew, John Maurice, the supposed occupant of the room on the night of the murder. The actual murderer was the tool of a person more skillful—who had a private vengeance to gratify. This tool was bought, and under orders, probably from his employer, arranged everything to throw the guilt upon an innocent man—Henry Ducis. The plot fully succeeded, and the real, unknown author of all was never even suspected. It is for the jury to say who they think he is—as to his tools, they defied conviction; the whole had been too well planned. Arrested on suspicion, they were discharged for want of evidence. There was absolutely no proof of their guilt. One only was shown to have been present at or about the time of the murder, but that person was a woman, and women rarely murder men—they may rob, but shrink from bloodshed."

"Well, that is tolerably plain. An unknown person planned the crime, but this particular unknown did not personally commit it. Who did?"

"I can only recall to your mind the testimony of the witness Jean Baptiste Maurice as to what he overheard at the house in the hills—my own as to the bullet fired at me—and the identification of the messenger who carried the letters written to and by Miss Burns."

"Well, that does look rather ugly," said Mr. Dunn, "and all the parties are equally responsible. Of course, if two persons were actually present at the time of the murder both are guilty as principals whether the crime was committed by one or both. That's law, I believe?" said Mr. Dunn to Mr. Shirley.

"Yes, sir," said that gentleman.

"In the absence of evidence," added Mr. Dunn, "there is only one course to pursue—to procure a pardon for one of them and summon him or her to testify to the facts."

Mr. Dunn looked at Wilkins and the woman. On their stolid countenances it was impossible to observe the least traces of emotion.

"But all that can wait. We are in no hurry and have the whole term before us," said Mr. Dunn. "I have only a few more questions to ask the witness. You say that you had then made up your mind on the subject of the murder, Doctor?"

"To a certain point—yes."

"That Mr. Ducis was absolutely innocent, and certain other persons were guilty?"

"Yes."

"Well, it seems to me that under these circumstances the time to act had come. You had been shot at—you had information of that night visit in the hills—you had been denounced in anonymous letters—you found that garrote in the bed, a peculiar instrument for the commission of murder, which necessarily pointed to some person familiar with the methods of death employed in Spanish countries—you had all this to go upon, and as you have explained had an ardent desire to bring the real offenders to justice. Why, then, I say, did you not take steps leading to a judicial investigation?"

"The steps were taken."

"To connect specific people with the murder of Mr. James Maurice?"

"Yes."

"What steps?"

"I procured warrants for the arrest of three persons—Col. Ross, Wilkins and his wife, the former servant or housekeeper at Mauricewood, who was seen coming out of the room on the night of the murder."

"That was during my absence from home attending the Circuit Court, I suppose. The warrants were issued, you say?"

"Yes, sir; by Prof. Lesner, a magistrate of the neighborhood."

"Prof. Lesner—that fine old fellow? I thought he was a retired scholar. Yes, I remember now that he was elected a justice recently. Well, I am glad party politics still allow us a few honorable magistrates. So the old Professor did issue the warrants?" :

"Yes."

"Why was no action taken?" ..

" The parties were warned and escaped."

" Warned ? Escaped ? "

" Yes," said Dr. Haworth, " the officer to whom the warrants were addressed was either suborned by some one having an interest to avoid the inquiry, or had private reasons of his own. The fact remains that the return ' not found ' was made by the officer, or his deputy. The three persons had disappeared."

" Well, that is rather a serious charge, Doctor, against an officer of the law."

" The charge is just. I was present when the return was made to Prof. Lesner and can testify that he was extremely indignant."

" A serious matter. If constables are to warn people there is an end of justice. Are you sure of your statement ? "

" Prof. Lesner will corroborate it. I am aware that it is serious —to the accused as well as to the constable. Innocent people do not fly from justice."

" I shall ask for a subpena for Prof. Lesner, your Honor," said Mr. Dunn ; and, as I wish to avoid delay, I want it served to-night, so that we may go on in the morning. If a constable warned the accused, and they avoided arrest, it will be an ugly thing for all parties."

The subpena was then made out, and placed in the hands of an officer, who was directed to deliver it at once to Prof. Lesner. He would be examined the first thing when the court met in the morning.

Mr. Dunn then said to the witness :

" I understand you to state that you procured these warrants for the arrest of the parties, and they fled from justice ? Col. Ross did not fly—or if he did he flew back."

" Yes," said Dr. Haworth, looking fixedly at Col. Ross, " after the arrest of his confederates."

" I heard he was called to Washington to testify before a committee, and returned at once after getting through—I throw out the remark for the benefit of the defense, and hope they will not object to it as hearsay evidence ! "

" He was in Washington for that purpose," said Dr. Haworth, " and returned—for a purpose."

" What purpose ? "

" Ask him. An accused can testify under certain circumstances."

" Not in this Commonwealth—certainly not in this case,"

"Then I decline to testify for him—others may do so if they wish—Mr. Maurice or his family."

Col. Ross suddenly flushed. His instinct of gentleman doubtless revolted from a public exposure of the incident of the death register and the scene at Mauricewood.

"Very well," said Mr. Dunn. "Prof. Lesner, I have no doubt, will tell us whether there was or was not an evasion of justice. Such a thing is *prima facie* evidence of guilt, of course. As you say that Mr. Timothy Maurice or his family can throw some light on Col. Ross' return to meet this charge, I will summon them all to testify to-morrow. I have no further questions for the witness, gentlemen."

Dr. Haworth was subjected to a cross-examination which lasted until nearly midnight. Every link in his statement was subjected by Mr. Shirley to the most determined attack, and Mr. Dunn, who was generally so careless, was observed to lean forward and listen with absorbing attention.

He was studying his profession. A master of criminal law was teaching him *viva voce* more than he had ever learned in books, and when Mr. Sparrow chirped and hopped, interrupting the master, Mr. Dunn scowled at him.

At last the cross-examination ended—Dr. Haworth's testimony had not been shaken in the remotest degree. If the jury were to decide the case upon it, they at least knew what weight to attach to it.

Mr. Dunn then rose and moved an adjournment, which seemed to be a welcome proposition to everybody; and the court was accordingly adjourned to meet at 11 next morning.

As Mr. Dunn was putting on his hat with a yawn Judge Bootlack descended from the bench.

"It's too late to-night for that game of poker, Judge," said Mr. Dunn, "but I have a question to submit for your Honor's decision."

Judge Bootlack looked puzzled and smiled uneasily—Mr. Dunn was always quizzing.

"Is it ever too late at night to indulge in—a nightcap?"

Judge Bootlack looked radiant.

"Never!" he exclaimed; "the court is with you there, sir!"

XII.

COL. ROSS EXPLAINS.

WHEN the court adjourned it was nearly midnight. That portion of the audience residing outside of Abbeyville prepared to return home, and among them were Dr. Haworth, Mr. Tim Maurice and Jean.

As Dr. Haworth was about to mount his horse a servant came up to him and handed him a note, written in pencil. It contained only these lines:

"I should be glad to have a few moments' private conversation with Gen. Ducis on matters of some importance. He will find me awaiting him at the town jail.   FERDINAND ROSS."

The messenger was waiting for a reply, and going into the tavern in front of which the note had been handed him, Dr. Haworth wrote:

"I will visit Col. Ross at once as he requests.
        "HENRY HAWORTH DUCIS."

The servant took back the reply, and Dr. Haworth then informed his friends of Col. Ross' request.

"We will wait until you return, Doctor," said Mr. Tim Maurice.

"It will be unnecessary. I may be detained."

"Don't send *me* away, Excellency!" said Jean.

"It is useless for you to remain. I wish you to return with Mr. Maurice."

And as Jean Baptiste never argued with his master when he spoke in that tone, he set out for Mauricewood in company with Mr. Maurice.

Dr. Haworth then went straight to the jail, which was not far from the court-house, and knocking at the door, which was heavily studded with iron, found it open immediately.

"Col. Ross wishes to see me," he said.

"Dr. Haworth?" asked the man.

"Yes."

"All right, sir. I'll take you to the Colonel's room—the very best room in the house."

The jail was a *house*, it seems, and the prisoner occupied a room. which was an indication of the fact that Col. Ross was not regarded as a common criminal to be confined in a vulgar cell.

The room was really a room—not a cell at all. In fact it was the jailer's own. He and his wife had promptly vacated it on the appearance of their distinguished lodger ; had done far more indeed —for, prompted by feminine sympathizers, they had draped the grimy windows with white curtains. Easy-chairs had been provided. There was a handsome table, covered with books and newspapers, and in the fireplace shone a cheerful blaze. The floor was carpeted, and everything was neat down to the snow-white bed, looking very inviting with its fringed pillows in the light of the argand burner.

Col. Ross was seated in an easy-chair, smoking a cigar. His appearance was elegant, and he was perfectly composed. At the entrance of Dr. Haworth he rose and bowed :

"I am pleased to see you, Gen. Ducis," he said. "You will find the seat opposite an agreeable one."

Dr. Haworth bowed and sat down, Col. Ross also resuming his seat.

"I regret to put you to inconvenience by requesting an interview at so late an hour, as you must be fatigued," said Col. Ross.

"I am not at all fatigued, sir," replied Dr. Haworth formally, "and the hour is of no importance."

"You were probably surprised at receiving my note?"

"Yes."

"The surprise was natural."

"It had not occurred to me that you would take pleasure in a personal interview with myself," said Dr. Haworth in the same cold and formal tone.

"To be frank," said Col. Ross, "up to a certain moment I should have desired nothing *less* than such a personal interview."

"Up to a certain moment, sir?"

"Up to the moment when you informed the court that your real name was not Dr. Haworth, but Henry Haworth Ducis—the son of an innocent gentleman convicted through my agency, as you suppose, of a cowardly murder."

Dr. Haworth looked at the speaker with an air of cold surprise. Was this effrontery or trick?

"I do not understand you, sir," he said.

Col. Ross had thrown his cigar in the fire, and was leaning back thoughtfully in his chair. After a moment he said, looking coolly at his visitor:

"I see you regard me as a wretch and the real murderer of your father. Well, you are mistaken. I had nothing to do with the murder of James Maurice, nor the miserable plot of fixing the crime on Mr. Ducis."

Dr. Haworth said nothing; his fixed look was the only indication that he had heard the words.

"I understand perfectly," said Col. Ross, preserving his deliberate tone; "you do not believe me. Very well; before you go away to-night you will be satisfied. The object of this interview is to satisfy you. As long as I regarded you as an unknown stranger—an enemy pursuing me in order to destroy me—I owed you nothing. From the moment when I discovered who you really are, I owed you everything. Your answer in court to-day, 'I am the son of Henry Ducis,' struck me like a blow. I was not aware that Mr. Ducis had a son, and I trust you now begin to understand. I am not altogether the wretch that you think me, and even venture to call myself a gentleman, in spite of appearances. I give you the proof. I will tell you everything connected with the murder of James Maurice, if you think it will interest you."

"I shall be glad to hear your statement, sir," said Dr. Haworth, unable to conceal his emotion.

Col. Ross leaned back in his chair and said in a composed voice:

"Suppose I say a word first of myself. The subject may not interest you or excite your sympathy to any very great extent, but it is necessary to inflict a sort of preface upon you to make myself understood. We are not in a court of justice now, and I can say whatever I care to say. I see you are interested—you will find that my brief narrative, egotistical as it may appear, will elucidate this whole affair. I will therefore speak of some events of my life, and hope to remove a few impressions from your mind which are not flattering to me."

Dr. Haworth bowed, gravely fixing his eyes as before upon those of the speaker.

"I was born in this country and went to South America as a midshipman, and afterward became a lieutenant," said Col. Ross. "My ship was detained at Callao, which is not far from Lima, as you are aware, and after the habit of young naval officers I visited the place for amusement. A traveling opera company was perform-

ing at the time in the City of Lima, and the prima donna was a
beautiful French girl, Marie Antoinette Lascelles. To be brief, I
fell very much in love with her and had reason to believe the sentiment
returned—when she made the acquaintance of Mr. John Maurice and
began to cool. He was a young man from my own neighborhood
here and at the time was *attaché* or secretary of the American legation. He was extremely handsome and had a certain glance and
tone of the voice which women cannot resist; and, not to make a
long story of it, he supplanted me with poor Antoinette. I say poor
because she is dead, and I never had the remotest ill-feeling toward
her. I cannot say as much of my sentiment in the direction of Mr.
John Maurice. To be frank, I hated him—as a man will hate another who robs him of the love of a woman. I said nothing, however, at the time. Things took their course. I went on a cruise,
and when I got back to Lima they were married.

"Well," continued Col. Ross, "I had, of course, nothing to say
to that, and said nothing. I did not regard it as absolutely necessary, however, that I should completely drop the acquaintance of
Mrs. Antoinette Maurice, as we had formerly been friends. She
herself indicated no desire that her old friends should give her up.
She was fond of admiration, though one of the best and purest persons in the world, and accepted an amount of attention from gentlemen more customary in France, perhaps, than in America. As I
was among these gentlemen, our former relations, unfortunately,
made people talk, and Mr. John Maurice, still more unfortunately,
had one great fault—he was jealous and suspicious to the echo. In
a word, he grew angry, offered me a gross insult, or to be more precise, slapped my face—and in a duel which followed nearly put an
end to me. I had a long and dangerous illness, and some time
afterward heard curious intelligence. Mr. Maurice had grown
more and more jealous of everybody, and at last convinced himself
that his wife was unfaithful to him—in consequence of which he
had deserted her and South America together. She also had disappeared—none of her old friends ever saw her—and it was only
long afterward that I heard that she had died at Lima in some obscure part of the town where she had lived unknown after her deser-
tion by her husband.

"That is all of that part of my story, sir," said Col. Ross. "It
was necessary to state the facts, since a great deal hinges upon
them. Right or wrong, the result with me was a good wholesome

hatred for Mr. John Maurice who had supplanted me, outraged me, painfully wounded me, and left a good girl, whom I loved, to die in poverty and misery. Whether natural or not, I had the sentiment— a genuine hatred of the man, and a very strong desire to be even with him. Is that intelligible ? "

" Yes, sir," said Dr. Haworth.

" Very well ; that was the state of affairs when I found myself back in this country and neighborhood. Mr. John Maurice had re- turned some time before and was paying his addresses to Miss Ellen Maurice—his first wife being presumably dead. I say presumably, as to myself, for I did not know the fact at the time. I met him now and then, and had half determined to select the opportunity to insult him and force him to fight me—it would be an excellent time, just as he was going to be married—for that fact was soon an- nounced. I did not do so—it really looked too scandalous ! Or say, if you prefer, that I was afraid—that he had taught me a lesson at Lima. It is not true, as I have never been afraid of anybody, but you may adopt the theory if you fancy as an explanation of the fact that I did not interfere with his marriage or himself in any manner.

" What I did do, however, was injudicious and had unfortunate results. I will state the whole case against myself in the plainest and fairest manner, leaving you to believe me or not as you choose, and to form your own opinion.

" At the time when Mr. John Maurice paid his addresses to his cousin, Miss Maurice, she had another suitor who was crazily in love with her. It is unnecessary to tell you his name at present—call him Brown or Jones if you fancy—it will save trouble. It was said that Miss Maurice had been engaged to him—*he* said so—and had jilted him for the handsome John Maurice. I do not believe that, but it is unimportant. He so stated, and as I knew Mr. Brown in- timately and had a sympathy for jilted people, we exchanged views on the subject of Mr. Maurice, whom I liked no better than he did, and often talked about the approaching marriage and festivities at Mauricewood. These conversations took place generally at my house, which I had inherited on the death of my father—and Mr. Brown would walk up and down the floor raging and grinding his teeth. He was a cowardly cur, but, like that sort of animal, very dangerous if it was made plain to him that he could use his teeth without personal risk. Another of his traits was that drink embold- ened him, and I often amused myself by urging it upon him in order to listen to his oaths and threats of vengeance. One day I remember saying: 'If you hate him so, why don't you fight him? He is a brave man and will not refuse you an opportunity to right your wrongs.' 'Because he would kill me!' was the reply. 'Then go and murder him,' I said, laughing, 'on the very day of his marriage —stab him to death—put arsenic in his porridge, or steal on him in slumber and *garrote him*—it is a pleasant death, they say.' He said nothing and went away, and on the next day had occasion to write to me on some matter of business. The note found me dining with some friends—we were all a little elevated with champagne—and, begging my friends to excuse me for a moment, I went into my library and scribbled off a hasty reply to the note. Having answered the business portion I wrote these words. I remembered them afterward, and have never ceased to remember them since:

"'How comes on our affair? Are we going to submit to everything? Never—we will do for him with knife, bludgeon, hammer, or poison. But, on the whole, I think we had better garrote him in his sleep. That will put a quietus to our dear friend at Mauricewood!'

"I signed the note with my name," continued Col. Ross, "and a day or two afterward rejoined my ship. You know what followed. On the night of Miss Maurice's marriage some one entered the chamber supposed to be that of the bride and groom and committed the murder there. In the darkness Mr. James Maurice was taken for his nephew, and first garroted and then finished with the hammer. The hammer was really the property of Mr. Ducis, and had been accidentally left by him at Mauricewood on a recent visit, and secreted by the assassin. Finding that it had been identified, and that his own glove, which dropped, was also supposed to belong to Mr. Ducis, the wretch hastened to destroy the proof of the alibi at Sinclair's, which he effected without discovery while the back of the merchant was turned. Then all duly followed as I afterward ascertained. Mr. Ducis was arrested, tried, and convicted on the circumstantial evidence, and the real criminal has never been discovered."

Dr. Haworth had listened without uttering a word—his eyes still fixed upon the face of Col. Ross. He now said coolly:

"You have not told me the name of this real criminal, sir."

"I wish to reserve it for the end, as a pleasant finale," said Col. Ross. "I have nearly done now, and will proceed to explain a few matters of more recent date which must have puzzled you."

XIII.

THE MAN.

COL. ROSS carefully removed a speck of dust from his coat sleeve with the point of his white finger and said :
"So much for the events which occurred in this neighborhood twenty years ago. I was not present at the time of the murder and knew nothing of it or of the trial of Mr. Ducis until some months afterward. I had been ordered on a cruise and my ship sailed for the Pacific before the catastrophe took place. Upon this question of dates you are not obliged to accept my statement, as the records of the Naval Department will satisfy any doubt you may have on the subject.

"Well, to come to latter times now and what has recently taken place in this neighborhood. I will stop a moment, however, to say that I really had nothing whatever to do with that torpedo-boat affair in Callao harbor. I was only informed of it at the moment when the boat drifted toward your steamer, and remonstrated against it as utterly indefensible, but without avail. Of course you can believe me or not, as you please. I am speaking the truth. I can understand why you thought it my own device with your theory of my character, and that you placed to my credit that shot fired at you in the hills by Wilkins. I was not the author of the torpedo project, of the shot, or even the anonymous letter sent to Mauricewood, despised as it ought to have been.

"I did employ that girl to watch you and ascertain your movements—that is to say, I commissioned a rascally valet brought with me from South America to keep me advised of all your proceedings. He engaged the girl Burns through her friend, Miss Larkins, and I made no objection, so I say I employed her. The object was to ascertain who you were and why you were so curious about the old affair of the murder. The anonymous letter, I repeat, was the ingenious device of Miss Larkins in response, it seems, to Miss Burns' suggestion. I declare upon my honor—you are at liberty to believe me or not—that I knew nothing about it."

Col. Ross paused. A slight depression of the corners of Dr. Haworth's mouth made him flush.

"You doubt my statement!" he exclaimed. "You are disposed to laugh when I speak of *honor!* You are thinking of that leaf from the death register containing the date of *Antoinette Mau-rice's* death. Well, sir, I have nothing to reply to that. I bow my head with shame, but not as low as you think I should, perhaps—for I did not falsify that record. I did not lay a plan to deceive and carry it out. The date *was* printed incorrectly in the commissioner's report, which I found at Washington—you may go and look at it. I telegraphed at once to Lima to ascertain the truth, and my agent, the subtlest of Spaniards, must have conceived that I wished to have the mortuary register support the public document. He made the erasure and substitution, beyond a doubt, as he abstracted the leaf —*after* you had obtained your certificate."

"Well," said Dr. Haworth briefly.

Col. Ross looked at him and said gloomily :

"After all, you are right! It *was* a low business to offer that paper as the price of Miss Maurice's hand! I believed it to be genu-ine—that Antoinette Maurice died in October, 1860, *after* her hus-band's second marriage—that Miss Maurice was not born in wed-lock! I meant to burn the record in Mrs. Maurice's presence! And if I attempted to make my profit of it before doing so, *you*, at least, sir, ought to have some charity for my weakness!"

Col. Ross looked down with contracted brows ; then he resumed moodily :

"I regret that—if it were to do over again I would rather cut off my hand! To return to the main affair. You came to this country to unearth these old matters, and I saw from the first that you were a dangerous adversary. I was in the real murderer's power and he was in the power of the Pitts-Wilkins woman, who had reached Mr. Maurice's room in time to see him as he escaped, and to steal the money. She had it beneath her apron when she came out into the hall. I say that the murderer—he was not Wil-kins—had me in his power, or at least my good name. He had kept the note in which I had spoken of the murder of ' our friend at Mauricewood ' with a hammer or by garroting—and that note, meant as a jest, was signed with my name. It might not hang me as an accomplice—it would fix an ineffaceable stain upon my name. Do you wonder then that I was interested in shielding all these parties who could point their fingers at me as their confederate? The murderer denied having kept the note—I knew that he lied. He had not only kept it, but informed the woman Wilkins of it, and the price of her silence was the enjoyment of the stolen money. Thus

I was tangled in the detestable net—took night rides—was watched in my turn, until one day, weary of all this, you did what the son of Henry Ducis had the right to do—you obtained warrants for the arrest of the whole crew, myself included !

"I was notified that the warrants had been made out and that they would be served on me in the morning; and yielding to cowardly apprehension found that I had business in Washington ! The other wretches were also warned and disappeared. I only differed from them in one thing, that shame and my pride of gentleman made me come back here to face the charge ! I was innocent, in intent at least, of the death of James Maurice and Henry Ducis. As I had never meant to advise anybody to commit murder, I had at least the luxury of a good conscience ! I intended to fight it out to the end, and keep back that foolish note if possible ; but I never intended to *hang* in place of my worthy friend, the real murderer, who evidently means to sacrifice me ! "

" Is he living ? " said Dr. Haworth, looking at Col. Ross intently.

" Living ? Certainly. You are acquainted—I believe intimately acquainted—with him."

" *I* acquainted with the murderer of James Maurice and my father ! "

" Necessarily, since you have applied to him to assist you in your laudable object of relieving your father's name from the stain upon it."

" *I* appealed to him ? "

" And he promptly aided you, and issued the warrant for my arrest—only he privately informed me an hour afterwards that I had better have business elsewhere. In other words," said Col. Ross coolly, "the wretch who murdered James Maurice and your father, Henry Ducis, was the excellent Prof. Lesner."

XIV.

COL. ROSS ON THE SUBJECT OF RATTLESNAKES.

DR. HAWORTH looked at Col. Ross with the profoundest astonishment.

" Prof. Lesner ! " he exclaimed.

" Certainly—Prof. Lesner. I did not tell you his name before, as

I thought it would interfere with my narrative," said Col. Ross composedly. "The real murderer, I repeat, of James Maurice and Henry Ducis is the respectable, the amiable, the excellent Prof. Lesner, who finds in birds and bees the tranquil enjoyment experienced by men of simple tastes in their home surroundings. You know the Professor? He is a model man. He would not hurt a fly. He is wrapped up in his books and bees—smiles sweetly on everybody— and holds the commission of *Justice of the Peace!* In other words, he is a living lie—a whited sepulchre, as the Good Book says —a cowardly murderer, gray before his time, for he is scarcely more than 50—and feeds on opium to drug his conscience!"

Dr. Haworth said nothing. It was doubtful from the expression of his face whether he believed Col. Ross.

"That is a strange statement," he said at length.

"Which I see you do not attach any importance to," replied Col. Ross. "In other words, my dear sir, you think my whole narrative is a tissue of lies—that I was the real author of that murder —and that I am simply adding a crowning lie in charging another person with the offense."

Dr. Haworth made no reply.

"It is rather unpleasant to feel that one's word is doubted," said Col. Ross, coolly, "but I suppose it is natural. I allow that after that death-register business you have the right to think ill of me. So be it. And yet you will soon find that I am telling you the truth. I shall denounce Prof. Lesner to-morrow in open court as the murderer—and the woman Wilkins will be offered a pardon and put on the witness stand. There will be no trouble about that, as she is, in reality, only a thief. She only *saw* the murderer as he was escaping and will testify as to his identity. Is that plain?"

"Yes," said Dr. Haworth.

"There will be no trouble whatever," repeated Col. Ross, "and I rather enjoy the new phase of things, since my dear friend Lesner forces my hand. To be plain, I did not know the extent of the evidence you had collected against me, and thought a simple denial of any connection with the murder would suffice. You have been more skillful than I thought—and in fact since yesterday I have been meditating this *coupe de main*. Lesner will, of course, produce my jesting note to him, and that will be unpleasant—but it will not be so unpleasant as hanging, or spending the rest of my life in the State Prison."

" Prof. Lesner the murderer!" said Dr. Haworth with a last remnant of doubt.

" Yes, he was the real and actual murderer of James Maurice," said Col. Ross in a matter of fact tone. " I see you find it rather difficult to believe, but it is nevertheless the fact. Human nature is a curious affair, and this man is a curious specimen of it. I have known him a long time, and have often made him the subject of reflection. He is a cowardly cur, as I have said, and as full of venom as a rattlesnake. He had strong passions, and was not held back by any sentiment from gratifying them, for he never had any religious belief of any sort, or the least trace of what gentlemen call honor. He was quite poor at the time when he paid his addresses to Miss Maurice, who was an heiress. As to his love, it was no doubt only the love of an animal. Hate was his mainspring, however, and I think the gratification of that weighed more with him than success in his suit. But the subject is not particularly pleasant. It has been your luck to see only one of these traits—his hypocrisy."

" Such hypocrisy is incredible ! "

" Well," said Col. Ross, " it is curious how many things are incredible to us until they are plain to our eyes. This man I say has been a real study to me. He seems to have enjoyed life since the murder. He is a scholar, fond of books—appears to derive real happiness from his birds and bees—is the model of a kindly host, smiles on everybody and seems to love the whole human race. Perhaps he lives in an atmosphere of opium."

" Yes."

" That may explain things. I have never tried the drug, but it is said to make a man oblivious of the real world, to produce forgetfulness. I suppose a cobra or rattlesnake under its effect would forget how many victims he had bitten ! I have not seen our friend much of late years—in fact, since *his* friend John Maurice died so suddenly."

" *John* Maurice ? You mean *James* Maurice."

" I mean *John* Maurice. His death took place a year or two after his marriage, and under very peculiar circumstances. He was a little unwell and sent for Dr. Seabright, who was absent from home. Luckily, or unluckily rather, Prof. Lesner happened to be at Mauricewood, and prescribed for him—he had been a professor of medicine once."

Dr. Haworth looked at Col. Ross, recalling the words uttered by Dr. Seabright during his first visit to him.

"All this is rather scandalous," added Col. Ross negligently, "since there was no proof. Something was said of a *mistake* having been made in the medicine by Prof. Lesner—one preparation of antimony was administered instead of another. One was harmless, the other an active poison—unfortunately, Mr. Maurice swallowed the poison."

"It is impossible—!"

"Well, I see that you do not like to listen to these scandalous imputations on the character of so estimable a gentleman as your friend the Professor," said Col. Ross, "and it is rather unfair, perhaps, to allude to them. Ask Dr. Seabright. Mr. John Maurice certainly died very suddenly from one cause or another—from what he swallowed, Dr. Seabright said. Let that pass."

Dr. Haworth listened to this appalling charge without comment, and a long silence followed.

"Well, sir," he said at length, "it is only necessary for me to say now that I believe what you have stated. To-morrow will show whether I am right or wrong."

Col. Ross bowed, and said coolly:

"I am pleased to hear that you believe my word, sir. You are not effusive in your assurances, but I suppose I ought not to expect you to say more. Whether you believe or disbelieve my statement, it is the truth. That jesting note to the wretch Lesner was a fearful imprudence—it was no more. If I had dreamed that it would have led to murder I would certainly never have written it. You will say that I should have spoken out and cleared the memory of your father on my return. Yes—I should have done so, but I was told that no human being believed that he was really guilty. I ought to have exposed the murderer—yes, but the result would have been a stain on my name. I have often resolved to do so, but I had not the courage. You see I am frank. I say as frankly that the threat to proclaim the fact that the present Mrs. Maurice was never lawfully married to her husband was disgraceful, but a threat only in appearance. I swear to you that I meant to burn that paper before her eyes, under any circumstances, and return to Washington and take steps to declare the date in the commissioner's report an error. If I was guilty of an offense which no gentleman should have been guilty of—if I believed the record was true, and said to Mrs. Maurice: 'There is the proof that you were never married, and that Miss Maurice is not legally your daughter—give me her hand as my wife,' I am sorry for it and ashamed of it. I shall only repeat, sir, that you, my successful rival, ought to weigh my temptation and be a little charitable."

Col. Ross did not utter these words in any tone of feeling, much less of humility. He spoke coolly and with a certain pride.

"Men—honorable men—commit these offenses sometimes," he added, "and if the ladies come into court to-morrow and testify to everything I shall instruct my counsel to admit their statements without a word and permit them to go to the jury undisputed and unmodified."

Dr. Haworth bowed gravely.

"It was unnecessary to introduce that testimony," he said, "but it may be unavoidable now. The point of most interest is the probable evidence of Prof. Lesner, who has also been summoned."

"Yes," said Col. Ross. "Well, if he does not abscond the scene will be interesting. He will fight like a cat in the corner and deny everything, of course. When the woman is pardoned and the murder is brought home to him, he will, of course, produce my note and attempt to drag me down with him, but I shall anticipate all this and formally denounce him as the real murderer of James Maurice, on the opening of the court to-morrow."

Col. Ross rose and said:

"I believe that is all I wished to say. I am detaining you, sir. The hour is late and you have a ride before you. I need not again call your attention to the fact that if you had not stated that you were the son of Mr. Ducis I should not have troubled you with this long explanation. Your announcement of that fact produced a very painful impression upon me. Allow me to say once more that I regard myself as a gentleman, in spite of appearances, so I thought I owed you this statement. My silence when a word might have reinstated Mr. Ducis has been a lasting source of self-reproach to me. I can only repeat that everybody, including the very family of the murdered man, scouted the idea of his guilt and attributed the murder to some unknown person. That is all I have to say at present, sir."

Dr. Haworth had risen and the two men bowed to each other.

"To-morrow will probably convince you whether I have spoken the truth or not," said Col. Ross.

And so the interview ended.

XV.

MR. DUNN INDULGES IN A PROFESSIONAL WITTICISM.

PROF. LESNER had not absconded, but the summons to appear and testify found him so unwell that he was unable to attend court. He would be sufficiently strong, however, he said, to be present on the next day; in the meanwhile other witnesses might be examined, and perhaps the issue of the warrants, the return, etc., might be shown by other testimony.

When court opened on the following morning, this message was communicated to Mr. Dunn, and he said:

"Well, there's no real necessity for pulling the old gentleman out of his sick-bed for a small matter of that sort. If he is able to attend to-morrow we can examine him; if not, we'll swear the constable and get at the facts."

Mr. Dunn examined his notes and said:

"The next point is the return of Col. Ross, which was said yesterday to be *for a purpose, other than his trial.* Mr. Timothy Maurice and the ladies of his family, it seems, can testify upon this subject. Are they present?"

"Mr. Tim Maurice came forward alone, and any one looking at Col. Ross, seated as usual behind Mr. Shirley, might have seen on his face an expression of immense relief. Mr. Tim Maurice had not been present at the interview between himself and Mrs. Maurice, and the ladies were not going to appear.

He was quite right. Mr. Tim Maurice's testimony was unimportant. Col. Ross, he said, had visited Mauricewood on his return from Washington. His former relations with the family had been intimate, and the visit had been connected with family affairs. These did not concern the case before the court in any manner, and his niece and her daughter would prefer not to be compelled to make them public. He was authorized by them to say that the interview had no bearing whatever on the investigation.

Mr. Dunn bowed politely, and said that under the circumstances it would be unnecessary to insist on the presence of the ladies. But Mr. Sparrow suspected a ruse. This ready acquiescence was suspicious; and before Mr. Shirley could stop him he rose and insisted that the witnesses should be brought into court.

He did not like the look of the thing, he said, fighting imaginary windmills. The attorney for the Commonwealth had issued his summons; a summons was a summons; he meant himself to conduct this case in a straightforward manner; and Mr. Sparrow seemed about to hop over the desk before him, to the huge disgust of Col. Ross and Mr. Shirley, who endeavored in vain to restrain him.

Then he sat down and Mr. Dunn got up. His face was bland, and he smiled—but the expression of his eye was sanguinary. He proceeded to flay Mr. Sparrow, to rub vitriol figuratively into the wounds, and to cruelly demolish what was left of him. He then laughed and took his seat, leaving the Judge to decide the point.

Judge Bootlack endeavored to do so, but the judicial luminary was under the weather. He had partaken of so many nightcaps on the preceding night that his great intellect was clouded; he had a headache, he said, and would reserve his decision until the afternoon; and as the dinner hour was near he would adjourn court.

This was accordingly done in the midst of general hilarity, and the Judge, having descended unsteadily from the platform, disappeared in the direction of the tavern.

After dinner the court did not resume its session. Judge Bootlack was unwell. It was said that he had made every effort to regain strength to resume his official duties; that he had partaken of alcoholic beverages at the bar and retired to his chamber to lie down, and finding himself still indisposed had sent for additional tonics of the same description, about a dozen times in succession. This still having failed to revive him, there was no afternoon session of the court, and the witnesses in the case were bound over to be present on the next day.

Mr. Dunn then put on his hat and linked his arm in that of his friend Sparrow. They fought savagely in public, but were bosom companions.

"It's sad, very sad," said Mr. Dunn in a pathetic voice, "that our friend, the Judge, is stronger mentally than physically."

"It is, indeed," said Mr. Sparrow, laughing.

"One hope, however, consoles me," said Mr. Dunn, "I think he will meander into court to-morrow on the strength of old Coke's maxim."

"What maxim?"

"*Id certum est quod certum reddi potest.* Free translation: 'It is certain what a certain *red-eye* can do!'"

XVI.

MR. BURDETTE BESTOWS HIS BLESSING.

"I SAY, Haworth—no, Ducis!" exclaimed Mr. Burdette, walk-ing in the Mauricewood grounds on the same evening, "is this the way you do things in the South?"

"What things, my dear friend?"

"Murder trials and murder generally, secret assassination and that sort of thing! What do you mean? Don't you know that you are calling down on your heads the denunciation of the civilized world? This thing is going to get into the papers, Haworth—no, Ducis. You can't fool the press. Why not cover it up somehow and prevent the horror from being exposed as an evidence of the barbarism of the South? Such things never take place else-where."

"Well, elsewhere is lucky."

"In fact, I don't believe the thing took place at all! Prof. Les-ner concerned in it? Good heavens! that splendid old boy?"

"You have Col. Ross' statement. I have repeated it, as it was not made in confidence."

"Well, well," sighed Mr. Burdette, "if anybody had told me that I was publishing for a *murderer* I should have laughed in scorn! How lucky I got away from his hospitable establishment, and how unlucky his name is not on the title page of 'Psychology of Opium!' The whole edition would go off like hot cakes, though I should feel like putting the proceeds in the fire instead of into my pocket."

Having thus unburdened his mind, Mr. Burdette asked:

"Do you think he will appear to-morrow as a witness?"

"I think so."

"It will be a remarkable scene! And do you really think Col. Ross will publicly denounce him?"

"Yes."

"I'll be present without fail. And now let me repeat a question I asked the other day."

"What is that?"

"Are you literary? If so, I want you to write up this affair. It's a stunner, and would curdle the blood."

"I thought you said tragedy was out of fashion?"

"You might make it comic, you see; and get in a lily and a sun-flower!"

"I'm not literary, and there is not much of the lily about Prof. Lesner. Yes, you were fortunate in getting away from that den with your nice little *Miss Giorgione.* There she is yonder on the veran-da, and I think she has a companion—Mr. Jean Baptiste Maurice. Is she going to marry him?"

"I asked her yesterday," said Mr. Burdette, laughing, "and she proposed to box me, but as she blushed tremendously I suppose she is."

"Jean could not be more lucky. I thought he had made an im-pression upon her in Lima."

"They might be married at once. I never saw a boy so much in love! I said to him yesterday : 'I can't get a word with you! You are always poking about, looking for Giorgione!' He blushed worse than she did. Send for a parson and marry the young ones! I'll stand godfather—and it may be a double wedding."

"A double wedding?"

"You and the fair Miss Cary might embrace the occasion ; *em-brace* is not a bad word!"

As Dr. Haworth simply smiled and made no reply, it is possible that he did not regard Mr. Burdette's suggestion as altogether absurd.

"I have no time to think of such matters," he said quietly. "I have been quite busy this morning."

"Holding Miss Cary's fan or worsted?"

"No, purchasing an estate. I have bought back my family property—the Ducis estate in this county. I found no difficulty in doing so by offering more than its value. The deeds are executed and the place is again my property."

"You are not going to return to South America, then?"

"I am not."

"Well, well, I might have understood that! What a world, and how would it get along without woman? It would certainly get along differently. They pick a fellow up and set him down when and where they fancy!"

"A profound truth."

"And *you* are set down—twisted around a girl's finger! Poor old boy, or young man, whichever you prefer! No more haciendas, and mangrove trees, and delightful bananas! No more opportuni-ties of entertaining your friend Burdette—!"

"Why not? Come to 'Brierland,' the name of our home; there are no briers to scratch you. You know the door will always be open."

"I'll come!" said Mr. Burdette, "and divide my time between Giorgione and her husband at Mauricewood, and Gen. Henry Haworth Ducis and bride at the brierless Brierland."

On the same evening that wicked Mr. Burdette said to his charge:

"Giorgione, I think I will leave you here for a week or two, when I return day after to-morrow."

"Leave me here?" exclaimed the young lady, greatly outraged.

"With this young Apollo, Mr. Jean Baptiste Maurice—hadn't I better?"

"No, sir!!!" cried Miss Giorgione blushing crimson.

"He is not coming North, you know—he's going back to Lima."

"Miss Giorgione could not blush more deeply, but she looked down and played with the cuff of her dress, smiling.

"Well, I see it's all arranged, and he's not going back in the least."

And as Jean came up at the moment, and approached Miss Giorgione, Mr. Burdette yielded to a sudden inspiration, cleared his throat, extended his arms above the pair in the attitude of the stage father, and exclaimed in a faltering voice:

"Bless you, my children!"

Jean laughed and blushed, and Miss Giorgione was overwhelmed with confusion.

"I will now add a few words of exhortation, my young friends," said Mr. Burdette, solemnly; "a brief lecture on the interesting subject of matrimony, its drawbacks and attractions. Matrimony—"

But a stifled laugh behind him interrupted Mr. Burdette. He turned around and found himself face to face with Miss Cary Maurice and Dr. Haworth, who had come in from their twilight walk.

"You are just in time, Excellency!" exclaimed Jean, "Mr. Burdette is going to lecture. You and sister Cary can join the audience!"

"What is the lecture about, Jean?" said Cary to her new brother, laying her hand affectionately on his shoulder.

"About matrimony!" said Jean, looking at Miss Giorgione with all his soul in his eyes. "What do you think of that, Excellency?"

"I think he is entitled to lecture on that subject," said Dr.

Haworth. "His own experience has been charming—if I may judge from personal observation."

"Gracias, Senor!" said Mr. Burdette saluting, "and now as I am going to say adios to this amiable household I will not neglect the occasion to finish my good work. As my young friend, Mr. Jean Baptiste Maurice, has perspicuously observed, you have arrived just in time—if not to be present when I bestowed my blessing upon himself and this fair damsel, at least to hear their engagement announced. They are about to be united in the holy bonds of matrimony, and I have pronounced my paternal benediction. I think others will be gratified by that same, also."

Dr. Haworth was standing by the side of Miss Cary, and Mr. Burdette suddenly extended his arms above them.

"Bless you also, my children!" he exclaimed in a broken voice; after which, as the scene overcame him, the noble stage parent bent double with laughter.

Miss Cary escaped from the room, carrying Miss Giorgione with her in a state of immense confusion, and Mr. Burdette winked at his friend Haworth.

"Really, this thing is getting too strong!" he exclaimed. "Are the couples coming to the ark? Is all the world and his wife going to be married over again? I never saw such a love-sick establishment! Let me fly to Mrs. B.! If I don't I'll catch the contagion and make love to the widow!"

XVII.

THE END OF THE TRIAL.

DR. HAWORTH had not echoed the laughter of his friend. His thoughts were too much absorbed in the gloomy drama whose last scenes were now about to be played. The next day would doubtless witness the end of the trial at Abbeyville, and the curious spectacle would be presented of Col. Ross and Prof. Lesner confronting each other in open court and each charging the other with murder.

Would Prof. Lesner have the nerve to defy his old associate? It was probable. If Col. Ross had accurately described his character he would fight desperately when driven into a corner, taking the chances. There was little probability that he would attempt to abscond, and under any circumstances that would be impossible. He was watched by an agent of Dr. Haworth, whose whole soul was now bent on definitely relieving the name of his father from the imputations resting upon it.

The next day came and the party from Mauricewood reached Abbeyville before the opening of court. The streets were already thronged, and the crowd had already begun to flock to the courthouse. At 11 o'clock the room was packed, and by order of Judge Bootlack, who looked solemn and said little, the crier opened court.

Mr. Dunn was observed to be uncommonly grave, and uttered not a single jest. From time to time he looked at Col. Ross, who was seated behind Mr. Shirley, and with even more attention at Mr. Shirley himself, as if he were studying the demeanor of that master under peculiar circumstances.

Dr. Haworth had in fact communicated to Mr. Dunn Col. Ross' statement after an interview with the latter at the jail, and Mr. Shirley had received a similar confidence from his client, Col. Ross.

Thus it was known to the counsel on both sides that the whole case henceforward hinged upon Prof. Lesner—that from the character of a simple witness to an immaterial point, the return on the warrants, he had passed to the character of the real criminal, the murderer of James Maurice.

As soon as court was opened Mr. Dunn said in the midst of a profound silence :

" Is Prof. Lesner in court ? "

" He was sent for this morning, sir," said the officer addressed, "and it is time for him to be here."

Something in the tones of Mr. Dunn seemed to produce a vague impression upon the crowd. The silence was like death. In the midst of it the sound of hoofs was heard on the cobblestones of the street, and a constable pushed his way in a moment afterward through the dense crowd.

" Well, where is Prof. Lesner ? " said Mr. Dunn; "you served the new summons ? "

" Yes, sir," said the constable in a low voice.

" Where is he ? "

" He was found dead."

Mr. Dunn looked the man in the face for a moment without speaking. He then said :

" Dead ? You say that you found Prof. Lesner dead ? "

"Yes, sir; in his chair, with a book on his knees."

A profound silence followed the words—not a soul in the vast audience moved.

"Tell the court everything," said Mr. Dunn, calmly.

There was not much more to tell. The constable had gone to Prof. Lesner's with a peremptory summons two hours before and knocked at the door. No one replying to his knock, he had gone in, opened the door of the library on the right and seen the Professor leaning back with a smile on his lips in a large arm-chair. Some pet birds were singing, everything looked peaceful, and he supposed the Professor was taking a nap. When he called, the Professor did not open his eyes, however, and after shaking him the officer touched his face. It was cold. Prof. Lesner was dead.

For the first time, the great audience stirred and murmured, moving to and fro as if overcome by the tragic report of the constable.

"That is all, then?" said Mr. Dunn.

"I found this paper in his hand, sir."

"A paper? Give it to me."

The constable handed Mr. Dunn the paper, which was an ordinary leaf of note-paper, upon which were written these lines in a bold and firm hand:

"I murdered James Maurice, taking him, in the darkness, for John Maurice—a man I hated. I also altered a date throwing the guilt on Henry Ducis. His son has discovered everything, and a woman who recognized me at the time of the murder will probably be called to testify. All is over, therefore, and an easy death by opium is better than a death on the gallows.

"It is not much, as there is no hereafter. Life is a dream, and I only wake from it, to fall asleep not to wake. All my trouble came from a woman. I was a fool to murder two men for such a nothing, when I had my birds and bees. LESNER."

Mr. Dunn read this note slowly, and then passed it across to Mr. Shirley. That gentleman perused it with similar calmness, and simply said:

"I presume you will direct a *nolle prosequi* to be entered, sir, under the circumstances?"

"As to Col. Ross, of course. I will indict the other accused persons for grand larceny, and misprision of felony."

Mr. Shirley bowed and rose. He and Mr. Dunn exchanged looks. It was probable that they regretted not having crossed weapons as adversaries worthy of each other.

An hour afterward the court-house was deserted, and Col. Ross, cheered by sympathizing friends, was driven home.

On the next day it was announced in the "Abbeyville Gazette" that our respected fellow-citizen, Col. Ferdinand Ross, who had been subjected to great inconvenience by a groundless charge brought against⋅ him, had returned to Washington on public business. Every respectable citizen rejoiced at his success in repelling the calumnies circulated against him, and he was followed by the good wishes of the entire community.

A month afterward the same paper announced that its favorite had left the United States for South America, where important interests demanded his presence.

As to the sole written document which might have cast a shadow on the fair fame of Col. Ross—that had either been destroyed by Prof. Lesner as amounting to nothing; or if carried in his pocket was buried with him.

XVIII.

AT PRESENT.

As the event here related occurred in the year 1880, they do not mount to a very remote antiquity, even in an age which lives as fast as our own.

They nevertheless seem very far away already from the actors in them.

After the storm comes the calm; after struggle, peace; and whatever any one may say, peace is better than war.

General Henry Haworth Ducis is married to Miss Cary Maurice; and Mr. Jean Baptiste Maurice has discovered that Miss Carry Fenton, otherwise Miss Giorgione, had never meant to send him away from Lima in that heartless manner. They have just been united and reside at Mauricewood, which it is reasonable to suppose will become their property at Mrs. Maurice's death. As to General and Mrs. Ducis, they live at the old Ducis estate, and, as far as any one can perceive, the young lady with the blue eyes and banged hair has never regretted the result of her horseback accident.

Mr. Burdette has been back twice. He says he is fond of the South, because the people there laugh out in a natural manner when anything amuses them, and take life easy, which he thinks is the best way to take it. He himself always does—he is never in a hurry, as he never rejects a manuscript under any circumstances. He also never allows business to annoy him in any manner—and especially avoids all connection with it when he is traveling.

Gen. Ducis is always extremely glad to see him, and he always stops, on his flying trips. When he goes over to Mauricewood to interview the young couple there, he invariably recalls the scene when he bestowed his benediction, and says to Jean:

"Are you as fond as ever of poking around Giorgione?"

Judge Bootlack is still an ornament to the bench, and has but one thorn in the flesh—Mr. Dunn. As to the Wilkins people, they were convicted of larceny, and are in the State prison.

Of the person who has passed in this history under the name of Dr. Haworth, it may be said that he is quite a different person now. The result of the trial lifted a great weight from him, and he is ten years younger and altogether happier. He has disposed of his property at Lima and become a citizen of the United States, which he thinks is a better country than South America.

THE END.